Klaus Berger   Odilon Redon

Klaus Berger

Odilon Redon

FANTASY AND COLOUR

Translated by Michael Bullock

McGraw-Hill Book Company

New York · Toronto · London

Frontispiece: Vase with Japanese Warrior 1905–1908   P   (498)

Dedicated in homage to
Dr. Franklin D. Murphy

Contents

I Symbolism

Redon's Isolation

Do pictures arise from ideas or from the interplay of colour and form? This is an old controversy. It may appear senseless when we consider how often both elements operate in conjunction. Everything depends upon how their inter-relationship is seen. There is John Ruskin, who states: "The art is greatest, which conveys to the mind of the spectator, by any means whatsoever, the greatest number of the greatest ideas," (*Modern Painters* I, 11) coming down very definitely on the side of ideas in his assessment of both the nature and the value of art. And on the other hand there is Maurice Denis's famous definition: "Never forget that in its essence every painting is first of all a picture surface upon which colours are arranged in a particular pattern and only then is it a warhorse, a nude or some anecdote." (*Theories*, p. 1). Artistic achievement is in one case means, in another end; behind this distinction, of course, there lies a profoundly different approach to art as a whole that is accompanied by quite concrete differences in the attitude towards particular artists and works of art. Here the stress is placed on expressive form, there on literary illustration.

Odilon Redon's work affords a good example of the dilemma that may spring from a confused critical standpoint. For a long time his art was measured by its ideas, its content, by the feelings and moods which can be deciphered, above all, in his prints; critics were either filled with admiration for the visions of his daemonic dream world or with repugnance against his impenetrable, indeed terrifying hallucinations. Both friends and foes are agreed that we are dealing here with an entirely isolated figure; he is like a stranger in his epoch, at most distantly related to poets like Poe and Baudelaire or to remote fantasts like Goya or Bosch. Are not the very titles and dedications of his work proof enough that he really comes from 'another' world and has almost nothing to do with the art of our and his time?

André Mellerio, his friend and essential biographer, already laid the foundation stone for this conception when he wrote that Odilon Redon deserves a special place in the art of the present. Why? Born in 1840, he belongs, in terms of his generation, to the Impressionists, with whom he has almost no affinities in respect either to his art or his ideas. Where they perceive the beautiful appearance and glittering surface of sunny landscapes or gay figures, Redon presents a shadowy dream-picture that rises from the depths, a vision that embraces a second, invisible world. Where the Impressionists rely upon the sensory impression of external nature, Redon gives the symbols of a spiritual, inwardly-directed experience. These, roughly, are Mellerio's arguments, and they are correct, but they remain bogged down on the plane of ideas. Not only are profound ideas often artistically dangerous, but they are no indication whatever as to the character of a work of art. How many bad works of art have been created with good ideas!

Another route altogether would appear to offer a better means of approach to Redon's art and its magical aspects. We must consider its plastic elements, must see what means come to his aid in giving cogent expression and vivid shape to his 'invisible' ideas. His productions are certainly unique and in the highest degree creative. But are they really totally isolated? How can his style be explained, if not in relation to the visual forms current during the period in which he lived? His originality does not run counter to them; quite the reverse, it becomes visible precisely to the extent to which it rises out of the soil of the style of the day and carries it beyond its evident potentialities. A work of art may remain misunderstood and unacknowledged in its own epoch, surrounded by all sorts of obscurity—this is almost the rule—yet the unprejudiced observer must draw it into the light and put it in the place that properly belongs to it in the history of artistic evolution, in order fully to appreciate its values and its essential nature. The work of art in isolation and the artist in isolation yield only half the story. Redon is no exception.

The Style of the Period

The Maurice Denis referred to above, who was undoubtedly more influential as a theorist than as a practising artist, painted in 1901 a picture entitled *Homage to Cézanne* (Pl. 6). Round a still-life painting by the great Post-Impressionist are grouped several painters of the Nabi group, Vuillard, Bonnard, Denis himself, and others, with Odilon Redon in the place of honour. This is an important piece of historical evidence, the first step towards drawing Redon out of his isolation and setting him in the context of the art of his period. Contact with the Nabis was purely artistic. Redon never belonged to the group and with certain of its members had only a fleeting acquaintance. To establish a relationship between Redon and Cézanne, as part and counter-part, so to speak, certainly opens up an audacious vista, but it is very difficult to maintain if we hold fast to biographical fact, psychological motivation or intellectual outlook. It is impossible to build any bridges from one to the other.

The Linear and the Painterly

Only if we free ourselves from the old imitation theory and turn to the true problems of the creation of form, can we discover aspects common to Redon, Cézanne and others of their contemporaries. Both maintain a critical distance from the optical theories of the Impressionists. When Redon complains that the Impressionists had "too low a ceiling" for him, he is tending in the same direction as Cézanne, who said of his friend Monet: "He is nothing but an eye, but what an eye!" The purely painterly sensory impression is to be supplemented by another, spiritual element better expressed through drawing, through line and structure. This tension between colour and form, and all that goes with it, was not new; it was characteristic of the whole of the 19th century, but during the last two decades it reached its culmination and became a matter of particularly intense significance to its proponents, the Post-Impressionists.

If we survey the evolution of style from the early Renaissance to the late Rococo, we see a slow transition from 'linear' beginnings to 'painterly' end-results, as Wölfflin has put it. In each individual situation it was a question of more or less. Then with the French Revolution the whole cycle seems to begin all over again: Neo-Classicism simplifies colour and once more adheres rigidly to the linear scaffolding, the three-dimensional roundness of the individual form. But from the beginning the new period presents a very different picture from the course of development that took place over the previous four centuries: contemporaneously with Jacques-Louis David, we see Goya at work; alongside Ingres (till 1867) there appears Delacroix (till 1863). The sequence of different phases was replaced by a co-existence, indeed a kind of competition. Each individual artist had, in a sense, to decide whether to pursue the linear or the painterly tradition.

Our histories of art have frequently greatly simplified the major trends of development in the 19th century and created the impression that there was only the Neo-Baroque of Goya and Delacroix and that the road led from there straight to Courbet, Manet and the Impressionists. The existence of all kinds of variations and stages was certainly admitted, but by and large only a century tending towards the painterly was seen. But the facts do not support this interpretation. If the classical idea is more comprehensive than the mere ability to reproduce things in three-dimensional roundness, we must expand the concept of its rebirth in painting so as to include David, Ingres and his large school, Chassériau, Degas and also Puvis de Chavannes, Marées and Hildebrand in Germany, while admitting all their mutual diversity. Only then shall we become aware that the linear tradition too—the representation of visible reality by means of tangible outlines instead of by patches of colour—never surrendered its right to life.

Synthesis

Because the Impressionists conquered the favour of the public and the art market, it is easy to overlook the counter-currents, not only the awful official art of 'coloured photographs.' We forget the really fundamental split in the artistic situation of that century. How else are we to understand that in every generation there were those who broke out of one camp and crossed the fissure that runs through the ages, in order to see what was taking place on the other side? The search for equilibrium, synthesis or conversion between two divergent standpoints is linked with the names Géricault, Chassériau, Corot, Millet and Manet. Each of them, not out of weakness but under various circumstances and with very varying results, flirted both with one side and the other.

For several generations there had existed a longing for a more comprehensive view of the work of art: as order and freedom at the same time, as everlasting and living, as complete and unending, as unity of composition and wealth of painterly colour, as eye and mind coordinated. This longing operated underground, so to speak, until it made itself felt in the great breakthrough of the Eighties. (Memory of the old masters, especially Poussin, served as an aid towards a possible synthesis.) Here is the beginning of our modern art, here stand the figures of Cézanne and van Gogh, Gauguin, Renoir and Seurat. Here also stands Odilon Redon. Of less importance by comparison are the labels that have been attached to them, whether it be Symbolism or Neo-Traditionalism, Post-Impressionism or Synthetism, Divisionism or Pre-Expressionism.

In his excellent study of this epoch, Bernard Dorival has advanced the opinion that the great transformation in the Eighties is attributable to two factors. On the one hand the philosophical turn towards Neo-Platonism with its contempt for the deceptive world of sensory perception and predilection for the display of symbols. On the other, but linked with this, the Realist and Impressionist painters had so wearied the public with their endless copies of nature that a change was absolutely essential. In analogy with the last days of antiquity, he sees here too a fundamental metamorphosis "from Roman realism to Byzantine abstraction." It is certainly correct that new trends in philosophy, as in poetry and music, created a favourable climate for art. But how can we imagine that they could have influenced or actually caused the new painting, if the preconditions for a new vision had not already existed within art? It turns out that Redon's 'Symbolism' preceded rather than followed the literary movement of the same name.

And what about the sudden breakdown of Naturalism? Is a surfeit of one kind of art sufficient in itself to explain *in which direction* the new departure takes place? And does not even crass Realism (a piece of nature seen through a temperament) contain within it a good proportion of form-creation? The mere 'imitation' of Nature only exists on paper. The transposition of three-dimensional reality into a two-dimensional picture is already an interpretation. Are Degas or Courbet, for example, second-class artists because they clung to physical nature?

Again and again we are thrown back upon the one basic question. A new art is crystallized in a new vision, grows out of changed formal processes. The consequences may be very far-reaching: interest in different aspects of the world, different ideas, a different taste and many other things. Without creative vision no new art is possible; the breakthrough of a new vision is the decisive criterion; it has almost nothing to do with the handling of techniques.

Dissatisfaction with a one-sided naturalistic Impressionism does not of itself imply the elimination of Nature. Nature, Delacroix already declared, is to the artist merely a dictionary from which he takes elements for his style. To combine the natural with the spiritual through artistic creation became the real endeavour of the generation of 1880. Thus it is not primarily a question of mastering a new domain of subject matter or realm of ideas. In this respect Redon has nothing in common with, say, Cézanne. What links them is the craving for an expansion of Impressionism and its painterly elements, so that structural, 'classical' components can enter into the construction of the picture. A more comprehensive image of the world thereby becomes possible. The competition between colour and linear form is overcome by their interplay. "When the colour is richest, the form reaches its highest degree of clarity," is Cézanne's striking way of putting it.

The new synthesis is justified by its results, magnificent pictures as well as a tremendous upsurge in the decorative arts, architecture and book illustration. It is also justified on another plane through its invocation of 'synthetic' features in the arts of other peoples and ages. It was not from outward eclecticism, but from inner affinity that the founders of the new art turned their attention to important forerunners: Gauguin learning from the primitivism of Cambodia as well as from Giotto; Seurat and his followers studying Ingres as well as Delacroix. The later Renoir sought to integrate Raphael and the wall paintings of Pompeii with Impressionism, Cézanne turned to Poussin, and Redon looked at Leonardo and Rembrandt, but also at Delacroix and Corot. He needed more witnesses to his misunderstood art; his path, artistically speaking, was more complicated than that of his companions. By the time he reached his first high-point, at the end of the Eighties, when almost fifty, he was stylistically in the front rank of Post-Impressionism. But how much longer the journey was for him than for anyone else, because he set out even before Impressionism and never let himself be carried by the latter.

Another circumstance contributed no less to this delay. The visionary apparitions, to which he had to turn out of an inner need, now became more difficult of access to the visual arts because they were commandeered by literature. E. T. A. Hoffmann and Edgar Allen Poe seemed to have exhausted the possibilities of the fantastic. In the pictorial sphere there was only the pale reflection afforded by the minor 'romantic' illustrators: Tony Johannot, Grandville, Boulanger. Of course a return to Goya would have been possible but there is almost no sign of it.

Stylistic Constellation

The sum total of these factors produced the artistic constellation of Redon's graphic art, which falls for the most part within the last two decades of the last century. What they lead up to is easily appraised. The sequence *The Temptation of St Anthony* (M 90 Pl. 37) is probably among the best of all his graphic works, and it is a convincing expression of the 'new vision'. These visions are actually monochrome pictures with a 'colourful' charm and a rich orchestration. Black, white and grey are no longer gradations of tone between light and dark, they have become stages in the colour scale and give the figures a chromatic existence. The light is no longer diffuse, it has no representational value (to use the phrase coined by Hans Jantzen); it is organized into a firm structure that transforms the figures into arabesques of hieratic power. There are sonorous black areas, the ground-bass so to speak, in opposition to which are set the white and grey areas of varying density and intensity. Outdoor light, an essential element of Impressionism, has been done away with, cast shadows have been lost, the picture has become a vision from which the last remnants of perspective spatial depth have been banished and the (two-dimensional) picture plane alone dominates. Hegel already knew that it is creation with abstract elements and not the illustration of spiritual events which spiritualizes style, when he stated that the inwardness of art depends upon respect for the 'optical plane.' Similarly Maurice Denis, as a spokesman for the new art, claimed that objective as well as subjective deformation must be present in every picture, i. e. a decorative conception of colour and form as well as personal sensibility and feeling for nature.

Further, we must stress the extent to which Redon's pictorial ideas may be reduced to a few elementary shapes—circles, spirals, triangles, verticals and horizontals; his compositions appear to be the result of a process of clarification and look like the final, immobile reflections of an inner order; they render him, in this respect, akin to the classical styles with their demand for the crystallization of forms: 'abstract' pattern-like shapes are made to conform over wide areas with the distribution of light and hence are made subject to the same rhythmic play. There are no natural sources of light any more, no more cast shadows and no more space, as we have seen. Light itself has become unnatural or spiritual, in a certain sense it is the substance out of which the visions are formed.

The Overcoming of Romanticism

How powerful is the synthesis out of which Redon created his new vision—parallel with Cézanne, van Gogh, Seurat or Gauguin—may be measured by a comparison with his 'Romantic' forerunners. Sven Sandström has carried out an iconological investigation into the themes which Redon borrowed from the Romantic illustrators, e. g. I. I. Grandville (Pl. 38a). There is a beautiful girl, in the true reportage manner, surrounded by a whole host of admirers, all in the elegant costume of 1844, the date of the work, only instead of heads they have a grotesque thistle-like growth that looks like an upturned eye. The portrayal is entirely naturalistic and it is only when we read the title *Making Eyes* that we come upon the joke and its possible deeper significance. It lacks plastic quality. But Redon reached the precision of his graphic expression step by step and thus transformed the confusion of the dream world into a genuinely symbolic, not merely allegorical existence (M 34, Pl. 38).

The story of artistic vision in the 19th century has not yet been written, in particular we lack any exposition dealing with the development of free drawing and the making of original prints closely bound up with it. If it is one day written, it will confirm how little isolated Redon was and how closely he approached in an early work of 1879 the stage which Seurat reached three years later (cf. the drawing *The Black Bow*, Pl. 73).

New Visual Form

Here the question arises: how did Redon's visual form come into being? His first sequence *In the Dream (Dans le rêve* 1879) shows him already so securely set on his path that we are almost inclined to regard him as a miracle fallen from heaven. Redon himself, with the right of the creative artist, never particularly liked to show his hand. He never made any statement regarding the sources of his inspiration, and only late and reticently did he say anything about his artistic ancestors, really not until he had already finished with printmaking. He deeply loved Rembrandt, but what graphic artist does not admire him? The copying of Delacroix occurred at an early stage, before he had found himself, and left little mark on his art. His first real teacher in Bordeaux, a man named Gorin, made no name for himself in art history. His brief encounter with official painting in Gérôme's studio ended in fiasco.

Much more concrete, however, is his relationship with Rodolphe Bresdin, as whose pupil he expressly describes himself and to whom he frequently refers in his *A soi-même,* his 'notes on life, art and artists'. Admittedly it is only in his early etchings, which precede the lithographs, that we can directly perceive the hand of the teacher; indirectly, however, a lasting influence arises from "these strange, mysterious and legendary effects" (*A soi-même*, p. 160), derived from Bresdin's 'archaic style' (Pl. 71, Bresdin: *Caesar and his Legions*).

Here, I believe, at the age of twenty-four and fifteen years before his first work was published, Redon found a main source of his fantastic art and the impulse to translate it into graphic signs.

Millet as a Point of Departure

This first beginning must have been decisively reinforced by contact with Jean François Millet. Two years before the appearance of *Dans le rêve* he spent a summer painting at Barbizon. Mellerio dismisses this in a single sentence. But we need only look at a charcoal drawing produced by the older man during this decade (Pl. 69, *The Fisherman*), to discern striking similarities in the treatment of space in planes, the handling of light, the silhouette-like isolation of the figures and so on. It was particularly fortunate for Redon that during the years around 1870, so decisive for him, he was scarcely touched by the avant-garde of Impressionism and in his provincial and backward Bordeaux was exposed precisely to the works of the Barbizon School as 'modern' art. Among the pictures which he saw there he mentions first and foremost the name of Millet. Why, therefore, should we not assume that a decade later he came into personal contact with him at Barbizon or at least became familiar with his drawings?

Millet's magnificent drawings and pastels (Pl. 70) are little known even today and almost obscured by his sentimental and overloaded paintings of the *Angelus* type; in the former the 'synthesis' between the linear and painterly tendencies of the pre-Impressionist era finds excellent expression; they constitute, as it were, another, minor path to Post-Impressionism that casts additional light upon the main route. To combine the individual with the typical is characteristic of Millet and distinguishes him from his Barbizon friends Th. Rousseau, Daubigny, etc. For just this reason Redon found in him, stylistically and in outlook, a kindred spirit, an important draughtsman, a man who observed nature with imagination.

Moreau the Antipode

At the same time, however, Gustave Moreau, in every sense his antipode, cast his spell upon him. "I believe neither in what I touch, nor in what I see. I believe only in what I do not see, but feel," Moreau said of himself. The combination of over-intensified imagination, acute intellectuality, a mania for the microscopic reproduction of precious detail and a 'primitive' perspective borrowed from the early Italians did not merely make his art the emblem of all anti-naturalistic trends; it also gained for him the admiration of the poets and thinkers who were craving for meaning. This poet of extravagant impotence and sterility became the hero of the decadent movement. His sensational visions have connexions with the English Pre-Raphaelites at the beginning of

1 Redon 1867 self-portrait O (1)

2 Redon 1875—77 self-portrait O (2)

3 Redon c. 1888 self-portrait D (551)

4　Redon　1894　Ph

5　Redon　c. 1894　self-portrait　D

Homage to Cézanne   1900
by Maurice Denis (in the left foreground Redon)

7   Odilon Redon   1901   oil by Edouard Vuillard

8 In the studio 1909 Ph

9 Redon 1904 self-portrait D (750)

10 Redon 1910 self-portrait D

11   Redon   1914   Ph   12   Redon   in May 1914   Ph

his career as well as with the *fin-de-siècle* outlook of Huysmans and Oscar Wilde at its end. Here, perhaps for the first time, dubious aesthetic elements helped a whole artistic culture to its feet (Pl. 68, Moreau: *Alexander's Triumph*, detail). Did even his contemporary Richard Wagner ever evolve a bolder programme than "to render the visual arts more eloquent than speech and music put together"? (Léon Deshairs: *Gustave Moreau*, p. 8). Moreau is important not as the creator of a new style, but as the inventor of a 'poetically' bizarre modern iconography. He made no studies from nature but merely noted down fragments, which with the indefatigable minuteness of an engraver he combined together to form a picture. "He tries to make us believe that the antique gods wore heavy gold watch chains," Degas aptly said of him. Nevertheless, the resuscitation of classical and Christian mythology during this naturalistic epoch filled a vacuum; hence all those tendencies which sought an outlet for imagination, for the fantastic and evocative, grouped themselves around him.

Looking back over a quarter of a century, Redon relates how *Oedipus and the Sphinx* (Pl. 66), Moreau's first sensational work, "soothed him," almost put him under a spell. It is clear from his early charcoal drawings and first lithographs how influenced he was by the older man, down to small details. Only in the course of the Eighties did he find his own individual style, increasingly renouncing detail in order to advance to a symbolic form of expression. He developed a stricter coherence of his composition with abstract elements, pictorial 'equivalents' of the spiritual—to speak in the words of Gauguin, the new friend he made just at this time. The difference between the urbane theatrical producer and the inspired embodier of dreams emerges especially clearly in those cases where both of them, Moreau and Redon, dealt with the same subject—*Orpheus, Saint Sebastian, Jacob and the Angel, Phaeton*, etc.

The Rôle of Puvis de Chavannes

Puvis de Chavannes shares with his diametrical opposite, Moreau, derivation from Chassériau and hence from the Renaissance tradition of Luini as seen by Ingres. If ever an inheritance was split into two unequal parts, it was here. One took over the by-product, an accumulation of glittering coloured jewels, the other the principle of the monumental use of flat areas as practised in mural painting. Puvis's art remains as little influenced by academic salon painting as by the naturalistic-impressionist avant-garde and unfolds in the organic sequence of four decades a classical vision, if the combination of traditional forms with contemporary sensibility may be described as classical. Where his German contemporary Hans von Marées ate his heart out in isolation, Puvis was carried along by the secret classicism of his countrymen. He was able to throw a bridge across into a new era, in which the simplicity and grandeur of his form was hailed as liberating, as a way out of the dead-end of Impressionism. His bias towards the artificial and intellectual has often been noted. Is not the fresco itself an art form imported from Italy? Do his figures resemble those seen in the streets of France? Only when naturalistic criteria are applied can such objections diminish his art. Anyone looking at his work from a greater distance and hence with more objectivity, will be able to say that "his ceiling is not set too low," that he can even afford to make excursions into the dangerous realm of allegory with his supra-temporal ideal figures, because his dream, as Léon Werth expressed it, magically goes hand in hand with the design. He does not give himself up to the trivial episode, nor to the vibrant colour with which he models his figures, nor to any individual details. Everything is subordinated to the decorative order that arises out of respect for the wall: space organized in layers. The figures are there to clarify the pictorial space; space is not there to be filled with figures (Pl. 72, *Summer*). Therefore colour has to be, not suppressed, but neutralized.

It is well known that he was set right on this point by his admirer Gauguin. Purity of colour was no less important to him than form. But Puvis's importance lies in the fact that in an epoch subservient to the quick impression, without lapsing into literary painting, he found his way back to essentials: meaningful content, wholeness of composition, balance of the elements, decorative unity. Out of a classical tradition known of old and long forgotten, he created something living. On the dissolution of Impressionism, he was able therewith to make a very relevant contribution to the next phase. The generation of 1890 looked upon him as a precursor. Few were able to escape his influence. Van Gogh, Gauguin, Toulouse-Lautrec, the Nabis, even the young Picasso had to come to terms with him.

How much Redon's drawings and subsequent lithographs owe to him is difficult to prove in detail. No direct path leads from the monumental wall paintings of the one, meant to be looked at from a distance, to the 'shortsighted' intimate fantasies of the other. The influence was more a normative one: here was the example of a great artist who was able to give pictorial expression to fantasy and ideas. Perhaps the sight of stylized space, the enchantment of space, inspired the younger man. All we can say for sure is that Redon knew and often praised Puvis's work. In a note in his journal (of 14 May 1888) he ranks his work with that of Giorgione and Correggio. In a picture like Manet's *Le déjeuner sur l'herbe*, he remarks, the naked female figure has a wretched existence, "she is in a hurry to get dressed again after sitting uncomfortably on the damp grass with the unidealistic gentlemen who surround her and are conversing with her. What are they saying? Nothing fine, I suspect." But "Puvis's women do not get dressed again ... The painter of understanding places a naked woman free from shame in Paradise and allows her to be gazed upon by eyes that do not belong to us, but to a spiritual world, a world of the imagination created by the painter."

The Flight into Egypt   c. 1902   P and gouache   (362)

Imagination

This imaginary world created by the painter is at the same time a good description of Redon's own art. The word imaginary must be underlined and distinguished from bizarre and fantastic. In the latter case we are dealing with the confusion of the impossible, in the former with an extension of the natural, with a second existence. Moreau points in the former direction; he merely illustrates a chimerical world of private vagaries by highly naturalistic means. But for Redon the visions seem to rise up out of memory. He must have recalled his study of Baudelaire, in whose *Le Salon de 1846* we read: "Memory is the great touchstone of art. When art springs from the recollection of the beautiful, memory is spoiled by outward imitation."

But how is imagination connected with memory? Is it the mere product of memory? Once more the answer is to be found in Baudelaire *(Salon de 1859):* "The whole universe is merely a storehouse of images and signs to which fantasy, imagination, assigns place and value; it is a kind of raw material which imagination has to work over and transform." Carrying neo-Platonist ideas further, the whole realm of art, whether naturalistic or spiritualistic, whether it deals with inner or with outer reality, is encompassed by imagination. Imagination, promoted master over nature, is no longer restricted to a particular domain but can penetrate everywhere as a transforming, creative force. "Without actually taking refuge in opium—as Poe recommended—who has not known those glorious hours, festal moments of the brain, when the better sharpened senses perceive fuller sensations, when the sky breaks through in an improbably transparent blue to infinite depths, when sounds take on the ring of music, colours begin to speak and scents tell of the world of ideas?" (Baudelaire, *Exposition Universelle).* This is imagination, seen in all its power and in the central position now assigned to it in the visual arts.

Instinctively, of course, its rôle has always been felt, especially since the Renaissance. Without imagination nothing of an artistic nature can come into being. But there is a difference between regarding it as one desirable component among others and hailing it as the *fons et origo* of all artistic activity and making it the central element of a world-view. There seem to be three reasons for the enormous effect of Baudelaire's ideas, which, incidentally, were printed in quite obscure periodicals. First, the recasting of the Romantic heritage of ideas to transform it from an esoteric doctrine applying to philosophy and poetry into an open-minded way of looking at the visual world, is fundamental. Baudelaire's reinterpretation of Delacroix's rather literary definition of imagination so that it becomes universal imagination, and his commendation of Guys as the "painter of modern life", show the direction. Second, the triumph and misuse of Naturalism during the Fifties positively provoked a counter-manifesto, justified an inquiry as to when art is *not* imitation. Baudelaire's ideas were evolved at precisely this time. They fall in a late period when a common denominator was required to comprehend the widest range of artistic tendencies without lapsing into pale eclecticism. Third, they are magnificent formulations from the pen of a poet and this explains why the Salon reviews, written for the day, have survived a whole century and revealed fresh aspects to every generation.

In fact Baudelaire's writings on art were posthumously collected in one volume in 1868 under the title *Curiosités esthétiques* and since 1884, the date of the real beginning of modern art in Post-Impressionism, have embarked upon the rôle that has made them almost the 'book of hours' of modern art from this year down to Surrealism.

There can be no doubt that Odilon Redon entered very early into the orbit of Baudelaire's world. At the age of seventeen, on their first appearance, he read *Les fleurs du mal*. Twenty-three years later he was still using them as the inspiration for his eighth series of prints. In the artistically still vacillating period of his apprenticeship, with its tendency towards the literary, no other influence can have had such a far-reaching effect on him. Traces of the *Curiosités esthéthiques* are to be found at every step in his journal *A soi-même:* in his general trend of thought, in the evaluation of various contemporary painters, even in individual turns of phrase, which may, of course, have reached him indirectly and second-hand. It would be worth while investigating to see whether a number of the ideas for his pictures were not derived from the poems of the admired master. However that may be, there was no artistic figure in young Redon's environment so congenial to him in the concord of image, sound and language, in the love of dream, symbol and imagination, as Baudelaire.

Inspiration

With this discussion of the forces that might have had a stimulating or deterrent effect upon him we have more or less covered the ground from which Redon launched his attack on art. Grandville, Bresdin, Millet, Moreau, Puvis, Baudelaire stand round him in varying relationships. Their presence around him provides a desirable means of access to the artist's symbolism. One question remains: what was the immediate source of his inspiration in the 150-odd lithographs which, from beginning to end, disclose a vision that is in the highest degree individual in both handwriting and content? What was the substance from which a semi-dilettante of almost forty began to produce, year by year and month by month, one print after another until suddenly, after two decades, he came to a stop and turned in quite a different direction? During his lifetime no one was able to draw from him any hint regarding the how and why. (See the letter of 16 August 1898 that appears on p. 129). Once only did he admit indirectly that everything came from the unknown depths of his own self. All those works with titles and captions that contain a reference to Edgar Allan Poe, Goya, Flaubert, Baudelaire or Verhaeren were not created as 'illustrations' and, seen clearly, have nothing to do with the text; the titles merely serve to conceal the true, obscure source of the images.

A solution of this riddle has been attempted only recently by a depth psychologist. And even though the questions he has posed lie on a different plane, that of medical biography, his findings run so 'parallel' with the problems of Redon the artist that they also cast light on the latter's artistic personality and work. The deep and hidden roots of Redon's experience according to the view advanced by Pierre Roumeguère (*La Vie Médicale*, Christmas 1956, pp. 64—77), lie in a traumatic infantile shock on which the artist was fixated. "Odilon Redon bears the oppressive weight of a secret childhood knowledge of events and extremely violent scenes which remain for him a mystery, which were at one and the same time seen and not seen, for they took place by night and he must not wish to understand them." The reference is to the time when he was growing up on the lonely estate in the heathland, Peyrelebade, separated from his father and mother, shut out from family, school and world, left to himself, and to the deep wound that was there inflicted upon him. A man who has been banished from the world, an almost pathological introvert, seeks to come to terms with life. This suffering has been translated into concrete images drawn from unconscious memories in the charcoal drawings and lithographs. They relate to scenes of anxiety, horror and terror from which the setting and the precise event are missing. Instead we see compulsive imaginings that revolve endlessly around the enigmatic act of violence, the downfall; we see a strange darkness, the 'third eye' of the spirit that looks shyly away, and—death.

Thus through sublimation and self-analysis he not merely kept sickness at arm's length, but effected his own cure. The colour, the flowers, *The Birth of Venus* (cf. Cat. 179, p. 105) in his late work announce the victory. The true crisis, says Roumeguère, occurred in the Nineties with a severe illness in the winter of 1894/95. After this he had mastered his unconscious and the ascent to light, gaiety and *joie de vivre* lay open.

Quite right. The dates show a striking correspondence with the change in his artistic output. Nevertheless the psychological 'liberation' provides a basis for the change only from a negative point of view; the true pointers to the new style are to be sought elsewhere. "Temperament alone does not make an artist until it is joined by clarity of vision," says Wölfflin. 'Repression' of colour during Redon's black and white period is an inadequate explanation. Did he not paint in colour simultaneously with, and even prior to, the prints? But these carefully concealed little nature studies have virtually nothing in common with his coloured style after 1900. His late work, as with Rubens or Dürer, grew out of an insight into other, richer means of expression.

Formal Equivalents

Redon was undoubtedly right when he stated: "I have endured the martyrdom of the imagination." But he omitted to add that with his best prints he created symbols of firm validity; they have lasted for generations and remain effective even today; we need neither to be familiar with the difficult experiences of the

Jeanne Chaire   1903   P   (395)

artist, nor to live through them ourselves, in order to assess their importance. Therefore one can only agree with Maurice Denis who declares: "Redon occupies a position at the point of origin of Symbolism, if by this is meant the *pictorial* expression of the ideal." (*Théories*, p. 254). No dream dictated the elements of which his pictures are composed, made him turn to printmaking as a medium or advised him as to the degree of abstraction he should adopt. In another part of this essay I shall show how his pictorial imagination crystallized out over the years and then developed. Here I shall content myself with pointing out a few of its basic principles.

In order to express the mysterious and 'invisible' character of his experiences, the artist made effective use of stylization, abstraction, even distortion of natural perception. It is a question of finding equivalents. Redon mastered them and recognized the field of graphic art as his domain. Today, standing under the sign of non-representational painting and sculpture, it is very easy to assert that all types of art are open to abstraction, the Middle Ages, the primitives and the present day bear witness to this. But not everything is possible at all times in the history of art. In the nineteenth century the naturalistic, imitative tendencies were actually so strong that everything became subordinate to them. Even the decorative arts became 'concrete' and included photographic elements. It took Redon's indomitable courage to batter down the locked door and win the right to abstraction, at least for the 'inferior' art of engraving. Did he not again and again have to assure obtuse critics that he had no intention of portraying or defining anything, but merely of 'suggesting' and hinting? Again, when he boasts of having been "born on a musical wave," he is invoking his right to free, abstract composition.

Flat Plane and Arabesque

The capacity for abstraction is expressed in Redon in two ways. First, in his flat-plane conception of space. Second, in the decorative treatment of the arabesque.

Starting from a conception of pictorial space as being composed of various planes rising perpendicularly behind the picture surface in parallel layers and neatly delimited from each other, in other words from space as conceived by Raphael or Ingres, he quickly reduced both the depth and the number of relief layers, so that space became flatter and flatter. Soon we find ourselves moving within a very narrow 'stage.' Then followed the decisive step: the various planes are all united in one. As in the early woodcut, the third dimension is missing; but whereas at that time perspective space had not been discovered, now it has been discarded and at the same time expanded into infinitude. Redon's *White Woman's Body with Death's Head* of 1888 (M. 89, Pl. 39) is entirely filled with space, it is the all-embracing and no longer tangible space of the night, which has now become the vessel of his immaterial visions. In his own words, the invisible is portrayed by means of the visible. The emergence

32

Nude   ca. 1911   P   (381a)

of the apparitions out of darkness is for him not merely a symbolic expression,
but the appropriate artistic equivalent. Every generation of graphic artists after
him, down to the present, has sailed in this channel; whether Seurat's magnificent conté drawings of about the same period were directly influenced by him
or produced independently—the two artists met as early as 1884—need not be
decided here. Even if the second hypothesis were correct, it would only show
how ripe the stylistic situation was for an immaterial conception of space. It
may be remarked in passing that the growing admiration for Japanese prints

33

during those years, and his friend Gauguin's interest in primitive art, both point in the same direction.

And then the arabesque. Analogously to the transformation of space, the world of figures moving within it shrinks from three-dimensional modelling to a flat pattern, to ornamental simplification. An extremely dangerous tendency, because it is derived from the 'grotesque' wall decoration of classical antiquity and the Renaissance and is therefore bound by tradition to the sphere of the frivolous, lascivious and obscene. On the face of it, there can be no better method for expressing the superficial. All Redon's intuition is shown in the fact that he reversed this function into its opposite and conquered the arabesque for depth of ideas as well as for depth of drawing. Whether in this connexion he made use of stimuli received from the circle of the French Pre-Raphaelites need not be investigated here. As early as 1833, in fact, Victor Orsel, a distant adherent of Ingres, painted a chapel in the Paris church of Notre Dame de Lorette in which arabesques as symbols of the Litany play no small part, and links can be traced back to medieval miniatures. (Cf the present author's lecture on 'Ingrism and Pre-Raphaelitism' at the 19th International Congress for Art History). In any case, it can only have been a question of stimuli, for it is impossible to put one's finger on any direct borrowings, from the point of view either of style or iconography.

There is nothing comparable to the reality portrayed by Redon, simplified to a silhouette and reduced to circles, spirals and other curves, to his world of masks, death's heads, bells lucarnes, shells, disks, serpents, flying heads and petrified profiles. The way in which an enormous face grows like a fruit on a thin stalk (Cat. 614, Pl. 51) of course leaves all 'natural' criteria and possibilities of comparison behind. Just as there is no longer any horizon, so nothing large or small exists any longer. Constructed of elementary and precise components, a second world rises up in full lucidity. This lucidity, a spiritual lucidity, is reinforced by the contrast between light and dark. The more mature his visions become, the more forcefully the illuminated arabesques thrust out into the darkness of space surrounding them. The black achieves at times a velvety richness and tonality unknown since Rembrandt, or at least since Goya; the interplay of the white, grey and black tones leads finally to a symphonically intensified colourfulness (see *From the 'Haunted House'*, M 164, Pl. 64), in which the objective elements move even further into the background in order to show the envelope of the marvellous. From the world of symbols there has developed a symbolic world. The objects have in the process become quite commonplace: a hand, a sheet of paper, the corner of a table.

Transition to Colour

Works like this already belong to the phase in which the martyrdom of the imagination and the nightmares of the fantastic are on the wane. After the struggle, the victory. The transition to colour, to pastel and oil, increasingly

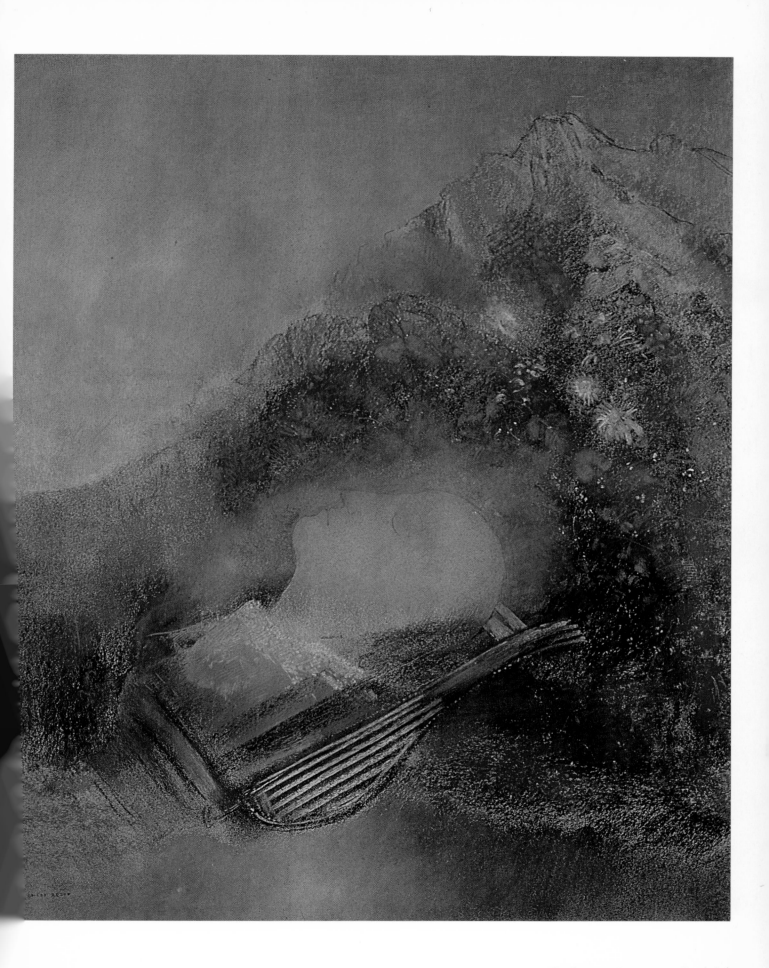

Orpheus   after 1903   P   (365)

evident after 1890, may represent both psychologically and iconographically a perceptible break between the first and second Redon. Artistically, the second is inconceivable without the first. The flower-pieces (Pls. pp. 89, 93, 115, 119), *Apollo's Sun Chariot* (Pl. p. 95), *The Birth of Venus* (Pl. p. 105) contain as many marvellous and symbolic elements as the visions of the earlier lithographs. They are spiritual in their own way, just as much transformation of the phenomenal world, only in a different direction; they no longer avoid sensory perception but permeate it.

From the Daemonic to the Magical

If, speaking metaphorically, we see here a new and powerful branch sprouting from an old tree, we must also not overlook the fact that the principle of development present in the first half of Redon's creative life is also confirmed in the second. After he embarks upon his religious, mythological and 'botanical' works, the object is more and more dissolved in a growing orchestration of colour, rhythmic fullness of graphic devices and the abstract tautening of form and composition. The flower-pieces are less and less tied to realistic, existing models; in their intensity they create a spiritual order for which the fine products of our flora only provide pretexts, though very charming pretexts. The late decorative wall screens and wall panels, with their content that is merely hinted at, leave just as much scope for fantasy and the symbolic as the early prints dedicated to the 'dream,' the 'conjuration' of Goya or Edgar Allan Poe or the *Haunted House*, only in a different manner. A daemonic symbolism has been replaced by a magical one. We thus follow the dictionary, which defines magic as "the art of producing miracles on phenomena that are really derived from natural causes" *(Petit Larousse)*. Whether Redon employs white or black magic, whether he had made a pact with divine or evil powers, are questions we must leave open. At all events, the results are the achievement of a magician.

His works in colour are even more closely linked than his prints with the style of the age. After the procedure followed by Cézanne from the beginning of the Eighties, an all-embracing change in artistic vision took place shortly before 1890: the turning away from Impressionism (pictures as a mere delight to the eye) to a conception aiming to do more justice to the essential. In *La Grande Jatte* (Pl. 74) Seurat portrayed a scene in which, with the aid of pure, integrated colour and strong, structural drawing, time has been brought to a standstill, petrified, eternalized. Gauguin painted his *Vision after the Sermon* (Pl. 75) and overcame the illustrative nature of the theme by an imaginative distortion of colour and form. The meadow cannot be green, because it is not in nature but in the world of the supernatural and marvellous, consequently it is red, the complementary colour, as red as paint can produce. He is concerned above all with the 'synthesis', the permeation of meaning by

36

Homage to Gauguin   1904   P   (396)

form, of the composition by pure colour, of unbroken flat areas by expressive patterns. The Nabis, his successors, developed the decorative side of this tendency and are heralded in Redon's work.

Art Nouveau

A second movement followed on the heels of the first. 'Art Nouveau' in Western Europe and 'Jugendstil' in Germany began as attempts to breathe new life into applied art and architecture and hence have for too long been looked upon as specialized fields that merely run alongside that of painting. In reality, however, we have here, for the first time since the Rococo, a total style that touches in some way or other vertically all the arts from building via painting to book decoration, and horizontally almost every country in Europe. It is the convergence of the English Arts and Crafts movement, with roots that reach back to Blake and the Pre-Raphaelites, and French Symbolist and Post-Impressionist painting, which made Belgium its focus and radiated outwards to Germany, Vienna, Holland, Norway, Barcelona and France. What is the substance that held such diversified products together for about fifteen years? Nikolaus Pevsner states in *Pioneers of Modern Design* (London 1936): "The long, sensitive curve, reminiscent of the lily's stem, an insect's feeler, the filament of a blossom, or occasionally a slender flame, the curve undulating, flowing, and interplaying with others, sprouting from corners and covering assymetrically all available surfaces, can be regarded as the *leitmotif* of Art Nouveau" (Revised edition, Penguin 1960, p. 90). Who can fail to see that van Gogh's *Cypresses* (Pl. 77), Edvard Munch's *The Cry* (Pl. 76), Toulouse-Lautrec's *Jane Avril* poster (Pl. 78) or Redon's *My Irony Exceeds All Others* (M 97, Pl. 40), the disparate products of a single decade, are bound together by the ornamental flamelike line?

It thus becomes clear that when Redon's daemonic symbolism changed into a symbolism governed by the decorative, he thereby placed himself in the front rank of modern art. The one-time outsider now stood in the centre. It is certainly no coincidence that the Art Nouveau phase marks the beginning of wall painting and decorative folding-screens, nourished by Japanese models and similar works by his Nabi friend Vuillard. It is certainly no coincidence that he now abandoned his reserve towards other artists and established friendly relations with Gauguin, Emile Bernard, Maurice Denis and other Nabis, that in 1899 he really became the centre of the Symbolist Exhibition. It is also certainly no coincidence that in 1894 he was invited to Brussels, the starting point of Art Nouveau, to exhibit in the Libre Esthétique alongside Gauguin, Ensor, Beardsley, Maillol, Denis, Toorop and William Morris. There, for the first time, the international aspects and ramified perspectives of the new style were publicly demonstrated.

Spiritualized Nature

All the same there was another delay before Redon's decorative stage reached its highest glory in 'magical' symbolism. The religious themes with which he wrestled have proved rewarding to few modern artists. Not until around 1905, simultaneously with the decline of Art Nouveau, did the road to freedom open up to him. Now there appear the sun chariots of Apollo, the pictures of Venus and the full flower-pieces (pp. 89, 95, 105, 115, 119), masterpieces in the taut organization of an almost geometrical order and symphonic colour. He now gave shape to a spiritual world in terms of sensuous perception, not in opposition to it. It was the new wave in modern art, the Fauves, with which he now sailed. Their leader Matisse became his admirer—and a purchaser of his works; in the Basle Museum we can see a landscape by Matisse, *The Riverbank*, of 1907, which, in the interplay of two blues with tones of lavender, is very reminiscent of a pastel by Redon that is hanging in the same room and was drawn four years earlier. An additional factor was his meeting with Cézanne, the full range of whose work was demonstrated for the first time in the memorial exhibition of the same year. Not that the master from Aix came closer to him—Redon never managed to feel enthusiastic about Cézanne, as he says himself—but if we look at the *Venus* or the *Pandora* alongside earlier works they display a fuller weight, a hitherto unknown richness of form that can be described as Cézannesque, even if we are inclined to think rather of a Japanese, decorative Cézanne.

Thus the ring of Redon's symbolic art closes. From the beginnings, in which the fantastic motifs seem to hang over him and he has to seek his way by borrowing Moreau's themes or Millet's drawings, the path leads to the prints in which dreamlike visions rest in equilibrium with their pictorial equivalents. With the transition to colour a new domain is introduced into the 'synthesis' between form and content. The decorative element becomes more all-embracing, the fantastic gives ground, the thematic shrinks. From ordinary visual impressions, flower-pieces, female figures, sea-pieces there finally develop compositions which can only be called magical and are based on textural colour, a disciplined, rhythmic use of flat areas, and abstract patterns: a new Symbolism in which the daemonic content is replaced by spiritualized nature.

This is Redon's path into the art of the new century.

II Works and Life

A Literary Art?

In the middle of his life, at thirty-eight, Redon was still unknown. As an artist, he had not yet found himself. A few years later he showed his first charcoal drawings in modest surroundings. As little notice was taken of them as of his recently published series of lithographs *Dans le rêve* and *À Edgar Poe*, which appeared in an edition of 25 and 50 prints respectively—and found hardly any purchasers.

Nevertheless, two voices made themselves heard reporting the exhibition. Emile Hennequin, a relatively little known critic, discovered here *"un nouveau frisson artistique*, the grandiose, sensitive and subtle vision of a master". But whether this *feuilleton* in the *Revue Littéraire et Artistique* (of 4 March 1882) had any further echo is doubtful.

The judgment of another visitor, Joris-Karl Huysmans, was of an entirely different significance. The young novelist had already made a name for himself in the domain of naturalistic social criticism mapped out by his mentor Zola; his powerful language and pregnant phraseology made readers prick up their ears. Having reached a crisis, he sought new attractions, adopted the way of life of an over-refined aestheticism, in a word began to live the life of a cultivated dandy, from which point, incidentally, he soon found his way into the bosom of the Catholic Church. His experience of Redon's work took place precisely at the borderline between the first two periods and was perhaps a decisive factor in the change. After a brief note on the exhibition, there appeared in 1884 his novel *A rebours*, the sensation of the year. What can more deeply satisfy the hero of the story, washed in all the waters of sophisticated pleasure, than to be able to show off among other items in his gallery of "fantastic, uncanny, violent and wild" works of art the drawings of a still unknown contemporary? "These drawings" (Redon's)—we read at the end of a longish description of the recently exhibited items—"were outside of any known category; most of them leap beyond the boundaries of painting, innovating a very special fantasy, a fantasy of sickness and delirium."

This book, the first signal of literary Symbolism and again and again reprinted, stood for a whole generation between the artist and his public, set a stamp upon him and drew him into a 'decadent' literary world against which he could defend himself only inadequately. Thus at the outset of his career he became the victim of a *littérateur* and for many years his reputation suffered as a result. But perhaps Huysmans was right? Certainly he only put into his sensational description what he believed he could see in Redon's work: a monster who was aiding Symbolism. Whatever we may think about it, he saw in Redon only the means, and Redon was on firm ground when he protested against this interpretation and expressed the desire to be evaluated above all as a visual artist. In a letter dated 21 July 1898 (quoted in full on another page), that is to say right at the end of his graphic period, he raised objections to his friends' errors in construing his artistic intentions, saying that his works were created spontaneously and owed nothing to literary ideas picked up second-hand. He describes his method of creating even more vividly in *A soi-même*: "It is only after making an effort of will power to represent with minute care a grass blade, a stone, a branch, the face of an old wall, that I am overcome by the irresistible urge to create something imaginary. External nature, thus assimilated and measured, becomes, by transformation, my source, my ferment."

Redon's art has entered into history under these two aspects. For the first, entirely under the sign of black and white drawing, literary Symbolism had stood godfather: from Huysmans to Mallarmé, Verhaeren and the Brussels circle round Edmond Picard and Octave Maus. It stood firm up to the turn of the century, indeed in some domains right up to the present. The other aspect emerged only gradually, became acute shortly before 1890 through contact with the Post-Impressionist artists Seurat, Gauguin, Bernard, the 'Nabis' and Japanese art, led to the awakening of the decorative element as of colour and found its true fulfilment during the last fifteen years of his life.

The First Albums

Apart from the early etchings, which were produced under the influence and the eye of Rodolphe Bresdin in the mid-Sixties, Redon's graphic work begins with the powerful prelude of the lithographic album *Dans le rêve* of 1879. If we ask ourselves whether the ten prints of the series are homogeneous, whether they represent, so to speak, the various aspects of a single great vision, the answer must be a clear no. There is no link, either iconographic or stylistic, between *False Friendship* (M 33, Pl. 41) and *Sad Ascent* (M 35); they mark rather the two poles of quite distinct pictorial ideas, the beginning and the end, between which come the other prints: four with sharply cut profiles, four others with rotating, flying or resting heads and spheres seen from in front, then again, in complete isolation, the *Three Tree Trunks with the Dice Bearer* (M 31). The first, with its adding together of small elements, minute, almost realistic rendering of detail, and above all the three-layered space and the representation of cast shadows, is still strongly reminiscent of the vision of the minor romantic illustrators such as Grandville. The tree scene too is governed by a perspectivist spatial stage that clearly moves back into the picture. All these are characteristics of Redon's early style not to be found in his later sequences except on rare occasions, when they suggest the insertion of early work.

The Representation of Space

Vision (M 34, Pl. 38) goes a step further. In the foreground there is still the clearly-defined, measurable scenery with two tiny figures; they lead over into the background, of indeterminate depth, which shows the entirely abstract shape of a sphere encircled by a garland of rays. Is this a cosmic eye floating through space, or an image of almighty God, or the sanctuary of marital communion, which biographically the artist was just approaching? All these have been conjectured, all may have played a part in the composition on various pre-artistic planes. The crucial fact is that here, for the first time in Redon's art, a breakthrough has taken place to his own individual graphic style: a basic geometrical shape, here a disc, later a spiral, pointing symbolically to a second, abstract, spiritual world. And at the same time the 'symbolic' space is created out of the darkness by graphic and purely graphic means. The theme is no doubt inspired by Moreau's *Salome with the Apparition of John the Baptist (The Apparition*, Pl. 67), as Sandström has shown, but a comparison between the two drastically demonstrates the fundamentally different orientation of the creator and the illustrator.

The print *Sur la coupe* (M 36), in which the theme of John the Baptist's head is interwoven with that of Orpheus, simplifies layered space still further and condenses the content to a single arabesque in the interplay of the dark charger with the light head. In the remaining six prints the desired 'spaceless' space is then completely realized; there is no longer any forwards or backwards, but only, as in dreams, the floating interpenetration of lost elements, submerged in the darkness of the night, a velvety black. The shadows have vanished, the heads are flying, the petrified profiles standing still, the wide-open eyes fixed upon something transcendental. Here is the true beginning of 'Symbolist' art, if Symbolism does not mean, or does not merely mean, the use of fantastic themes but the unfolding of the imagination in such a way that the content acquires its equivalent, its correspondence in artistic form. Thus there is created by purely visual means the zone of the still vague, of the veil of mystery, the basic theme of a new vision of the world.

On the Bottom of the Sea   1904   P   (435)

The Rôle of the Charcoal Drawings

A study of the charcoal drawings produced during the same period is of great assistance in establishing the order of the various prints in a sequence. There are a whole series of instances in which the drawings are to be considered as a first draught or preliminary sketch for the prints, others where they are almost identical, others again where they differ considerably, and yet others in which the charcoal drawing is entirely independent and has absolutely no parallel among the prints. Numerically—six hundred according to his son's estimate—the drawings exceed the prints several times over, but no small number have been lost and hardly any of them are dated. Nevertheless, there is sufficient evidence for the date of certain drawings, while the latest possible date for the prints is established by the publication of the sequence. Thus, by comparing charcoal drawings and prints, it is possible to establish the main stages of development and to differentiate the earlier from the later prints even within one lithographic series. We know from Redon's own account that the drawings were all produced at his lonely summer residence of Peyrelebade in the heathlands of south-west France (Pls. 42, 43, 44), whereas the 'working out' with the lithographic crayon was reserved for the following winter in Paris.

If, with these thoughts in mind, we study the early charcoal drawings, the earliest of which goes back a full seventeen years before *Dans le rêve*, we observe a remarkable fact: not a trace of the 'symbolic' representation of space is to be seen before the mid-Seventies. Prior to this Redon produced no small number of landscape drawings with trees and occasionally with tiny figures that would have done honour to any nature-lover from the Barbizon group, but nothing more. Then, step by step, one new motif is introduced after the other: the outsize eyes rigidly staring into the beyond, the achievement of the deepest black, the regular geometric bodies, and finally the shrinking of pictorial space. The available material is sufficient to show how each of these features was developed over a period of four years with an almost logical consistency and how then, when the first lithographic sequence appeared in 1879, all the elements are integrated, at least in some prints, into a new vision. The graphic work, far from serving merely to reproduce the charcoal drawings, becomes the true pacemaker of the new style, although the printer's hand is introduced into the process.

The Broadening Out of Redon's Imagination

The second graphic sequence of 1882 bears in its title a dedication to Edgar Allan Poe. An admirer, perhaps Huysmans, had pressed a copy of the *Tales of the Grotesque and Arabesque* into the artist's hand, and if he was not exactly overcome by reading them, what could he do but accompany his prints by captions *à la* Poe, in the same way as the movements of a symphony are headed with the mood and tempo? That he had allowed himself to do this was something Redon later regretted, saying that he had thereby lost his innocence. Of the six visions that make up the series, at least three are striking in their monumental simplification: *The Eye like a Marvellous Balloon, Before the Black Sun of Melancholy* and *A Mask Tolling the Hour of Death* (M 38–40, Pl. 48). The element of mystery is all the more convincing here, because the drawing is firmer, simpler and less stiff, but fundamentally the new series adds nothing fresh to the advanced works of the first sequence. In their dissection of the layers of space, the other three lithographs represent a return to earlier compositional ideas and are doubtless to be looked upon as belated repetitions.

On the whole, the artist's imagination broadens out to an astonishing degree during these years. He easily turns to new subjects and impresses upon them the *cachet* of his and their mystery. *The Masque of the Red Death* (Cat. 609, Pl. 49), a charcoal drawing with no counterpart among the prints and bearing the date 1883, is an evocative composition in which four figures produce such an atmosphere of fear and horror (without a spark of satire or irony, hence entirely unliterary) that we are not surprised to learn what an impression they created at the Brussels Exhibition three years later.

Surrealism

At the same time another lithographic album appeared, *Les origines*, the original edition of which bore no title. Redon declared that he might just as well have called it *Les monstres*, to satisfy his usual customers. It is rich in thematic ideas, enormous eyes rotating on plants, in the firmament or on a cannibal's skull, fabulous horses with wings and the body of a woman, half-humans with fish-tails and a naked man in flight. The whole atmosphere of Surrealist horror is here anticipated and has made this work in particular the favourite of the younger and youngest generation. In his own day, however, Redon had to defend himself against quite a different reproach: having regard to his friendship with the biologist Armand Clavaud, he was suspected of merely exploiting the results of looking at things through the microscope or of having furnished an interpretation of Darwin's theory of evolution. Is he really *engagé* in this sense, as Svenström has recently supposed? Is he really interested in such problems as how life arose on the earth, where the animal is in morphological contact with the plant? The references to Greek mythology in *Pegasus* (M 51), *Centaur* (M 50) and *Siren* (M 48) do not fit in with this thesis at all and merely underline Redon's desire to let his imagination range freely where it will.

It would be interesting to ascertain what constitutes the intellectual significance and unity of the next sequence, to which *Homage to Goya* belongs. No commentary is to be found on this sequence, obviously because neither the relationship to the grotesquerie of the great Spaniard nor the inner unity of the series is immediately evident. Apart from the astonishing print *A Strange Juggler* (M 58, Pl. 50), which continues the earlier 'Surrealism', the other five designs seem to have been taken out of an old portfolio and put together to provide a survey of thematic and stylistic possibilities, old and new.

Tachist Elements

The year 1886 saw the beginning of a revolutionary change. Whereas till now darkness had been the true leitmotif of Redon's compositions, impenetrable darkness against which sharply profiled light forms stand out here and there (or occasionally the other way round, as in *Orpheus over the Waters)* and the design is dominated by the linear pattern of contours and arabesques, this was now radically altered. A soft, pearly, diffuse light without a precise source trickles along the outlines, making them elastic and pliable, forces its way into the dark areas and there forms 'islands of light,' bright arabesques on a black ground that often become independent and by no means always coincide with the shapes of objects. The result is a composition that is more tonal in character, tending towards the painterly; the envelope of light develops within a system of modelling that includes the most brilliant white through all gradations of grey to the deepest velvety black and can almost be called coloured. In contradistinction to the early tree studies (cf. Pl. p. 51) form is not merely seen on a much larger scale, more monumentally, but above all the structure, the building up, from the tiniest detail to the fitting of the figures into the total composition, is much tauter and more consistent. The *Light Profile* among the lithographs (M 61, Pl. 52), or the corresponding charcoal drawing (C. Roger-Marx Collection, Paris), compared with *Orpheus*, show very clearly the changes that had taken place during these five years.

Here we also see with full clarity the stylistic device that has ensured for Redon recognition of his great originality right down to the present: the organization of the picture surface in rich textures or, as they are called today, graphisms. A whole generation of 'Tachists' can find here a model going much further back than Monet's *Waterlilies*. In fact this combination of the decorative with the structural is not only a good way of overcoming the dangers of the objective, representational, illustrative element, it was also, precisely during these decisive years, Redon's most important contribution to Post-Impressionism; it is his own version of the 'synthesis'. Later he enormously enriched this type of composition with pastel, watercolour and oils. Then it became visible to everyone, but the germ was already present here. There can be no doubt that here already he drew inspiration and stimulus from Degas's pastels or Japanese prints, or both together.

HOKUSAI, *Ghost of an Unfaithful Servant.*

In 1883 the large scale exhibition of Japanese prints took place in Paris. A print like this would indicate that Redon was already receiving strong impulses from this source in his own graphic fantasies. His cycle 'Origins' appeared that very year.

Maturity

The series entitled *La nuit* (1886), and even more strongly the seven prints for Edmond Picard's *Le juré* from the following year, together with all the accompanying charcoal drawings still extant, show the new Redon reaching out to a fresh range of imaginative subject matter and at the same time employing incomparably richer means for the orchestration of his graphic work. Unity of theme is even harder to find here than in the preceding sequence. Apart from the not very powerful scene with the waiting priestesses, which has apparently been worked up out of earlier components, all the inhabitants of the night are single and lonely figures, the old man with the features of Leonardo, the priest by the tree, the fallen angel, the terrified chimera, the questioning researcher. They almost all look like old acquaintances whom we have already met in earlier works, and yet each and every one of them is different: from the documentary nucleus, from what the author, the spectator or any sentient being has seen or could see, gruesome, bitter, painful, astounding, or whatever it may be—from this nucleus all obtrusiveness has gone and it is presented in greater purity and increased richness of artistic form. No one need read Picard's book in order to feel the immense magic emitted by Redon's 'illustrations,' and perhaps most strongly where the subject is the most artless, in the print *The wall splits open and a death's head appears* (M 78, Pl. 53). *The Man of the People* (M 75) and the three final prints (M 79–81) are undoubtedly among Redon's most powerful lithographs.

By chance we are in a position to follow the genesis of one of these visions through its various stages, to wit the one captioned: *Must there not be an invisible world?* (M 79, Pl. 57). In a sketch book of 1880, now in the Chicago Museum, there is a sketch made up of elements most probably taken from observations in the Jardin du Luxembourg, Paris: *A Balloon Seller* (Pl. 54), the naked figure of a girl meant to be the genius of truth, a figure taken from some monument, and the stump of a column ornamented with masks (cf. Pl. 55). The artist's imagination immediately transformed it into an 'embryonic' vision. The third step is the charcoal drawing executed several years later (Cat. 654, Pl. 56). A single mask is left, greatly enlarged, stylized in the manner of Gauguin (long before Gauguin's journey to Tahiti, incidentally), the naked girl is enveloped in darkness, and the balloons are now distributed all over the paper and guided by a spiral arabesque. Finally we have the lithograph (Pl. 57), in which the coalescence of the forms under the domination of a painterly approach has gone so far that the synthesis of imagination and natural perception leaps to the eye. The plastic equivalents of symbolic vision, to use the language of the period, are here superb.

48

Scene with Two White Girls   c. 1905   O   (93)

The End of Isolation

The change of style in 1886 must be understood within the wider context of two biographical events of that year: the meeting with Gauguin and relations with the Les XX circle in Brussels. Both mark the end of Redon's isolation and the opening of a door to freedom.

As to Redon's isolation up to this point there can be no doubt. Apart from the tiny group of subscribers to his prints, he was known to the art world almost exclusively through Huysmans's description as a moonstruck outsider. He was, so to speak, the prisoner of the novelist, whose ideas he did not share. True, an acquaintance with Mallarmé, a kindred spirit, had opened up the milieu of the avant-garde to him; but here too he could not help noticing that the titles of his works aroused greater admiration than the compositions themselves.

Meeting with Gauguin

With Gauguin things were quite different. Redon made his acquaintance when they were both exhibiting at the last salon of the Impressionists and he found in him, for the first time, a painter to whom he was linked by the same visual attitude. Certainly, Gauguin had not yet come into contact with van Gogh nor made the decisive breakthrough of his Pont-Aven period, but already everything in him was in ferment. He was already discarding Impressionism, already seeking to fade in the magical image of a second existence over the fleeting sensory impression and the portrayal of nature. The meeting was fruitful for both partners, for they came from opposite directions and met in an intermediate region. Gauguin set out from 'sensuous' colour and wished, like all the Post-Impressionists, to complete it with 'spiritual' structure, order and drawing; in the graphic artist, now and even much later, he admired precisely these qualities, in his spiritually orientated art he discovered a guiding exemplar. Redon, on the other hand, was seeking a way out from his intellectual, private visions; he found the painterly envelope in which to wrap his visions, in a short time colour broke into his work. Which of the two gained more from the encounter is hard to determine, since the effects did not spring from direct influence but from indirect stimuli. All that can be said for sure is that they were strong and reciprocal.

Affinity with Seurat

Although their personal relationship is shrouded in obscurity, Redon's approach to Seurat's work at this juncture is even more tangible. In the previous three years the two artists had twice exhibited together, in the Salon des Indépendants (1884) and now in the last exhibition arranged by the Impressionist group.

Tree   D

As in the past, it was the drawings of the younger man with their sparkling areas in which the contrasts of form are not marked by contours but by varying intensities of light and dark, which attracted Redon. A comparison between *The Dream is Consummated in Death* (M 81, Pl. 58) and the preceding charcoal drawing (Cat. 655, Pl. 59) best shows the direction in which he was advancing; but for the fantastic subject matter, the former might almost bear the signature of the Pointillist himself. Seurat's *La Grande Jatte* (Pl. 74), with its pure colours, complementary contrast and geometrical composition, was at this moment in the forefront of the avant-garde. One might have speculated that it would convert its admirer Redon to colour, but he was not ripe for this until four years later, and more than a decade had to pass before pure colour appears in his work and the objects portrayed undergo a complete transformation.

Le Salon des XX

Even stranger is Redon's relationship to James Ensor, or rather its complete absence. For no artist of that quarter of a century came as close to Redon as the Belgian. The bias towards the fantastic, the predilection for graphic expression, the avoidance of 'Impressionist' atmosphere, these are just a few of the features they have in common in spite of all differences. They must have seen one another's work in 1887. Was Redon not invited to take part in the famous Salon des XX, and did he not come to Brussels in person as the guest of Edmond Picard? Is the explanation to be found in Redon's excessive reserve?

Together with Octave Maus, Picard was the real instigator of this group, which transferred the capital of European Symbolism to Brussels and later, up to 1914, provided a first asylum for most of the modern movements. From Renoir, Cézanne, Seurat, Gauguin, van Gogh, Toulouse-Lautrec, from Monet to Denis, Ensor, Munch, from Liebermann to Hodler, from Marquet to Matisse, from Rodin to Minne, from Vuillard to Derain, all enjoyed here an early chance to present their work before an understanding and prepared community. Here the poets, the critics, the musicians, the architects, the creators of the Art Nouveau style met for joint presentations, here was the nucleus of so much that still seems to be determining trends today, here the synthesis of the modern style was born. The report given by Madeleine Octave Maus in her book *Trente années de lutte pour l'art 1884–1914* is a truly astonishing document.

For Redon contact with Les XX had several decisive results. Overnight, so to speak, he became famous throughout Europe; hitherto he had been notorious only in France and among readers of the 'decadent' literature. His drawings were acquired by collectors; the Belgian Symbolist poets Jules Destrée, Ivan Gilkin, F. Herold and Verhaeren, following Picard's example, wished to have their works illustrated by him or at least furnished with a vignette. The press notices, long reviews, piled up. According to Mellerio's carefully compiled list

Red Boat with Blue Sail   1906–07   O   (220)

thirty criticisms appeared in the one year 1886/87, twice as many as all those that had appeared in the preceding quarter of a century. A Belgian publisher took the initiative and commissioned Redon to produce a series of prints revolving round Flaubert's *Temptation of Saint Anthony*. This was to become the true crown of his work in black and white.

The misunderstood outsider of yesterday had suddenly become one of the forerunners of modern movements which, under the name of Symbolism, came into the foreground in literature, art and music. But he did not take up the rôle of champion and leader that lay at his feet. If he had been capable now of fully mastering abstract colour and its organization into decorative compositions, instead of suggesting them in the black and white of lithography, if, in other words, his later works had been produced twenty years earlier, he could have gone down in history as a pioneer of modern art. In any case it is fruitless to speculate about this; an exceptional reserve gave his early work a special *cachet* and subsequently prevented him from extending his range. It was his fate to be both too early and too late.

Redon's Belated Rôle

We can thus understand how it came about that he was present at the decisive breakthroughs of this decade—Gauguin's 'Cloisonnisme', the revelation of the principles of Japanese art in Paris and the unfolding of the flat-pattern style of Art Nouveau in Brussels—while the fruits of these new developments did not ripen in his own work until very much later. To begin with, he was content to remain for a long time a lithographer and, when we look at his output as a whole, we find that at this stage he had only completed eighty graphic works out of a total of two hundred and six. The greater part still lay ahead of him, but from now on everything seemed to go more easily. He no longer had to supply a pound of his own flesh with every lithograph he let out. His visions are more pictorial, he is less personally involved in them, the how is just as interesting as the what. Are we deceiving ourselves if we observe that the cruel, grim and bitter faces of the past have now grown milder?

In the eleven prints composing *The Temptation of Saint Anthony* (1888) at least three (M 85, 92/93) represent a return to earlier ideas and forms. The eye rolling through the cosmos, Christ encircled by the nimbus, and the Devil with the little creatures in his arms, are old friends. The *Astral Fantasy* (M 91), *White Woman's Body with Death's Head* (M 89, Pl. 39) and *The Green-Eyed Chimera* (M 90, Pl. 37), on the other hand, point to new paths. They are velvety and colourful, in so far as a black and white work can be colourful; there is nothing left of the wiry rigidity of the first works. They are totally immersed in the medium of the print; all arabesque, all texture, all flat areas, they no longer rise up out of the picture surface; thus they are completely decorative, no longer expressive and disquieting, entirely under control, entirely classical.

54

Already the following year the sequel appeared under title *To Gustave Flaubert*. This series contains the famous print showing Death, who declares: *My irony exceeds all others* (M 97, Pl. 40). Its great wavy line, exactly contemporaneous with van Gogh's starry sky furrowed by curves, has rightly been singled out as one of the earliest symbols of the newly arisen Jugendstil or Art Nouveau. The very next one, *Bodies like Pictures* (M 98, Pl. 60), with its bold texture and free arrangement, seems to prefigure the automatism that was to become such a feature of the art of our century, suggesting a Paul Klee *avant la lettre*. A single print, *Pegasus as a Prisoner* (M 102), bears witness to the relaxation of tension that was just beginning to make itself felt and points to a range of subject matter that unfolded to the full fifteen years later. With *Woman with closed Eyes* (107), dated 1890, the point was reached at which the black and white print was transmuted into colour. A few oil paintings (Pl. 17) and pastels represent variations on the same theme. No break is to be observed, we have rather the impression that the deep black of the past has turned into a paler violet, for a little while longer the paint and the chalk retain their graphic character.

Many charcoal drawings of this period have recently come to light; after 1893 those that had not already gone to foreign, mainly Belgian and Dutch, collections were bought up lock, stock and barrel by the insatiable young art dealer Ambroise Vollard and until his death in 1939 remained more or less permanently in his archives. Compared with the prints of the same period they show less perfection and discipline but a greater range of ideas, experiments, new twists. The 'thaw' that took place after 1886 is here demonstrated in the most various directions. We will mention just a few. *The Resurrection of Lazarus* (Pl. 61), which can probably be dated 1885, is a highly interesting piece tending towards what the French call *l'esprit de géometrie*. Not very far from Seurat, and yet completely a Redon, it contains elements of which, unfortunately, there are no traces in his prints. *Tree Face* (Cat. 639, Pl. 62), from the copious and particularly high-quality Redon collection in the Art Institute of Chicago, leans towards the other pole, is vibrant with light and a triumph of *l'esprit de finesse* over the brittle material of the charcoal. The *Woman with a Snake* in a door shaped like a uterus and resembling the letter R will perhaps be of especial interest to psychoanalysts as a document of sexual distress (in the Rijksmuseum Kröller Müller). A *Woman Inhaling the Scent of a Flower* (Roger-Marx Collection, Paris) anticipates a large part of Gauguin with its charm of 'primitive' drawing and wild, exotic approach. In short, a more universal spectrum of people and events is revealed than ever before.

Crisis

The next phase, the Nineties, has been interpreted by medical and biological criteria as a period of crisis. This is also true from an art historical point of view when we recall the wide variety of aspects under which Redon's output

now appears: the gradual drying up of his printmaking, his illness and religious impulse, his outward success and popularity with art lovers, and his difficult changeover to colour.

First the graphic works. The sets now appear in larger editions and at a faster rate. In 1891 *Songes (Dreams)* in six prints, in the next three years sixteen single prints, then in 1896, after his illness, the last instalment of *The Temptation* with twenty-four prints, and *The Haunted House* (Pl. 64) with six, and finally *The Apocalypse* (12) bearing the publication date 1899 (Pl. 65) but worked on and discussed with the instigator Vollard at least two years earlier. If we survey the whole group we are struck by two facts. On the one hand we find here the most mature works ever to come from Redon's lithographic crayon: the style based on the use of light, which he had embarked upon earlier, appears here more and more velvety, richer in tones, simpler in drawing. His relationship to his subject becomes more and more free, his

56

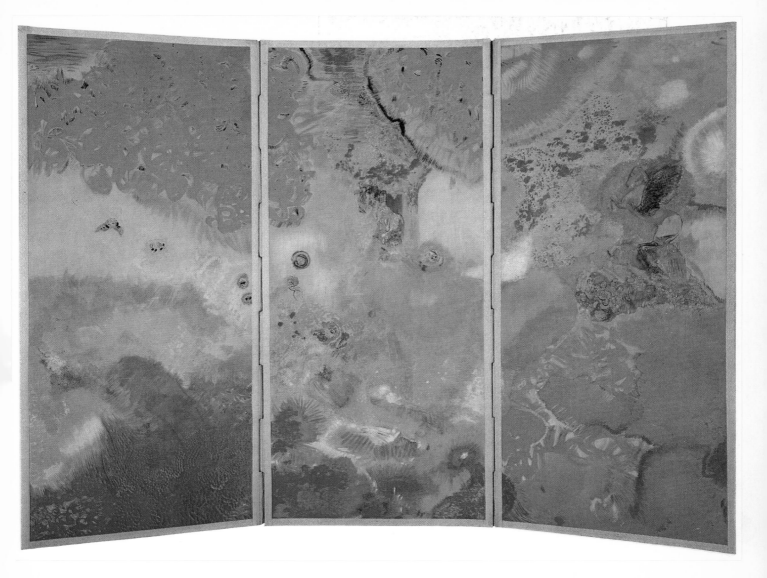

The Red Screen   1906–08   O   (324)

vision of the immaterial world more and more magnificent and precise (*Pegasus*, M 122, *Ear Cell*, M 126; from *The Temptation III*, M 138, 147, 148, 149, 154, 155, 156; from *The Haunted House*, M 161, 162, 164; from *The Apocalypse*, M 178 (Pl. 65), 179, 181, 182, 183, 184). It is like a last magnificent fanfare of trumpets.

Alongside these, a new trend becomes visible after 1890—the vignettelike drawing composed of flourishes with the charm of Art Nouveau but light in weight (M 131, 134, 145, 146, 159, 160, 166, 167, 172, 173, 186, 187, 188, 198, 200, 202). The rich 'colour' is over and done with.

A third group includes unassuming, more or less personal pen sketches, which are reproduced in simple graphic fashion (M 110, 115, 120, 121, 125, 129, 130, 133, 137, 144, 150, 157, 163, 168, 169, 170, 171, 199). The remainder, an appreciable remainder and by far the majority, appears to be brought together from remainders of all previous periods with their ideas and ways of seeing. Are we not reminded in some cases of charcoal drawings dated a quarter century earlier?

Thus, however highly we evaluate Redon's late prints, we must not forget that disintegration had already been preparing under cover for a long time. Hence the switch over from black and white to colour is not to be construed either as a psychological miracle nor as a break in the world of his ideas—although this is also involved; artistically speaking it is a matter of abandoning one phase for the next, or better, of thoughtful, consistent development.

It is difficult to judge from the published letters what part Redon's illness of 1895 played in stimulating or letting loose the new phase. The long-desired one-man show in such an esteemed gallery as Durand-Ruel's, a fresh invitation to Brussels to the Libre Esthétique, the successor to Les XX, and a further invitation to The Hague could only have helped to raise his spirits. He was now an artist who had arrived; he could count on any number of foolish voices in the press and one or two intelligent ones; a first catalogue of his prints appeared and from now on he could scarcely escape the fate of classification. On the other hand, the destiny of Peyrelebade hung disquietingly over his head. The unviable estate in the gloomy 'Celtic' heathland had been the scene of his lonely childhood, full of difficult and important experiences; for the last two decades he had found there every summer the inspiration for his strange charcoal drawings. The loss of Peyrelebade that now threatened tore asunder his last link with his mother and brothers, joint owners with him, and literally pulled the foundations of his imagination from under his feet. Is it then so extraordinary that after the loss of Peyrelebade the 'daemonic' Redon had played out his rôle and could never produce another piece of work in black and white?

Religious Disquiet

If the religious unrest of the decade that began in 1895 had been solely Redon's personal problem, it would be fairly easily dealt with. In reality it was a part and an expression of a social crisis that cast a shadow on the 'Gay Nineties' in almost every sphere of existence throughout Western Europe. Perhaps it was caused, directly and indirectly, by the painful transformation wrought by the increasing bureaucratization and technicization of life. Symbolism, with its claim to the realm of creative imagination, must be understood first of all as a healthy reaction against the malpractices of Naturalism. But then the situation came to a head. The Belgian Symbolists, Picard, Henry van der Velde and others, allied themselves with the Socialist opposition and began to take an interest in the social aspects of the crafts. Their French colleagues, on the other hand, looked in the direction of a strict Catholicism, mysticism and even esoteric occultism. As early as 1889 Schuré's study *Les grands initiés* had given a tremendous impetus and an intellectual backbone to all esoteric trends. After Huysmans had set the example, it was the order of the day for intellectuals to be converted and even to explore the mysteries of the Black Mass. Sâr Péladan was then a great spiritual power in Paris. In 1892 the Rose-Croix Salon was founded as a centre for artists sympathetic to the Rosicrucian idea. In 1894 the Affaire

Dreyfus broke out and drew people from all walks of life and spheres of activity into the vortex, into the struggle between the two sides of France that did not end in an armistice until eleven years later, with the separation of State and Church. Who then can be surprised that Redon too felt himself under pressure, especially as in his immediate environment his friends and patrons Maurice Denis, Emile Bernard, Paul Sérusier, Francis Jammes, Gabriel Frizeau, one after the other, returned to the bosom of the Church?

Prior to the publication of the correspondence (see Bibliography Nos 4 and 17) and Roseline Bacou's well-informed commentary, this aspect of Redon's career remained in darkness. Now we can see more clearly that although he could certainly not exclude the religious element from his conception of art, he could equally certainly not surrender himself to any restrictive communion, not even that of the Catholic Church. His independence was his dearest possession. It had obviously taken him many years to be able to see clearly in this field. Only when Frizeau's conversion raised the question for him too, did he draw a clear dividing-line, not in their friendly relations, but all the more sharply in regard to the philosophical standpoint. This moment was for him the end of his religious crisis and of biblical themes. Buddha and Apollo were the victors.

It must be clearly stated here that it would be altogether mistaken to attribute to Redon a religious message that affected his art. The essential thing for Redon was his art, everything else was subordinate to it. In this respect he was entirely European, entirely Western. Wisely, he never trod the path that led to Schuré, the subsequent translator of Rudolf Steiner, and to Eastern mysticism. His spiritualization of art is something quite different from the confusion of art with abstraction so popular today. Abstraction has been since the beginning an effective method of composition; to raise it to the status of an end in itself, to turn it into a pseudo-religion, was left to a late century that replied to the march of the machines with a progressive breakdown of values.

The Friendship of Emile Bernard

One more word regarding his friendship with Emile Bernard. There was no other painter with whom he was on friendlier terms or corresponded for longer than with Bernard, a generation younger than himself, who formed a link with Cézanne, van Gogh and Gauguin; their first meeting took place in 1889, that is to say at a moment when Symbolism in art was being propounded as a system, a theory and a programme. Bernard and Gauguin were just quarrelling over their respective priority in evolving 'Synthetism'. Never did Redon find a more ardent admirer, and one moreover who several times took up the pen to explain

13 Seated Woman in the Forest   c. 1875   O   (10)

14   Cliffs at Ebbe   1880   O   (30)

15 At the Harbour of Morgat 1882 O (28)

16 The Heart of Jesus 1895 P (352)

17 With Closed Eyes c. 1895 O (56)

18 The Cyclops   1898–1900 (1898)   O   (65)

19 The House at Peyrelebade   1895–98   O   (44)

20 Ari in a Sailor Suit 1897 O (185)

21 The Astrakhan Coat. Marie Botkin 1900 P (392)

22   Madame Arthur Fontaine   1901   P   (593)

23 Eve 1904 O (169)

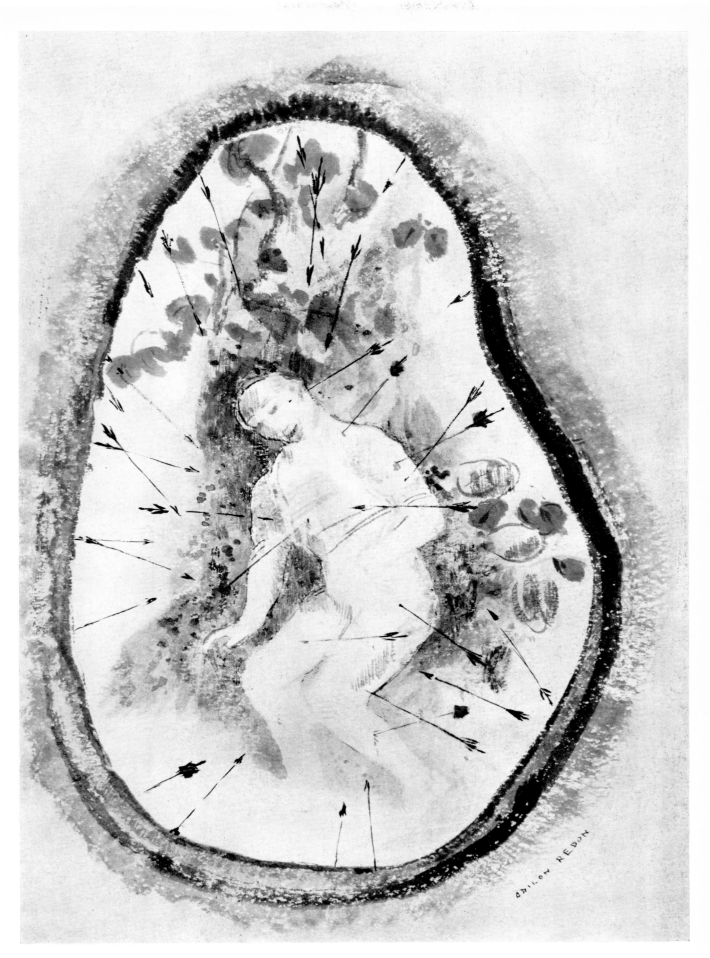

24   The Mystic Personality of Saint Sebastian   before 1910   W   (534)

25 The Green Rider   c. 1904   P   (372)

à mon ami Alfred Maille

ODILON REDON

26 Flower Still-Life   1866–68   O   (241a)

27   Saint George   before 1910   P   (363)

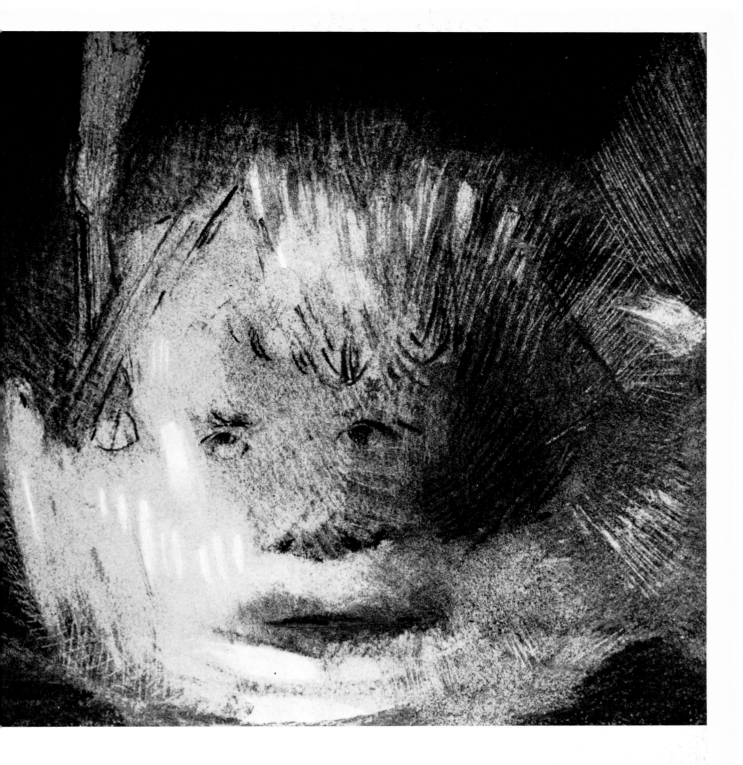

27a Detail from Pl. 27

28   Buddha Wandering among Flowers   1905   P   (369)

Homage to Leonardo da Vinci   c. 1908   29a   Detail from Pl. 29

30   The Prisoner   1910   O   (69)

31   Saint George and the Dragon   c. 1907 (c. 1910)   O   (134)

32   Three vases of Flowers   c. 1908–10   P   (475)

33 The Cathedral 1912 O (211)

34 Butterflies 1910 O (299)

34a Detail from Pl. 34

35 White Vase with Flowers 1916 P (497)

the older man's importance to a still hesitant public and to propagate his fame. Unfortunately he understood him no better than Huysmans had done in his day. There exist private marginal notes in Redon's hand to a longish article by Bernard in *L'Occident* that make mincemeat of one 'literary' argument after the other and really boil down to variations on the sentence: "All this is not true" (published by Rewald, see Bibliography No. 81). Emile Bernard, once a promising member of the avant-garde, then a disappointing academic painter, can be considered the *commis voyageur* of modern theories. His friendship with Redon continued so unclouded only because the latter preserved his usual reserve in artistic matters, because, as always, he kept quiet.

The same reasons explain his cordial relations with those whom he was accustomed to call *mes amateurs*. His friends in Belgium were joined by the Dutchman Andries Bonger, Théo van Gogh's brother-in-law, and in the South of France, besides Frizeau in Bordeaux, above all by Gustave Fayet in Béziers, one of the first collectors of Post-Impressionist art on a grand scale, and in Paris by Arthur Fontaine. No painter of his generation was on such intimate terms with his collectors as Redon, but with none of them did he enter into discussions on the theory of art. All the ideas about art which Redon expressed are to be found in the monologue of his confessions and intimate jottings.

The Nineties

The transition to colour that marks Redon's late works is the result of an increasing use of pastels, watercolours and oil paints and is accompanied by a steady decrease and finally abandonment of the use of charcoal and lithography. The Nineties are particularly interesting as the only period during which the two activities ran concurrently. In many respects the pastels may be looked upon as expanded charcoal drawings; both demand a non-transparent, opaque surface treatment, both set limits on 'open' form. In fact Redon took out a number of older black and white drawings and went over them with coloured chalk; but the graphic work from *The Temptation* to *The Apocalypse* with its painterly style, as well as the corresponding drawings, were searched for colour elements and religious themes and transposed with unaccustomed emphasis into the new medium. The image of Christ which he was looking for revolved round *The Crown of Thorns* and *The Heart of Jesus* (cf Cat. 352, Pl. 16). It contains more human empathy and more Expressionism than anything he produced either before or after. Did his acquaintance with the art of van Gogh and Rembrandt foster this advance precisely during these years? We can observe one typical feature: a pictorial idea, once found, is henceforth presented in several variations, in the same medium or in another.

Pre-Raphaelites and Primitives

Other themes, taken over in particular from *The Temptation* and developed further, are the sea monster, centaurs, Pegasus and especially the austere profile of a girl. This ever-recurring motif that undergoes every kind of transformation comes from the English Pre-Raphaelites and at the same time from their exemplars, the early Italians. In 1892 an exhibition of the works of Burne-Jones was held in Paris which drew much attention to this the best draughtsman of the group and made him appear very 'up-to-date'. Three years later Redon himself went for a short time to London and must there have gathered further impressions in this direction. His lively interest in the 'Florentine' primitives is clear from an entry in the sketchbook of 1880 now preserved in Chicago, in which the present author found a rather long list of artists of whom Redon obviously intended to make a special study in the Louvre or elsewhere. Along with Giotto, Gaddi, 'les Lorenzetti', Orcagna, the list includes Fra Angelico, Squarcione, Uccello, della Francesca, Masaccio, Botticelli, Gentile da Fabriano and 'Pesenillo'. Pisanello is missing; his important portrait of a princess, as may be ascertained, did not come into the museum's possession until 1893. There is no need to be surprised at the affinity which Redon felt himself to have with the 'draughtsmanly' painters. Redon was faced just then with similar problems.

Redon Begins to Paint

In the course of this decade Redon began only slowly to paint, following upon his adoption of pastels. Not that the artist was unfamiliar with the brush. After his death an almost countless number of small, intimate nature studies, on wood or cardboard, came to light, ranging from his earliest beginnings to the most recent past (cf *Cliffs at Ebbe*; *The Harbour of Morgat*; *The House at Peyrelebade*; Pls 14, 15, 19). Charming as they often are, these mood impressions reminiscent of Chintreuil or the Barbizon Group have almost nothing to do with new problems—namely to construct the picture out of authentic elements of form and colour as an object in its own right, rather than as a representation. No one pondered on this longer than Redon, but it is a somewhat different matter whether one seeks to exhaust the possibilities of the graphic idiom in relation to certain daemonic visions, or whether one is trying to extract a symbolic content from colour and at the same time remain in the world of the senses. All the same, he was no longer alone in this situation. The breakthrough of Gauguin and Seurat could serve him as a signpost, and his friends the Nabis were battling for the same things.

Hence it is highly remarkable and at the same time quite natural that in his new pictures he neither referred back to his early copies and studies after

Seahorse in an Undersea Landscape   before 1909   P   (438)

Delacroix, nor was greatly aided by free transpositions from his prints into oils (*The Thought on the Summit of the World*, *Head with Owls*, *Prayer*, *Caliban's Dream*, *Winged Demon*, *Despair*, *Oannes*, etc.), but scored his most successful hit in a portrait, *Ari in a Sailor Suit*, of 1897 (Cat. 185, Pl. 20). In the organization of the picture surface, as R. Bacou has noted, this portrait is reminiscent of the Nabis, particularly of Bonnard. In fact it is striking how the fragmentary abridgement of the figure to a few curves in the right-hand column, based on the arabesque of the collar, in counterpoint to the free treatment of the rest of the picture surface, here discloses the essence of the person without getting lost in psychological details. It is a new way of bringing out the pictorial equivalents. In contrast to the restrained colours of this picture we see the loud, impasto, dramatically contrasting colour complexes in *The Cyclops* (Cat. 65, Pl. 18) painted at almost the same time. The extended area in the centre, a strong violet, is flanked by two green areas; two yellow-gold passages on a different axis mark the silhouette of the Cyclops and of the naked woman; here Expressionism is at work again, merely muted by the flat-pattern effect. It is as though these two principles were pulling the picture in different directions. In more than one respect, this impressive work stands at a turning-point in Redon's career. Thematically it allows a backward glance to the exciting subjects of his early graphic years; it is full of daemonic tension; in the loose treatment of light it resembles the last charcoal drawings; in the bold colour effects it anticipates much of the coming decorative mode of composition.

Flower-Pieces

All tensions relaxed with the beginning of the new century. There was the experience of a trip to Venice, the beginning of the flower-pieces, the first decorative wall paintings, the emergence of light, transparent watercolours. The demons have retired. Never did he produce such a gay, almost coquette portrait as that of his young Russian friend *Marie Botkin* of 1900 (Cat. 392, Pl. 21). Even the religious motifs lose heaviness: the *Holy Women in the Bark*, from one variation to another, become smaller and smaller as figures; what remains and grows is the sea in its infinite deep blue and the red of a sail.

The flower-pieces afford the best means of studying the development of the period of colour that occupied Redon's last years; they constitute the red thread running through his late art (Pl. pp. 115, 119). Stylistic changes first show themselves in the pastels with their greater possibility of spontaneity, the oil paintings generally follow; the dating is not always easy, because the various phases partially overlap and interprenetrate, especially in the oil paintings. Virtually no attempt has been made up to now to arrange them in order from the viewpoint of artistic form. Roseline Bacou, for example, placed a whole

Woman among Flowers   1909–10   P   (516)

series of these works on one occasion at the beginning of this period and on another occassion quite near the end; the date varies as between her study based upon an earlier dissertation (see Bibliography No. 17) or her catalogue for an exhibition in Paris the same year.

In any case, three stylistic stages can be clearly distinguished. The first up to 1904, takes tangible forms and local colour as its starting-point, summing up as it were the flowers and their species, the leaves, the outline of the vase, a stand or table, and indicating space by cast shadows that create depth; this stage could be described as objective, if imagination had not cast over the composition a shower of improbable turquoise blue, orange, pink, violet, bottle-green. The second stage up to 1909/10 no longer starts from the object but from the decorative organization of the surface. Carrying on the style of the late lithographs and charcoal drawings, there is no longer any movement back into depth here, space has been reduced to a flat surface. Top and bottom also lose their importance, even when looked at from the side or stood on its head, the work retains its unity, which relies upon the interplay of textures, graphisms, arabesques. Choice flowers of fantasy that no gardener ever saw, abstract forms, underwater landscapes are combined with the ordinary flora into a fabric in which sharply outlined cloisonné shapes, structured stalks and the like determine the arrangement. The vases seem to be floating, the central axis is frequently abandoned, the shadows disappear, the juxtaposition of moist, opalescent patches of colour, all this suggests a fresh wave of Eastern Asian influence. Japanese coloured woodcuts helped Redon to gain his freedom. The great bunches of wild flowers of these years display simultaneously a degree of symphonic richness and harmonic purity never seen before in his work. On his second Italian journey he was drawn to Ravenna. A pastel entitled *In Memory of the Ravenna Mosaics* indicates the impression made upon him by the sparkling little stones and their abstract drawing.

In illustration of this point we may quote from the excellent analysis by Tristan Klingsor, the only writer up to the present to deal with Redon's style, though unfortunately too briefly *(La peinture*, p. 13): "What has perhaps up to now been less noticed in him is the striving after drawing. He rests his tones upon firmly outlined strokes. In portraying a flower he is not content with a vague patch (tache), he desires a highly significant contour. More than this, with the rubbing of the pastel he often mingles a decisive stroke, in order to mark out the form. A charming game in which the imprecise is associated with the precise. No other artist has presented us with such striking examples of this."

In this same period, 1908, fall the commissions for the Gobelins factory. Its understanding manager, the great art critic Gustave Geoffroy, a friend of Monet and Cézanne, recognized the possibility of filling the old tradition of an artistic handicraft with a modern formal content. With a sure eye, he called upon the artist with the greatest gift for decoration and thereby opened up a further field to his decorative style. At least eight armchair covers and tapestries were delivered as cartoons and then carried out. For Redon this work meant the necessity to further simplify his drawing and even his colour, but after all that had gone before it involved no change of direction.

The last phase constitutes a kind of synthesis between the first and second, the spatial and the decorative. He moved into a summer residence in the Paris suburb of Bièvres. Every morning he found the fragrant plants of the Ile de France on his table, this time they were cultivated garden flowers. A new realism may be perceived in his approach to his subject matter, but the painterly, shimmering vagueness and even the bold 'Japanese' assymetry vanish from his treatment. Instead a crystalline structure becomes the true bearer of the colourful radiance that has lost nothing of its luminosity, quite the reverse. If Impressionism gained richly hued colour solely from the reflections of light, a breakthrough has here taken place into an objective colour that is firmly based on construction.

Because at this stage he elaborates his compositions out of a coalescence of colour and graphic elements, Redon can afford to tread less warily in handling the objective content of the picture. The antinomy between abstract and concrete falls away. These works are comparatively more designed (abstract) and more object-related (concrete) than earlier ones. Here the artistic transformation no longer leads away from the object, but straight to it; these are no longer 'ordinary' objects, however, but are at the same time magically enchanted. With the imagination of the artist, we see these flowers as if we had never perceived them before, they are here revealed to us in their reality and introduced to us in their essence as colours, as forms, as order, as organisms. In a different way they are just as mysterious as the dramatic charcoal drawings of the past.

The New Climate of Art

There can be no doubt that the colour period with its lively development and so much richer output can only have come about in conjunction with the total artistic situation of the epoch. Up to the turn of the century, Redon was more or less an outsider. For each of his works he struggled on his own, even the Post-Impressionists who were closest to him were still fighting at isolated outposts of the avant-garde. But around 1900 the decorative movement of Art Nouveau, like the great retrospective exhibitions of Gauguin (1906) and Cézanne (1907), created a new climate of art. All those who regarded correct or pleasing portrayal as the basic condition of good painting were now forced onto the defensive. How else can Cézanne's triumph be explained? With the Nabis and the Fauves two trends developed which carried on the principle of structural colour in their own way and both of which had affinities with Redon. That the arrangement of colours comes before the warhorse, to recall Denis's phrase, has meanwhile become an axiom of contemporary art. Redon's late style is a fine example of this; it developed with such luxuriance because it was accompanied by the upsurge of the younger men.

Another question is where it developed from, where its origins lay. There are good grounds for concluding that a lone wolf like Redon evolved his colourful late style out of his own internal preconditions, that the style of the first pastels arises logically out of the last charcoal drawings, that the change of subject matter played only a secondary rôle, and that here we see an unbroken personality which should not be torn to pieces by analysis. Elsewhere I have placed this argument in the foreground. If we also take into consideration his rather stringent and by no means just judgment on Cézanne and Gauguin, this view becomes further reinforced. And yet we cannot overlook the fact that without Gauguin, Redon would have been a different artist. It was not the Gauguin of Tahiti who influenced Redon, but his much less well known period of Pont-Aven and Le Poldu prior to this. It was not the protesting Gauguin preaching the gospel of the primitive way of life, the Savonarola, the *engagé* accuser of his time and civilization, but the pioneer of a new mode of composition, the artist who reinterpreted Cézanne's structural approach to achieve a carpetlike decorative style. From the *Vision after the Sermon* (Pl. 75) a straighter path leads to the later art of Redon than to that of Gauguin himself. Or, looking at it from a different angle, must we not admit that in their use of pure colour and outline Matisse and the other Fauves draw upon Redon and Gauguin's Britanny period and could dispense entirely with his Tahitian paintings?

Japanese Influence

Without Gauguin, without the Japanese influence and without the decorative tendencies of Art Nouveau, Redon's late style would be suspended in mid-air. These three forces operate in the same direction and, each in its own way, help to overcome Redon's black, 'Surrealist,' anxiety-conditioned manner of the past. At the same time it must be said that what is involved is no direct dependence as to detail, no imitation that might restrict him, but a natural succession and an original synthesis that unfolds his own individual qualities.

In fact the rich development of his imagination in his seventh and eighth decade is an astounding phenomenon. The world of flowers with its never repeated, always new and creatively seen forms and colours is by no means the only theme of these years. For reasons of clarity and simplification it has been dealt with in advance. It remains to be shown how the 'light profile' (cf Pl. 52) was already in evidence at the time of the late charcoal drawings, continues to assert itself through the various metamorphoses, how it is combined with the flower-pieces, first stands out in depth, is then fused decoratively with the other elements or becomes 'magically' transfigured. At the same time one has the impression that the true imaginative accent rests upon the frame of flowers and that the face is rendered with little expression and at times sinks to the level of an almost stereotyped existence. A careful selection of the more power-

Black Vase with Flowers   c. 1909   P   (477)

fully inspired pieces, of which incidentally there is no lack, is entirely in place here. The same is true of the not infrequent girls' profiles under a vaulted arch, with or without the addition of flowers, a motif which had accompanied him ever since the 'mystic dialogues' of his religious period and which had a different significance in the phase before the turn of the century when Redon was dealing with ideas. A 'decorative' face is always in danger of appearing empty.

Wonders of the Sea

All the more convincing by contrast is another group of works which, starting in 1904, introduces a world that is new in both style and subject matter: the wonders of the sea. Fishes, shells, sea horses, strange plants growing on the bed of the ocean, seaweedlike growths, flowerlike abstractions, all of them as though swimming in confusion, are immersed with dreamlike preciseness in the most improbable tones, green, violet, pink, purple, white (Pls pp. 43, 87, 107). Everything seems to be floating and yet sits so securely in its position that one would not like to move it a millimetre. A fantasy without subjective arbitrariness, a reality without reportage-style indiscretion, an extension of familiar colours and shapes, seems here to be revealed. The immediate charm of the water-colour with transparent and opalescent tones, the pastel, often in an unusual, almost square format, taking in a whole cosmos, the oil painting in the mosaic of its areas of pure colour, all these reach an astonishing level of development. Perhaps we see these things with especial delight because in their modernity they anticipate the art of half a century and allow those who believe in abstraction as a means but not as an end in itself to demonstrate that art and the spattering of paint are not necessarily identical. Speaking strictly iconographically, some of these motifs are already to be found in *The Temptation of Saint Anthony* at the end of the graphic period. But what has become of them in the meantime, what colours and universal dimensions they have acquired! Biographically speaking it can be established that the inspiration is drawn from experience of the ocean, from the summer holidays which Redon had been spending and enjoying by the sea since 1900, and particularly from the many visits he paid to the aquarium at Arcachon. Artistically speaking, however, the inspiration was of course once more Japan with its long tradition of fish themes and the like.

From the same source there also flow the beautiful series of butterfly pictures (Cat. 299, Pl. 34), treated entirely decoratively and yet with an interest in the various species, shapes and textures, that is to say seen as 'magical' realities in just the same way as the last flower-pieces. Chronologically, they bring to an end the wonders of the sea, are to be dated after 1909 and belong locally to the Bièvres period.

94

Apollo's Sun Chariot with Four Horses and a Dragon   c. 1910   O   (164)

Decoration

Experiment with new formats, square in this case, has already been pointed to above as a sign of stylistic mobility. Even more striking are the high and narrow proportions which again are borrowed from the scroll paintings of the Far East and occur quite frequently. Sometimes they are framed pictures, at other times folding-screens or mural paintings. In them Redon's decoratively determined compositions in colour reach their true fulfilment. They number in all over a hundred, bearing in mind that the first of these commissions alone—and interestingly enough it really was a commission for a specific wall—for the Château Domecy in Burgundy, comprizes eighteen wall panels, each one 8′ 3″ high. This aspect of Redon's work, certainly not the least important, is the least known and deserves to be the best known. In the literature on the painter, with one exception, it is not mentioned at all; the format makes reproduction difficult, the fact that the works are attached to walls hinders exhibition. But even the more mobile folding-screens have escaped notice. Nothing would be calculated to afford a better idea of Redon's work in colour, of its compass, modernity and decorative foundations. They include all the themes already mentioned, all formats and all three styles (cf Pls pp. 56, 57).

One important theme must be added. This is the *Buddha* in many variations (cf Cat. 369, Pl. 28). It too is drawn from the last graphic phase, but it returns with the decline of the religious crisis. What Spinoza meant to the youth under Clavaud's influence was represented for the mature man by the Indian sage. When Redon the artist turned his eyes towards Asia this was more than a mere aesthetic titillation. The first signs of the crisis in Western culture, of which the rise of modern art is a healthy symptom, frequently led to eyes being turned towards its sources. For our Symbolist, Buddha was a favourite symbol of life, rebirth, creativity.

Tradition

It would, however, be quite wrong to see in Redon a deserter to Asia, in art or in life. His 'Japanese' orientation is counterbalanced by an equally important group of paintings and pastels in which the European heritage seeks its new mythological and physical embodiment. At the high-point of his decorative period, 1907—1910, we find the legend of *Phaeton's Fall* or of his triumph in *Apollo's Sun Chariot*, *The Drama of Pegasus*, *Pandora*, or *The Freeing of Andromeda*. We may consider such themes too literary and antiquated in the early years of Cubism, until we have really seen them in colour and on the wall. Then, in their decorative remoteness, we shall understand them better as the evening glow of a vanishing tradition to which Redon was just as closely linked as the majority of his artistically revolutionary contemporaries. It must

96

be clearly borne in mind that as a painter Odilon Redon did not become either a Japanese or a Tachist—this least of all—but he did take his own part, even if belatedly, in the magnificent artistic upsurge of the immediate past. It was the inclusion of the Japanese-decorative element that first clarified and enriched his own style, that ensured artistic livingspace for his almost innate Symbolism. In the breakthrough of modern art from the portrayal of sensory perceptions to the creation of a spiritual reality he stated his own message, alongside Cézanne, Seurat, Gauguin, van Gogh, a message that may be summed up in the words of Baudelaire as *luxe, calme et volupté*.

III Neglect and Posthumous Fame

Life

Nothing has been said so far about Redon's life story. According to his own wish it was to retire behind his work; apart from discreet jottings he never divulged anything. Sensational confessions and astounding revelations are not to be found among these notes; neither erotic debauches nor a wild Bohemian life, neither the thrill of Black Masses nor the mystic fervour of contrition are breathed from these pages. And yet from the beginning everyone guessed at a dark background in the work and life of this outsider. Not for nothing had his fame come from Huysman's milieu as portrayed in *Against the Grain*.

How great was the astonishment in Brussels when the exhibition with the flying heads and dancing skeletons had set minds in tumult and then the artist appeared in person: a solid citizen, no longer young, normally dressed, and with a well—kept full beard. A rebel, a dissolute genius had been expected; a patriarch in the making came.

His later visitors were surprised to find him not in a café in Montparnasse or Montmartre, but in a good bourgeois house by the Monceau Park. It must have been around 1912 when the Hahnlosers from Switzerland rang the doorbell of this house, had the door opened to them by a dignified old gentleman and on asking for his son received the reply: "If you wish to speak to the painter Odilon Redon, I am he."

In other words, Redon's life is devoid of all the dramatic incidents and daemonic features which nowadays people like to imagine in connexion with artists of his type. The outer events of his biography are quickly stated. He was born in 1840 in Bordeaux of a well-to-do family; his father had acquired a considerable fortune as a colonist in the south of the United States. His mother came from there, from the French population of New Orleans; he never seems to have been on good terms with her. Peyrelebade came to be of fateful significance for him. On this lonely wine-growing estate amidst the heath of Les Landes he spent the first eleven years of his childhood in the care of an uncle and later, from 1874 to 1897, the summer months of each year. He really grew up in Bordeaux. Not until he was thirty-four, on his father's death, did he leave the provincial city and settle permanently in Paris. Meanwhile he had tried in vain to become an architect; he found as little satisfaction in the rôle of a budding academic painter as in that of a soldier during the Franco-German war of 1870—71. At the age of forty he married a Creole woman, Camille Falte, who henceforth became the protector and shield of his delicate existence. Slowly the production of his charcoal drawings and lithographs got under way.

Since 1884 he had been known in avant-garde literary circles; Huysmans described his prints in a much-read novel as the pinnacle of the decadent style; two years later he became fairly well known through the Brussels exhibition of Les XX; his daemonic-fantastic prints aroused attention; Belgian and Dutch collectors took note of him. He entered into friendly relations with Mallarmé, Gauguin and Emile Bernard. Although he produced large numbers of prints during the ensuing decade, editions of his published sets never exceeded a hundred, and rarely fifty.

After 1890 he turned to colour and began to work in pastels and in oils. A trip to Venice helped the sexagenarian to launch out into a magnificent series of works that continued until he was on the threshold of death, in 1916. Shortly before the outbreak of the First World War he was still enjoying successes with his late works among collectors abroad, in Switzerland, Russia and Holland. At the Armory Show in America eleven of his flower-pieces were sold, fetching what were to him amazingly high prices of between $ 300 and $ 400. If prices are the criterion, however, he never achieved outstanding recognition in his own country during his lifetime. For a long time the esteem in which his lithographic work was held stood in the way of his works in colour.

The Early Critics

It was not until between the two World Wars that it became possible to gain any idea of the stages of Redon's work through various exhibitions in private galleries. Certainly, the municipal museum of Paris, the Petit Palais, after the donation of the Zoubaloff Collection, had a whole series of his paintings and pastels to show, but until 1950 the Louvre, the highest authority in distributing the accolade of fame, possessed only one picture by him.

There are many reasons for the long neglect of Redon. Unlike the Impressionists, who fought as a group and finally, around the turn of the century, all achieved success at about the same time, the next generation was not a homogeneous organism. Those who undertook the breakthrough to a spiritual art, in which the outward imitation of nature was no longer the goal, the Post-Impressionists and Symbolists, occupied solitary outposts. Even when Cézanne had long since won world fame, Seurat was still in obscurity, almost unknown. Recognition of the new art was more dependent upon understanding and well-informed critics than Impressionism with its immediate appeal to the senses. In Redon's case the story of his public acknowledgment is further complicated by the fact that his art has two faces. Graphic art is directed towards a different public than that of paintings, towards different collectors, different critics, a different artistic environment. The same Redon who was just beginning to achieve recognition with his 'daemonic' prints, had to start the struggle all over again with the works in his late decorative style. How many admirers of his lithographs believed that he knew nothing whatever about colour, and vice versa.

The triumph of Symbolist poetry in the ten years following 1886, the philosophical and theoretical discussions in small societies and periodicals, spread his name, certainly, but among Huysmans's followers he was seen solely as a literary illustrator, not as an artistic creator. They mistook the sign for the designation. Two artistically more receptive critics, Jules Laforgue (d. 1887) and Albert Aurier (d. 1891) passed away too soon to deal with Redon's work in any detail. Both were at home within the Symbolist movement and sought its equivalent in the sphere of visual art; but what Aurier has to say concretely about Redon's art gets lost again in philosophical generalities: "The artist's finger, it seems, tears through the veil of all oppressive mysteries in order at the end of every rent to show dark terror, shadows and again shadows, out of which baleful enigmas bubble, black, formless, invisible, and his mouth seems, entirely on the lines of Pascal, to announce that all human knowledge and thought leads only to a fearful trembling in the vagueness of the night." (Bibliography No. 60).

Quite different is Maurice Denis, the true discoverer and probably the first interpreter of Cézanne, Gauguin and van Gogh. He was also the first to see Redon in his proper context and to see that both his styles, the early prints and the late work in colour, both sprang from the same centre. "Already in his first works," he wrote in 1903, "Odilon Redon appropriated as his own the combination of formal stringency with the sadness of a sage wearied by knowledge and imagination, and now he shows bunches of flowers, portraits and scenes that look so freshly painted, so radiant and astonishingly youthful! For some years now he has been renewing and developing himself. Without regret, impelled by a mysterious force, he has turned his back on the rich black and white harmonies of the past and in their place creates the splendour of bright flowers in a joyful delight of colour. Through what miracle do these lush poppies and wild flowers nevertheless maintain the strange charm that once filled us with enthusiasm in the nocturnes and romances of his prints? The fact is, the attitude is still the same, at once simple and subtle, and whether chance, *gaucherie* or genius plays its part, whether the subject is a dream or a still-life, there is the same *resoluteness*, determined by an unalterably healthy conception of the work of art." (Bibliography No. 36). Here, for the first time, Redon's Symbolism has been clearly seen as an artistic and not as a literary

Aurora c. 1910 O (152)

phenomenon and at the same time his concord with modern tendencies has been recognized. And yet, this document was a solitary voice in the wilderness; nearly two decades had to pass before others were added to it. This utterance was made at a turning-point in the career of Denis, who soon afterwards subscribed to monarchism, the Catholic dogma and the rigorous classicism of Art Sacré.

Successes Abroad

No doubt under the influence of the great retrospective exhibition at Barbazanges, the tide slowly began to turn. At the beginning of the Twenties the number of judgments concerned less with his strange fantasies than with the creative power and structure of Redon's art in colour, in his contribution to a new, already fully unfolded art, began to multiply. Tristan Klingsor's impressive analysis, his understanding for the pervasion of colour with draughtsmanly structural elements, has already been quoted. The volte-face is almost palpable in the case of another companion of literary Symbolism. In his lively *Memoirs* André Fontainas describes the great evocative power that once emanated from Gustave Moreau and, so to speak, hypnotized the spectator. In his great panorama *Histoire de l'art français de la révolution à nos jours* (1922), however, he has to admit how sterile this power eventually turned out to be; by contrast, he regards Redon's star as in the ascendant. To be sure, Fontainas sees in him a "survivor from the Romantic era", but his "suggestions are founded upon truth" and "his art is therefore on a par with Cézanne, Renoir and van Gogh". This widely read work doubtless marks a decisive turn in the judgment of the younger generation. The rôle of Redon the 'odd man out' is at an end. His connexions with all the camps of the moderns were henceforth discovered, analyzed and emphasized with general agreement. Even André Salmon, a friend of the Cubists, announced his sympathy and recognized a "princely quality" *(principat)* in Redon's style (Bibliography No. 37). "Even if he is only painting a vase of flowers, it is always a complete picture, a composition, whereas the contemporaries of Matisse have for so long tried to satisfy us with ornamented fragments." The creation of an uninterrupted, coherent mode of appearance, he concludes, lends Redon's art a degree of completeness which he shares only with Cubism.

Prior to this the best description of our artist was that written by Hedy Hahnloser, the inspired Swiss woman collector. The following are a few quotations from her article, now, unfortunately, almost impossible to come by: "All the basic elements characteristic of the contemporary will to art are to be found in Redon's *œuvre*. Whether the young of today adhere to the Expressionist group or to the Symbolists, whether they operate with Cubist or Futurist theories, their formal idiom first took shape in the work of Redon. . . . Redon, himself having no suspicion of the place he was to occupy in the evolution of our art, perfected his work in quiet solitude. Even the circle of those around him, in spite of the great personal respect in which they held the artist and the man, never fully understood him in his lifetime. ... It is a characteristic of French art, which cannot be sufficiently stressed, that it is never the circle or the trend in which a creative artist stands that ultimately determines the value placed upon him. Talent alone is the criterion; talent never draws upon speculation, not even upon reflection, it is solely the expression of the essence of the artist, surrender to the artistic experience, vision is everything. ... Thanks to his roots in tradition, Redon is all the more reliable and valuable a pathfinder for modern art because its contemporary representatives, who stand under the sign of revolution that characterizes our whole age, run the risk of losing values that have always been indispensable imponderables of authentic artistic creation. ... The renunciation of the empirical in art, working without a basis of experience, without a study of nature, is far from being a guarantee of the evolution of a new style; without a doubt, modern art is in grave danger of sacrificing artistic truth to arbitrary fantasy. How much or how little metaphysical, purely spiritual element an art displays will always depend upon the personality and not upon the object. ... Confronted by (Redon's lithographic) prints, everyone will undergo the experience of first giving himself up purely to enjoyment of their artistic charm and only afterwards feeling called upon to read their subject matter. Every one of his works in black and white conveys a feeling of the infinite, the mysterious." (Bibliography No. 70).

These words were also accompanied by deeds. If so many of Redon's best works are today to be found in Swiss collections, this is largely due to the initiative of Hedy Hahnloser and her husband. With the sure eye of experts they gathered together at an early stage an exemplary selection of the works of living artists, developed out of human contacts, turned the little town of Winterthur into an art centre and as early as 1919 staged in the local museum the first Redon exhibition in Switzerland.

At the same time a kind of community of Redon's admirers sprang up in Holland. A generation earlier the artist had already found a great friend, admirer and patron in Andries Bonger, the brother-in-law of Théo van Gogh. His Redon collection is still unsurpassed. Other collectors followed his example, even if hesitantly. In no other country did Redon have so many admirers at the end of his life as in Holland. From 1909 Helene Kröller-Müller, the wife of an industrialist in The Hague, built up on a lavish scale a collection intended to give "an idea of the evolution of modern art". Van Gogh, Seurat and Juan Gris formed the axis. The Nabis and the Fauves, the real centre in the case of the Hahnlosers' collection, were entirely missing here. Thus two mutually complementary collections came into being, each on the initiative of a woman who was far ahead of the judgment of her day and who sought to justify her decisions in writing. Mrs Kröller-Müller acquired fifteen Redons, among which the fantastic-daemonic element was strongly dominant, but in her *Development of Modern Painting* the artist is mentioned only very marginally, because, as she believed, he was "uninfluenced by the *Zeitgeist*".

It was perhaps in America that Redon first found a few alert collectors, particularly of his late flower-pieces. Thanks to his 'discovery' by Walt Kuhn and Walter Pach he was splendidly represented at the Armory Show in New York, Boston and Chicago in 1913, found his way into the excellent collection of John Quinn and was actually never again forgotten. His reception by the public, however, was very mixed, as was only to be expected. Harriet Monroe saw in him "a really exceptionally original artist. These thirty-six pictures in colour and numerous lithographs add up to a magnificent and unusual sensation" (*Chicago Sunday Tribune* of 30 March 1913). But for the critic of the *New York Times* Redon's pictures entitled *Silence* was merely an example of "madness getting paid for."

His relations with Russia were of a different kind. In the very year of its first appearance the leading Moscow Symbolist periodical *Vesi (The Scales)* devoted two numbers to Redon's art. Alongside translations of earlier articles by Emile Hennequin, Gustave Geoffroy, Jean Lorrain, Francis Jourdain and Gauguin, there was an original contribution by a Russian writer then living in Paris who belonged to the Symbolist circle of Rémy de Gourmont: Maximilian Voloshin. He was manifestly the moving spirit behind the special numbers. Redon himself contributed a charcoal drawing which, as the cover picture of the first six numbers, actually became the periodical's symbol. Inside there are eighteen vignette-like ink drawings, charming arabesques, of which thirteen have been preserved in the original and are today housed in the Pushkin Museum. Six of them I have been able to publish here for the first time (pp. 39, 58, 97, 109, 135). Since the turn of the century, at least, the artist was in touch with intellectual circles among the Russians living in Paris. The *Portrait of Marie Botkin* (Pl. 21) bears witness to this. Finally, around 1908, the famous art patron Shchukin appeared in his studio, accompanied by Matisse, and bought two works which, along with countless Cézannes, Gauguins, Picassos and Matisses, entered what was perhaps the most magnificent avant-garde collection of those days.

It would be wrong to deduce from all these events that Redon must be considered as an export artist who was disregarded in his own country. In spite of his connexions with Vollard, however, he had very little to do with the art trade in Paris and thus deprived himself of easy successes. On the other hand, we must not overlook the fact that, at least from 1893, he could count on the assistance of his admirers, that is to say his collectors and friends. Without here going into details that occupy a great deal of space in Roseline Bacou's study, we will simply note in passing the date and order in which he entered the new French collections: 1893 Baron Domecy, 1899 Prince Bibesco, 1900 Arthur Fontaine, 1901 Gustave Fayet, 1902 Joseph Hessel, 1903 Maurice Frizeau, 1905 Olivier Sainsère, Albert Parent, Dr Sabouraud and Marcel Kapferer. All this was during his lifetime and before the First World War. It must not be forgotten that after this the number of new collections started in France was greatly reduced and could almost be counted on the fingers. At the same time, the foreign 'market' opened up to the triumphant Impressionists, Post-

Birth of Venus   1912   O   (179)

Impressionists and Cubists of the Paris School. So Redon merely shared, perhaps to a greater degree, the lot of all his colleagues, whose works were destined to emigrate, or perhaps one should say to spread France's artistic fame abroad.

In Paris itself the long delayed great monograph on Redon by the pen of his friend André Mellerio appeared in 1923. It has remained up to the present day the work that no one can ignore who is concerned with Redon, although it has little to offer from the point of view of art criticism and is a biographical account lacking any true perspective, classification or precision in the presentation of Redon's work; the whole body of work in colour of his late period has gone by the board.

No artist, no style, it seems, escapes the rule that directly after achieving maximum influence a period of weariness sets in; an incubation period is necessary before a kind of resurrection and transfiguration becomes possible. Between the two world wars Redon's reputation went to sleep or at least scarcely spread. Despite two remarkable exhibitions in Paris and others in London, New York and Chicago, despite tireless journalistic activity by a critic of the eminence of Claude Roger-Marx, despite the wave of Surrealist sensations in fashion and art, Redon has remained almost in shadow.

Belated Fame. Post-Impressionism

Then quite suddenly came the turning point. All doors seemed to be open to him. Post-Impressionism as an artistic phenomenon and its important figures achieved the 'status of true knowledge'; the connexions with tradition in art and with related cultural trends came under the light of research; vistas opened upon the history of its development and its style from the 'pathos of distance'. It was like the discovery of a new continent in the world of art that took place within the space of a few years. Between 1943 and 1947 there appeared the comprehensive studies by Dorival, Francastel, Bazin and Chassé (Bibliography Nos 46–49), a copious survey of the works themselves was provided by two mutually complementary Paris exhibitions, 'Gauguin' and 'Carrière et le Symbolisme'; in 1950 there followed Raynal's three-volume compilation on the history of modern painting, and finally Rewald's *Post-Impressionism*.

Fundamentally all these writings supplement one another, however much they may seem to contradict each other over details, particularly in their emphasis and evaluation. The metamorphosis of modern art from the representation of nature to a search for essentials is too vast for it not to tolerate and indeed demand clarification on many levels. The changed philosophical and ideological foundations, the different aims, programmes, doctrines, means of expression, the new experience of space, of structure, of colour, the reciprocal influence of groups and outstanding individuals, the appeal to related tendencies in the art of the past, finally the actual course of events and life stories, the

The Shell 1912 P (441)

contacts that sped things up and the disappointments that slowed them down, the incomprehension or interest of the public, the assistance or failure of the critics, the state of the market—all these things must be taken into account, and most of them, since the above works were published, are almost as clear to us as the art of the Renaissance.

But is this really so important? Is not the naive and elementary experience of the colours, the organization of the picture, the crucial factor precisely in modern art? Definitely. But since we are no longer living in a state of innocence we are surrounded, willy-nilly, by preconceived ideas that we have to see through, perhaps in order to break through them. The explanation of works of art, a second stage, will never be a substitute for direct experience, but it can test, can hold up a mirror, supplement intuitive judgment and hence be an aid to greater clarity. In an age of crisis, critical interpretation is almost indispensable.

Francastel's arguments afford a good example of this. Richard Wagner's music, his ideas about the total work of art, of mythological salvation, of the replacement of sensory reality by mysterious spiritual forces in nature have been accepted almost uncontested as the midwife of French Symbolism. Did not the *Revue Wagnérienne* supply the movement from the outset with all its slogans ready-made? And are not the traces of this visible even in the jottings of the painter Gauguin? "It is incontestable that some of his (Gauguin's) canvases painted in Brittany, such as *La lutte de Jacob avec l'Ange*, contain a large element of allusive Symbolism and that in certain works in his late manner, such as *Manao Tupapau*, he has again yielded to the same temptation. However, a close analysis of Gauguin's work makes it quite clear that the artist went beyond this formula of an art of literary allusion and created truly plastic symbols, clear in themselves and requiring no intermediary. ... The artistic Symbolism that began to develop in 1890 in the work of many of these painters is of a different kind. It is the work of men fully prepared to study reality and making no effort to impose upon the world the form of their own spirit; on the contrary, they wish to enrich the human spirit by a renewed knowledge of the universe. This Symbolism gives pride of place, not to dreams and passion, but to observation and serenity. Thanks to it ... the misty achievements of German musical poetry were counteracted by the will to analyse anew the fundamental data of the senses."

From this we can see that the art of Symbolism is a creative act tending towards a new way of rendering reality, which is not derived from the speculations and doctrines of philosophy, but developed in direct opposition to them, as an act of liberation. Neither the 'vogue' of Wagnerism nor literary Symbolism are any help in explaining modern art. "The creative achievement of Cézanne, van Gogh and Gauguin," our critic concludes, "lies essentially in a new way of seeing space which goes hand in hand with the scientific endeavours of that time. To regard painters as the epigoni of literature is the viewpoint of people who have never looked at a picture with their own eyes." (Bibliography No. 47).

Incidentally, Francastel did not include Redon in his discussions. If he had been better acquainted with his art, which was at that time not easily accessible, it would certainly have provided him with a particularly good demonstration of the way in which an artist could see himself surrounded on all sides by literary Symbolism and the Wagnerians and could yet retain his independence by evolving a purely visual, plastic Symbolism. In the last resort, it is the loftiness of the image itself which overrides the 'literature' produced by the artist. This contrast was first brought to light by Nietzsche when he wrote in *The Case of Wagner:* "It is not his music by which Wagner has won over youth, it is the 'idea,' it is the wealth of mystery in his art, its game of hide and seek beneath a hundred symbols, its multi-coloured idealism, it is Wagner's genius for fashioning clouds, his darting, soaring, wandering through the air, his ability to be everywhere and nowhere."

Here we touch upon the crucial point in the interpretation of Redon. Here there is a basic division of opinion. If the motive force of Redon's work is the 'idea,' then all that really counts is early output of fantastic works, then he towers above his age as an incomparable 'dreamer,' and the pastels and paintings of his late period must be regarded as no more than a deterioration into the decorative. Redon's achievement would then link up with that of the Surrealists of a later day.—But if the important thing is his 'form,' then the graphic and coloured works have much more in common and the 'solitary' Redon must be regarded as one of the originators of the style which, between 1880 and 1910, produced a new vision of reality in all spheres of art, then the decorative works of his late period gain the importance which they certainly deserve.

An equilibrium between these two viewpoints has rarely been attained or even striven for, no real balance has ever been struck between them. Perhaps this is simply not possible. Whether in a critical study or an exhibition, one aspect or the other is always stressed while the other is neglected. Certainly, during the last decade more of Redon's works have been exhibited, illustrated, discussed and seen than in the previous half century; from Canada to the Soviet Union, from Japan to Algeria, he has become a suitable artist to display in museums, and yet behind and above all this we are still seeking the true, the unfathomable magician of colour and imagination.

From a Soi-Même (Journal 1867-1915).
Notes sur la Vie, L'Art et les Artistes

I have created an art of my own. I created it with my eyes open on the wonders of the visible world, and, whatever people may have said, constantly endeavouring to obey the laws of nature and life.

I was also helped to create this art by the love of certain masters who introduced me to the cult of beauty. Art is the *Supreme Power*, vast, health-giving and sacred; it opens like a flower; in the hands of a dilettante it produces merely a delightful enjoyment, but in the hands of an artist it creates, in torment, the new grain for a new sowing. I believe that I have yielded docilely to the secret laws that have led me to fashion as best I could and according to my dream, things into which I have put my whole self. If this art has run counter to the art of others (which I do not believe), it has nevertheless gained me a public which has stood firm with the years and which includes valuable and helpful friendships that are dear to me and a recompense. . . .

So far as lay in my power, I have formed myself, because in the instruction from which I attempted to learn I failed to find my true creative method.

I did a year of sculpture at Bordeaux in the private studio of the municipal teacher. There I felt in my hands that exquisite, soft and pliable material clay, with which I endeavoured to make copies from the antique.

In Paris, at the so-called School of Fine Arts, in the Atelier Gérôme, I made a great effort to render forms; these efforts were vain, useless, without further significance to me. I can admit this today, after having reflected on my capabilities and powers throughout my entire life. In going to the Academy I was moved by the sincere desire to take my place in the historical succession of painters, a pupil as they had been, and expecting from others approval and justice. I reckoned without the artistic principle that was to be my guide, and thus I forgot my own temperament. I was tortured by the teacher. Whether it was that he recognized the sincerity of my serious desire to study, or whether he saw in me a shy individual of good will, he manifestly sought to inculcate in me his own way of seeing things and to make of me a disciple—or to make me disgusted with art itself. He overworked me, he was severe; he corrected my work with such vehemence that when he approached my easel my fellow pupils were moved with emotion. It was all in vain.

He ordered me to enclose within a contour a form which, for my part, I saw vibrating. On the pretext of simplification (and why?), he made me shut my eyes to light and neglect the vision of substances. I have never been able to force myself to do this. I feel only the shadows, the visible reliefs; every outline being without any doubt an abstraction. The teaching I was given was not in keeping with my nature. The teacher utterly failed to appreciate my natural gifts. He did not understand me in any way whatsoever. I saw that his eyes were voluntarily closed to everything which mine saw. Two thousand years of evolution or transformation in the way we interpret vision are a small thing by comparison with the divergence between our two opposed souls. There was I, young, sensitive and inescapably a child of my time, listening to obscure rhetoric based in some way or other upon the works of a past age. This teacher would vigorously draw a stone, the shaft of a column, a table, a chair, some insignificant inanimate object, a rock and the whole of inorganic nature. The pupil saw only the expression, the welling-up of feeling triumphing over the forms. Impossible to establish any link between the two, impossible to establish an alliance. Submission would have required the pupil to be a saint, which was also impossible.

Few artists have had to suffer as I suffered in the time that followed; patiently, without rebellion, in the hope of fitting into the ordinary line like the others. When I sent in works to the Salon following this teaching, or rather this confusion, in the studio, they naturally met with the same fate as my school work. I persevered in this dead end for too long; consciousness of being able to follow a direction of my own had not yet come to me. By this isolation in which I was left I was made different from the others and independent. Today I am very glad of this. Now there is a whole range of art, a whole stream flowing outside the channels of the official organizations. I was forced into the isolation in which I now find myself by the absolute impossibility of creating art otherwise than I have always done. I understand nothing of what are called "concessions"; one does not produce the art one would like to. The artist, day by day, is the receptacle of the things surrounding him; he receives from outside sensations which he transforms inescapably, inexorably and tenaciously in accordance with his own inner self. There can really be no artistic creation until one has something to say, a need for expression. I would go so far as to say that the artist is affected by the seasons; they stimulate or deaden his energy. Any attempt to ignore these influences, which will be revealed to him by groping experiment and experience, cannot but be fruitless.

I think that I have always tried to make the best of my abilities; I have conscientiously sought myself beneath the awakenings and the growth of my creative power; impelled by the desire that the products of my creative effort should be perfect, that is to say complete, autonomous, able to stand on their own. But had I the temperament of a draughtsman or a painter? What is the use of trying to find out now? The rather useless discrimination between these two modes of creation made by teachers is of little importance. And yet certain differences do exist. Practical skill in drawing came to me later, in response to my will, slowly, almost painfully. By *drawing* I mean here the power to find a means of representing things or persons objectively according to their own character. I have always striven after this as an exercise and because it is necessary to train oneself in the most essential element of one's art; but I was also obeying the stimulus that comes from line—just as I also yielded to the charm of chiaroscuro. At the same time I endeavoured to render a small piece of something, a fragment, showing as much detail as possible and bringing it into full relief. What attracted me was study, I was not concerned with the utility of what I was doing. These fragments have since frequently proved useful to me in reconstructing whole scenes, and even in conjuring them up in my imagination. Here we see the mysterious road marked by effort and achievement in the slow progress of a destiny. Sometimes and for some people it is compelling and firmly predetermined; in my case it was often troubled and restless; but I never lost sight of a higher goal and I did not resist the attraction exercised upon me by other arts. I was a regular attender at concerts and never without a fine book in my hand.

My capacity for contemplation made my search for a personal way of seeing things painful. At what moment did I become objective, that is to say when did I begin to look at things closely enough, to see nature in itself clearly enough, to proceed to the rendering of visible forms? It was towards 1865. Avant-garde Naturalism was in full swing; Courbet was producing real painting by free use of the palette knife. This misunderstood classicist was causing a ferment among the true painters of the younger generation. Millet was also giving offence to fashionable society by drawing peasants in clogs and portraying the rustic harshness of their bleak and suffering lives. I had a friend who initiated me, in theory and by example, into all the sensual delights of the palette. He was like the opposite pole to myself; hence our endless discussions. Together we painted landscapes, in which I forced myself to reproduce the real tones. At this point in time I produced studies that are beyond doubt or argument true painting.

This companion of my independent youth was useful to me; later, life with its vicissitudes, its harshness and the offence it offers to our tastes by the hard obligations of necessity, drew him away from painting. How many others richly gifted by nature give up and become submerged in the crowd! We are all born with another man in us, potentially, and the will either maintains, cultivates and preserves this other man—or it does not. We do not know, we shall never know, what makes of this man an artist, of that other a financier or a civil servant, although they both set out together encircled by the radiance of the same abilities. This is an unfathomable, insoluble problem. Fortune or poverty are no obstacle; we carry our souls with us everywhere and everywhere there is material for them to work on. It is a question of inner integrity, divorced from the weaknesses of vanity or the deviations of pride. There are artists of genius living in poverty, there are others living in opulence. The final goal of a destiny is contained within that destiny; it follows hidden paths of which the world knows nothing; they may be filled with flowers or with thorns.

What was it which, at the outset, made creation difficult for me and so delayed its accomplishment? Was it that I saw things in a way that did not accord with my gifts? A kind of conflict between heart and head? I do not know.

In any case, since the beginning I have always striven for perfection, including, believe it or not, perfection of form. But let me tell you now that no three-dimensional form, I mean form seen objectively, for its own sake, in conformity with the laws of light and shade, rendered by the conventional means of "modelling", will be found in my works. At most I often tried, in the beginning, and because one should so far as possible know everything, to reproduce visible objects in this way according to the artistic method deriving from the old way of seeing things. I only did it for practice. But I tell you today, in full, conscious maturity, and I insist on this, that all my art is limited solely to the resources of chiaroscuro and it also owes a great deal to the effects of abstract line, that power drawn from deep sources which acts directly upon our minds. An evocative art can achieve nothing without recourse to the mysterious play of shadows and of the rhythm of lines conceived in the mind. These elements never achieved loftier results than in the works of Leonardo da Vinci. He owes to them his mystery and the wealth of magical fascination which he exercises on our minds. They are the roots of the words that make up his language. And it is also by his perfection, his excellence, his reason and his docile submission to the natural laws of forms that this admirable and sovereign genius dominates the whole art of forms; he has mastered forms to their very essence. "Nature is full of infinite possibilities that have never been realized", he wrote. Nature for him, as no doubt for all the great masters, is the evident necessity, the axiomatic truth. What painter could think otherwise?

Nature also demands that we shall obey the gifts which she has given us. Mine led me into the world of dreams; I suffered the torments of imagination and the surprises which it presented to me under the pencil; but I guided and controlled these surprises according to the laws of artistic organization which I know, which I feel, with the sole purpose that they should exercise upon the spectator, through a process of attraction, all the evocative power, all the charm of the vague that lies at the extreme limits of thought.

Nor have I said anything that was not magnificently foreshadowed by Albrecht Dürer in his print *Melancholy*. It might be thought incoherent. No, it is rendered entirely in terms of line and the great powers of line. It is a serious and profound mind which here soothes us as though with the compressed, dense accents of a strict fugue. For our part we can sing only brief pieces consisting of a few bars.

114

Large Bouquet of Wild Flowers   1912   P   (487)

Evocative art is like the radiance of things seen in a dream which is also permeated by thought. Decadence or not, that is how it is. Let us say rather that it is the growth, the evolution of art so that it shall become the loftiest soaring of our own life, its expansion, its highest moral foothold attained through the necessary exaltation.

This evocative art is to be found entire in the stirring art of music, where it is at its freest and most radiant; but it is also present in my art through a combination of various allied elements, of transposed and transmuted forms, having no connexion with fortuitous circumstances, but possessing a logic of their own. All the mistakes that critics made about me when I started were due to their not having realized that there is no need to define, to understand, to limit anything, no need to be specific, because everything that is sincerely and genuinely new—like beauty itself—carries its own meaning within itself.

The titles given to my drawings sometimes add too much, in a sense. The title is justified only when it is vague, indeterminate and even tending to create confusion and ambiguity. My drawings *inspire*, and are not to be defined. They do not determine anything. Like music, they take us into the ambiguous world of the indeterminate.

They are a kind of *metaphor*, Remy de Gourmont has said, giving them a position all their own, far from all geometric art. He sees in them a logic of the imagination. I believe that this critic has said more in a few lines than all that was written in the past concerning my early works.

Imagine various arabesques or meanders unfolding not in a plane, but in space, with all that the deep and vague margins of the sky provide for the mind; imagine the play of these lines projected and combined with the most varied elements, including that of a human face; if this face has the features of the face we see every day in the street, with its completely direct, fortuitous truth, you will then have a combination of elements of which many of my drawings are composed.

They are, then, without the possibility of any more precise explanation, the reflection of a human expression, set, by the permissible use of the imagination, within interweaving arabesques; and I believe that the effects which they will exercise upon the mind of the spectator will stimulate him to invent fictions whose significance will be great or small according to his own sensibility and the capacity of his imagination to enlarge or diminish everything it lights upon.

And, further, everything emanates from the universal laws of life. A painter who did not draw a wall vertical would be drawing badly, because he would distract the mind from the idea of stability. He who did not make water horizontal would be doing the same (to quote only two very simple examples). But there are in the vegetable world, for instance, secret but normal currents of life which a sensitive landscape painter does not overlook; the trunk of a tree, with its character of strength, puts out its branches according to the laws of expansion and the movements of its sap, and this a true artist must feel and portray.

It is the same with animal or human life. We cannot move our hand without our whole being moving in obedience to the laws of gravity. A draughtsman knows this. I believe that I have obeyed this intuitive, instinctive knowledge in creating certain monsters. They do not come, as Huysmans has insinuated, from use of the microscope to observe the terrifying world of the infintely small. No. In creating them I was performing the more important task of devising their structure according to the laws of nature.

There is a way of drawing in which imagination is set free from troublesome concern with real details, so that it is at liberty to render things conceived solely in the mind. I have produced certain fantastic images involving the stalk of a flower, or the human face, or elements derived from the skeleton, all of which, I believe, are constructed and built up in a natural manner. They are constructed according to the laws of an inner organization. Whenever a human figure does not create the illusion that it is about, as it were, to step out of the frame and walk, act or think, truly modern drawing has not been achieved. I cannot be denied the merit of giving the illusion of life to my most irreal creations. My whole originality consists in bringing to life, in a human way, improbable beings and making them live according to the laws of probability, by putting, as far as possible, the logic of the visible at the service of the invisible.

Such drawing flows naturally and easily from the vision of the mysterious world of shadows, which Rembrandt revealed and endowed with a language.

On the other hand, as I have often said, the activity that has been most fruitful for me and the most necessary to my development, has been to copy reality directly, attentively reproducing the objects of external nature in their most minute, particular and accidental detail. After striving hard to copy with minute care a stone, a blade of grass, a hand, a profile or anything else in living or inorganic nature, I feel a welling-up within my mind; then I feel the need to create, to let myself be swept along to the creation of something imaginary. Nature, thus measured and assimilated, becomes my source, my yeast, my ferment. I believe that my true inventions spring from this origin. I believe that this is true of my drawings; and it is probable that, even taking into account the great proportion of weakness, unevenness and imperfection that characterizes everything recreated by man, no one could bear to look at them for an instant (because they are expressive of human feelings) if they were not, as I have said, fashioned and constructed according to the laws of life and of the transmission of a moral sense necessarily present in everything that exists.

1894

In the past, when I published my drawings and lithographs, I frequently received letters from unknown people telling me of their liking for this art and of the lofty emotions it inspired in them. One of them confessed that it had aroused religious feelings in him and brought him back to the faith. I do not know whether art has such power; but since then I have been forced myself to look with more respect upon certain of my pictures, particularly those executed at times of sorrow, of suffering, which for that reason no doubt are especially expressive. Groundless sorrow may perhaps be the outcome of a secret fervour, a sort of prayer uttered confusedly, as part of some act of worship, amidst the unknown.

So I carefully scrutinized my black and white works. It is above all in the lithographs that the blacks have their full, unadulterated brilliance; because the charcoal drawings which I made before and after them were always done on pink or yellow or sometimes blue tinted paper—a first hint of my predilection for colour, in which I later took so much pleasure, indeed delight.

Black is the most essential of all colours. Above all, if I may say so, it draws its excitement and vitality from deep and secret sources of health. The restrained vital energy that can be expressed in the charcoal drawing springs from a good diet and plenty of rest, or rather from an abundance of physical vigour. That is to say, charcoal drawing is likely to reach its best and fullest beauty at the very core of our life-span, whether it be long or short. Later, in old age, when we are less well able to extract full nourishment from our food, it becomes exhausting. When this stage is reached we can still spread black matter over a surface, but charcoal remains charcoal, the lithographic crayon does not transmit anything; in a word, matter appears to our eyes what it would seem to be in fact—an inert and lifeless thing; whereas at the happy hour of spiritual effervescence and abundant physical energy, an artist's essential vitality is expressed through it, his mind, his spirit, something of his soul, a reflection of his sensibility, as it were the deposit of his innermost substance.

One must admire black. Nothing can debauch it. It does not please the eye and awakens no sensuality. It is an agent of the spirit far more than the fine colour of the palette or the prism. Thus a good lithograph is more likely to be appreciated in a serious country, where inclement nature outside compels man to remain confined to his home, cultivating his own thoughts, that is to say in the countries of the north rather than those of the south, where the sun draws us outside ourselves and delights us. The lithograph enjoys little esteem in France, except when it has been impoverished by the addition of colour, which produces a different result, destroying its specific qualities so that it comes to resemble a cheap coloured print . . .

My first lithographs, published in 1879, were for the most part repetitions or variations of drawings which I had made long before, solely for myself, in the complete isolation of the countryside. Watching the peaceful labour of the fields was my only distraction. Nothing is so favourable to artistic creation as a series of distractions that have nothing whatever to do with art, just as mild physical activity brings about a certain productive effervescence in the brain. How often, in convincing proof of this, I have picked up the charcoal with a hand still brown from the soil which I had just touched while gardening. Holy and silent substance, source of revitalization and refuge, how much sweet solace I owe to you! What other balm ever exercised upon me, upon my mind and even upon my pains a more rapid, more beneficent effect than the sight of

Wild Flowers in a Long-necked Vase   after 1912   P   (491)

green grass or contact with other elements of unconscious nature. To leave the town and go out into the fields, to approach a village in its rustic tranquillity— such surroundings have always set my heart pounding, making me feel grave and suddenly bringing me back to myself, till I stammer that perhaps the true meaning of life would be to live in a place like this.

But regrets are vain. That which has not been, cannot be. And in any case, does not the past leave the present a margin in which the future can inscribe better days? And are there not also the consoling advantages of old age, that inescapable but lucid destination where we can more easily be wise, in the light of the good advice now given by memory?

In the same way one develops and improves one's talent.

The artist who sets out to achieve perfection—and by perfection I mean an honest, independent, satisfying work, a work in which his unique personality is revealed—will always feel some regret, some embarrassment in signing his name to it. And this conflict, this feeling of bad conscience, affords the chief incentive to quickly start again, providing the ferment for the next work through our desire to achieve something better.

So I have studied my productions. Oh, without pride, as a careful observer, rather as a scientist would study the visible phenomena of some natural process, in order to increase his knowledge of it. I have been aware of the sudden influence exercised upon me by various localities, or by the weather, the time of year, my dwelling place, the direction from which the light was entering my studio, so that I can say here with certainty how much we have to reckon with the invisible, moving world that surrounds and impinges upon us and bends our inner being under still obscure and unexplained pressures from without. Every bend imparted to our mind in one place is changed without our knowledge in another . . .

Apart from the influence exercised upon him by the people and places surrounding him, the artist also yields, to some extent, to the coercive demands of the medium he employs: pencil, charcoal, pastel, oil paint, printing ink, marble, bronze, clay or wood; all these substances are active participants which keep him company, collaborate with him and also have a contribution to make towards the work which he is creating. The medium reveals secrets, it has its own genius; it is through the medium that the oracle speaks. When the painter sets down his dream, do not forget the action of these secret elements that link and hold it to the earth; they work in conjunction with the lucid and alert mind and must certainly not be forgotten.

The lithographic crayon operates indirectly: it is the intermediary that transmits and duplicates the work; and the artist's sensibility, alas, must also take account of the necessary intervention of the printer. The artist entrusts to him the precious product of his spirit—he has no choice; but little that is good, little that is complete will be possible without the attentive co-operation of this acolyte, this simple craftsman, whose participation is invaluable when it is intuitive, disastrous and deplorable when it is unfeeling. The artist enters into a temporary but ill-assorted alliance with him, in which they must perforce reach an understanding and work together. But a work of art cannot be produced by two people. One of them must give way to the other.

My God, how I have suffered in the printing shops, what inner rages have seized me when I saw the bewildered incomprehension which printers have always shown towards my endeavours. I knew that my designs were unusual in form, not produced according to the customary methods of working on stone; but I was seeking new paths. And I believe that I set my imagination whole-heartedly and without restraint to demand of the resources of lithography all that they could give. All my prints, from the first to the last, have been nothing but the fruit of a curious, attentive, restless and passionate analysis of the powers of expression of the lithographic crayon, aided by paper and stone. I am astonished that artists have not made wider use of this supple and rich medium, obedient to the subtlest impulses of the sensibility. The times during which I have lived must have been very much preoccupied with direct imitation and naturalism for this process to have failed to grip minds given to the invention of fantasies and to lead them to exploit its rich potentialities of evocation. It positively calls the unexpected into being.

I am speaking here of the use of transfer paper rather than of working direct on stone. Stone is difficult, sullen, like a moody person given to attacks of nerves. It is impressionable, subject to all sorts of influences inflicted on it by the weather. Rain or snow, heat or cold, produce conditions in which the stone is helpful or unhelpful, a source of pleasant or unpleasant surprises, which determine the attitude one should adopt towards it when printing. The mono-tonous everyday events going on around the stone are likewise intolerable. It is better deliberately to neglect the stone and its grain, to forget it, as one neglects alas, through force of circumstances and despite all their virtue, certain elderly people worthy of respect in whose company one is bored, because they no longer share one's interest in life and the things of the present.

The whole future of lithography (if it has one) lies in the as yet undiscovered potentialities of paper, which so perfectly transmits to the stone the finest and most subtle motions of the spirit. The stone itself will then become entirely passive.

These reflections recall to me the memory of Rodolphe Bresdin who initiated me, with the greatest possible care for my independence, into etching and lithography. . . . He himself enjoyed gardening, which he did with the painstaking care of a Chinese. Subtle and meticulous in everything he did, he brought to it his delicate skill, and his keeness of analysis and observation. It was while gardening, more than at any other moment, that his mind was at its most alert; he used to burst out in a sudden and gripping flood of words that gave me food for thought. Once he said to me in a tone of gentle authority: "You see that chimney-flue, what does it say to you? It tells me a whole legend. If you have the power to observe it well and understand it, you may imagine the strangest, most bizarre scene and if it is based upon and remains within the limits of this simple area of wall, your dream will be living. Therein lies art." Bresdin made these remarks to me in 1864. I mention the date because that was not the way in which art was taught in those days.

Today I declare myself fortunate to have heard while young, from a very original and complete artist whom I loved and admired, these not very subversive words which I understood so well and which confirmed something I had already felt myself. In an apparently very simple form, they provide an introduction to a lofty teaching. They open the painters' eyes to the two worlds of life, to two realities which it is impossible to separate without diminishing our art and depriving it of what it can give that is noble and sovereign.

The artists of my generation, for the most part, certainly looked at the chimney-flue. And that was all they saw. They rendered nothing of all that can be added to the area of wall by the reflection of our own essence. Everything that goes beyond the object, illuminating or amplifying it and lifting up the spirit into the region of mystery, into the troubled zone of the unresolved and its delicious disquiet, remained totally closed to them. Everything that lends itself to expression through the symbol, everything that lends art a touch of the unexpected, the vague, the indefinable and gives it a hint of the enigmatic, they avoided, they feared. Truly parasitic upon the object, they cultivated art within the purely visual field and closed it to everything that went beyond this and might have introduced into the humblest endeavours, even into black and white drawings, the light of spirituality. I mean by this a radiance that takes possession of our mind—and defies all analysis.

In the face of these undeniable shortcomings one would be inclined to give oneself up to regret, if one forgot the great upsurge that took place during my youth. Those who, like myself, saw the course taken by art during that period will understand how much justification there was, alas, for the artists with closed minds of whom I have been speaking, and how much they were obeying, consciously or not, a law of necessary rejuvenation and revival. Everything that sprang from the influence of David, through his pupils and his pupil's pupils, was enjoying its official heyday: an imprisoned art, dry, destitute of abandon, arising out of abstract formulae, when it would have been enough for artists simply to open their eyes to the glories of nature to set this art free and give it new life.

Taking everything into consideration, we must nevertheless be grateful to those of my contemporaries who followed the right path in the forest, the path to truth. If the trees in that part of the forest are not lofty, if the sky is a little low and the clouds too heavy to let in our dreams, some of these artists nonetheless strode resolutely, manfully, along their chosen path, with the boldness of rebels convinced that they are holding for an instant a fragment of the true truth. If the building which they constructed presents no profound vistas, at least the air is pure and one can breathe. . . .

My first artistic difficulties, which I continued to experience long after my youth, were finally dissipated through a more exact concord between my

Rose, Marguerites and Cornflowers in Green Vase 1912–14 O (313)

ability and my wishes. By continually viewing myself objectively, and opening my eyes wider upon everything, I finally came to see that the life thus unfolded may also be joyous. If an artist's art is the song of his life, a melody that may be grave or melancholy, I first struck a gay note by using colour. . . .

1913

These are the final words that will explain and sum up my ideas.

The work of art is born from three sources, three causes:

Tradition, which springs from the primordial fountainhead and constant additions made by men of genius, who ceaselessly hand down to us the moral and intellectual life of the whole of Humanity, whose great book, written in living letters because it is written with their blood, is constantly open before us in our temples, on our walls, in every genuinely sincere and felt work of art, and through which we recognize our own nobility, our own grandeur. It is by tradition that we measure the respect due to those who teach. And I mean by these all the serious friends of beauty and the ideal, all those who admire and venerate it, a single word of admiration from whom can reveal to us new fields of truth.

The whole mission of art schools, including the Académie and the Institut de France, lies exclusively in their consciousness of guarding this truly sacred heritage. This, contrary to a whole contemporary school of thought, I frankly acknowledge as the justification for their continued existence, on condition, that is, that those who teach in them should be themselves the faithful and strict disciples of tradition.

Reality, or in other words Nature, which is a pure means for the expression of our feelings and their communication to our fellow men; without nature our will to create remains a mere dream, an abstraction, a simple vibration of life devoid of the perfect organ that will enable it to appear, forcefully, fully, in all the clarity and purety of its supreme expression.

Finally our own *personal invention*, the original intuition that combines and summarizes everything, seeking support in the past and in the present in order to give to the contemporary work a new organization, a temperament that is ceaselessly rejuvenated in the continuous development of human life, which incontestably progresses and unceasingly modifies the means of expression in art.

These three modes of speech, of the eternal speech of beauty, appear fully and constantly in the great epochs, when a civilization expands without hindrance and can seek unimpeded to rise towards its own truth. Example: Phidias, Leonardo da Vinci, sacred figures who raised art to the highest inaccessible peaks of plastic vision, which have now perhaps been lost forever and towards which the greatest minds continually turn in love, homage and rapt contemplation.

124

A genuine work of art appears only when its time has come. In order to be understood it needs the proper moment. Some great masters produced their work too soon, others too late; it is rare for a happy fame to spread freely around a genius, especially in our day, when every artist seeks his path alone, with no one to inspire his dreams but himself.

1887

Four letters by Redon

1

My dear Mellerio,

I don't want to keep you waiting, but it is impossible for me to answer all the questions you have asked me. Are you so concerned to know about the starting point of my work? Would it not be better to keep it somewhat hidden? Is it a good thing to watch a birth in this way?

However, I will tell you why I took up lithography. Previously, I had tried in vain to show in the official Salon the numerous charcoal drawings which lay buried in my portfolios. Then Fantin-Latour gave me the excellent advice to reproduce them with the aid of the lithographic crayon; he was even kind enough to give me a sheet of transfer paper in order to make a tracing. I therefore made my first lithographs *for the purpose of reproducing my drawings*. You can see how little grandeur there was about this initial source!

Since I wished to show my work, the idea of a set of prints naturally came to my mind; hence the first album was simply a collection of reproductions of various earlier drawings; but in the process of converting them into lithographs I became so enamoured of the method that finally I worked directly in the new medium.

The title came to me of its own accord and described the personal atmosphere within which I was living and working at that time. (People were then reading *L'Assomoir*, and the Impressionists with Degas had already made quite a breakthrough in the direction taken by Zola.)

This album is perhaps one of my favourites, because it was produced without the intervention of any literary element. The title *Dans le rêve* was really only intended to provide a key.

127

The declaration I have just made should tell you how awkward I find it to dwell on the subtleties which my later works may suggest to you through their captions, in which you are inclined to see too much. You attribute to me aims which I did not have. I should like to convince you that the whole thing is no more than a little oily black liquid, transmitted by crayon and stone to white paper, with the sole purpose of producing in the spectator a sort of diffuse but powerful attraction to the obscure world of the *indeterminate*, and to set him thinking.

This must be enough for you. All the reasons I could give you for the make-up of my albums would seem to you insignificant and puerile; they would deprive the albums of the magic which they ought to have. Once again, it is good to surround every genesis with a mystery.

When I undertook my second enterprise, *À Edgar Poe*, I had, alas, lost all my innocence. See how precise, almost dry, its execution is: the stone had already troubled me, changed me, by its harsh charm. I had been repeatedly advised to read the American poet on the assumption that it would provide inspiration for my art. This was a mistake, I think; his stories are not my favourite reading. Nevertheless, I put a few words under these new prints, skilfully I think, and the public fell for it. Obviously, this was nothing but a trick, though a perfectly legitimate, very permissible trick; the album was noticed, that was the essential thing for me.

And I saw that one does not touch the stone with impunity, not without being induced to burden it with the written word: all the great lithographers have done so. But in my case, as you can see, the situation is very different, it was not a matter of chance.

In *Les Origines* I tried in vain to rediscover the ease and spontaneity which I had shown in my first album. I did away with captions, because the title was already very heavy with meaning; you like it as it is. You would like it even more if you knew the captions that I added by hand at his request on the copy belonging to an Italian art-lover (Prince Primoli). But I was right not to print them. They would substantiate a hypothesis which it is not my intention to revive. The work gave me trouble enough as a lithograph, there was no point in making it appear more than that. Just suppose its title had been *Les Monstres*, and you will see how it fits into the pattern established by my other works.

The same holds good of my other series, in which I beg you to see solely an artistic aim, even in the vague words which ornament them and are comparable to the musical directions on a sonata.

I do not know what you mean by "homogeneous tendency" nor by the expression "a general current uniting the separate pieces". These isolated pieces are sometimes reproductions of earlier drawings, sometimes they were created spontaneously.

I have never used the misleading word "illustration". You will not find it in my catalogues. The right word remains to be found. Words like transmission or interpretation might be used, but even these do not exactly describe the process by which something I have read passes into my black and white drawings and prints.

As to Flaubert, it was my much lamented friend Emile Hennequin who brought me *La tentation de St Antoine* when he had seen *Les Origines*. He told me that I should find in this book new monsters. I was quickly entranced by the descriptive parts of this work, by the form and colour of all these resurrections of a past.

I would point out to you that the first series of lithographs which I made in connexion with this book were at the request of the publisher Deman. The designs for *Les fleurs du mal* were also committed to copper by this same publisher.

You ask me *why* I produced isolated pieces. Simply in order to make lithographs, following the example of all artists past and present; they did exactly the same. *La Gioconda* is a separate piece. So is *The Hundred Guilder Print*. These are fine precedents. I cannot analyse myself; the only thing I can analyse is the minute of my gestation and revelation. . . .

2

Peyrelebade, 16 August 1898

My dear Mellerio,

I still have in front of me your letter, the questions in which put me in some embarrassment. I cannot give a complete reply to them. What interest have you in finding out if I approach the easel or the stone with a preconceived idea in mind? People have been asking me this question for thirty years.

You cannot imagine how it shocks my sense of decency; I have never answered it. What use is there in revealing anything but the finished result? Those who watch me at work in the intimacy of my private life are no doubt better informed about these things, and Ari or his mother would probably tell you laughingly more about it than I.

If you wish, however, I can confide to you certain insurmountable features of my nature. Thus I have a horror of a white sheet of paper. It makes such a disagreeable impression upon me as to render me barren and take away my desire to work (except, of course, when I am intending to represent something real, to make a study, a portrait for example); a blank sheet of paper offends me so much that as soon as it is on the easel I am compelled to scribble on it with charcoal or pencil or some other medium, and this operation gives it life. I believe that evocative art draws much of its force from the stimuli exercised on the artist by the medium itself. A truly sensitive artist will not work out the same fantasy in different media, because they will exercise different influences on him.

This is to show you how relative and indirect is the action of the preconceived idea of which you speak. Very often, no doubt, it serves as a starting project that we abandon on the way in order to follow the charming and unforeseen paths of imagination, that sovereign who suddenly opens up to us magnificent, astonishing delights and subjugates us. She has been my guardian angel. Much more so in the past than today, alas! She loves restless and furrowed brows. Above all, she loves youth and childhood, and the wise thing is to remain always something of a child, in order to create.

Imagination is also the messenger of the "unconscious," that very lofty and mysterious personage. Her coming must be waited for in over-aware old age. She comes in her own good time, according to the weather, the place, even the season of the year. This will make clear to you how difficult it is to reply to questions as to "why" and "how", because everything in this fateful crucible in which art is brewed is dependent upon the precious caprice of this unknown.

A commonplace little aphorism:

Nothing in art can be done by will alone.

Everything is done by docile submission to the coming of the "unconscious." The spirit of analysis must be prompt to act when it appears, but there is little to be gained by remembering afterwards what happened, since for every work, every act of creation, the unconscious sets us a different problem. The unconscious is the wine of life, of a life that is divine and always new. I cannot put it to you in any other way.

As to what the professional lithographers reproach me with, I really don't know. They are wrong to bear witness against me, who have never practised nor wished to practise their craft. They have one point of view, I another. You are speaking, no doubt, of the official lithographers. All I know of what is going on in their minds is the effort they made in the past to elminate me from the exhibitions which they organized. After considering the matter carefully in my present maturity, I think I can say that they rejected my best lithographs. Since they are copyists, I could not be expected to work on the same lines as they. That was impossible. In the old days I saw some of their lithographs at Lemercier's printing shop; but we hardly exchanged a word about our respective working methods. Our contacts were mitigated by quite a frank atmosphere, which rendered them not unpleasant. I do remember that they used to speak with some mystery of the "grain", and I see from your letter that this also interests you.

All good lithographers know and respect this essential element of a good stone; but the results produced by it are not the true aim of art.

Transfer paper, with which you are also concerned, is excellent for improvization. I am very fond of it, because it is more obedient than stone. When I confide in you that the medium acts strongly upon my sensibility, you will understand that this grave, rough, hard flint is not conducive to my flights of fantasy. Paper yields, stone resists. I do not understand the stone until after the first shots have been fired, the hot smoke of improvization has spread over the paper.

When I see you I shall explain, with the help of examples, the differences between the two procedures or the combination of both.

Dante's Vision c. 1914 W (550)

I really cannot speak any longer now about technique.

The captions for the album to Edgar Poe and for all the others, apart from those devoted to Flaubert and Baudelaire, are of my own invention.

I know nothing of the use any other artist may make of transfer paper, because I am not he and he is not I...

3

2 October 1898
Still at Peyrelebade!

My dear Mellerio,

... The only cloud is that I have learned of the death of Mallarmé, which upset me profoundly and filled me with depression. After Huysmans's desertion, he was almost the only one left of my own generation, and I know that he never allowed anyone to smile about me; he was really an artistic ally upon whom I could rely absolutely. Such is the way of death and we shall never understand it.

But to come to the point. What you ask me this time is easier for me to answer, because everyone, I think, likes to talk, or at least to think, about himself even if they conceal the fact. Obviously it is a subject about which each person knows a great deal. The trouble is that it is not of the least interest to other people. However, *in order to cast light upon my art, and for no other reason*, and for the purpose of the catalogue you are preparing, I have made a start on the task I promised to carry out and, between your too rare letters, I have set down, in bits and pieces, by fits and starts, with no thread running through them—something of which I am incapable—a few notes in which you will find what you want; they provide further explanation of the questions you have asked me and my brief replies to them.

However, these notes exceed the scope of a letter by sheer weight of paper. As we are returning home in ten days or so, it will no doubt be better if I hand them over to you in person, rather than send them by post. I shall ask you to let me have them back when you have gone through them, because I add to them from time to time; the shapeless beginning makes additions easy. You will extract from them the information you require and I shall be there to supplement them verbally. I have not touched upon the war, a time when my vision was as though multiplied tenfold. Oh, the day of the 20th or 22nd of December when I took part in a battle near Tours at Monnaie (or Monay). I have described it at length with all my curiosity and excitement in one or two letters written to my brother Ernest Redon; I'm sure he still has them. They ought to be of interest, because they are scenes taken from life and written down on the corner of a canteen table at the base some days later.

They are an account of two days which I should like to re-read myself, I assure you.

But how to get hold of them! I am on such bad terms with him that it would be embarrassing for me to be in his presence, because of the harm done to me by the family quarrel which he engineered, the consequences of which still hang over my head and trouble me. I am afraid, my dear friend, that it will have an ugly end. In spite of all the red ink, or perhaps because of it, I see a great deal of black. The letters which we exchange between brothers and mother are not of a literary nature; they emanate from lawyers' offices and are on stamped paper. The putrefaction springs from too long a delay in dividing the inheritance and is now irreparable.

What can we do to get another look at these letters? It would be in order to ask for a copy, let us see if this proves to be necessary. Humanly, I should be glad if you could read these letters.

This brother, with whom my relations have now become so shadowed and dark, was at that time my confidant. He is now in possession of a collection of letters that would show me as I was then. I have changed a great deal! We ceased to have any confidence in each other, or at least I had no more confidence in him, since 1881 or 1882, after my marriage, a short while afterwards. I found in Madame Redon, like a sacred thread, my goddess of destiny, who enabled me to pass without dying through the most tragic and mysterious hours of my family drama. Without her, and without all the scales of black that I have laid down and poured out on paper, what would have become of me? My art alone, so inward looking, would not have saved me, I should have been done for. I believe that the *Yes* which I uttered on the day of our marriage was the expression of the most complete and unmixed certainty I have ever felt. A certainty even more absolute than my vocation.

In the meantime, you have the letter to my friend Picard, which he will publish in *L'Art Moderne*; it contains, in summary, everything which I could tell you endlessly. Have you got it? If not, I shall send it to you . . .

4   To Madame de Holstein

Paris, 29 January 1900

Madame and excellent friend,
The beautiful and moving translation of Pushkin's poetry has reached me and has reminded me of my debt. I would have written to you yesterday evening, but I was exhausted by a feverish cold; and as I have to go away for ten days or so tomorrow, in spite of this, I should like to talk to you a little, my dear, good friend, about our visit to the Moreau Museum. (cf Pls 66–68.)

This time I got back from the Rue de la Rochefoucauld without much trouble, and ready to take up my everyday life again where I left off. It was not like this the first time I saw *Oedipus and the Sphinx*; then I was young. At that time naturalism was in its heyday and how this work solaced me! I retained the memory of this first impression for a long time; maybe it had the power to give me the strength to follow a solitary path that perhaps ran alongside his, because of all the evocative element in both of them, so dear to men of letters.

But how different we are, Moreau and I. At this moment as I write to you, when I should be glad to believe that a fine gesture constitutes the whole of Art, this museum seems to me cold and to reveal nothing of the life of a man who had the opportunity to pursue his own endeavours throughout forty years. In short, he did not penetrate into himself; we know nothing of his mental life. It remains veiled beneath this essentially worldly art, in which the figures called to life are divested of their instinctive sincerity. Are these beings going to step forth from the canvas and act? No. They remain fixed in a sort of rhetoric of the eye, which has a beauty of its own, obviously, incontestably, but is not the eternal mirror in which mankind ceaselessly studies its own image. Without wishing to compare or judge two men, I like to recall how I felt on leaving the exhibition of Rembrandt's works in Amsterdam; what pity was suddenly aroused in me. That day, out in the street, I could not look at the poor or into the eyes of the people, they drew me too strongly. Art could not go further than that.

The Moreau Museum left behind an after-taste of hollow splendour, such as we see in the décor of *Alexander's Triumph*. Here, in this picture, Moreau is unique. There is something of India, with less sweetness and gentleness. It is the India of outward magnificence, not that of Sakuntala. The milk of mysticism does not flow here; there is nothing of the radiant and sacred fusion of past and future at the very heart of life. If I had devoted myself daily to the art of Moreau, it would have led me today to a worldly elegance. Would it also have led me to a *princely* brilliance of execution? However much one might wish this, I think there are too many jewels in his pictures.

But all regret is vain. Why should I express reservations when yesterday my eyes were delighted by astonishing surprises, quite independently of any search for skills which are no longer to be found? There are certain water-colours that are breathtaking for anyone who has ever handled a watercolour brush. They are scattered about, without having been sorted out, in the drawers of Boyer's original furniture. A great watercolourist without a doubt. A craftsman-painter who knew how to paint as did very few people in his day. He had made a profound study of painting; he was still learning at an age (between thirty and forty) when one scarcely expects to be still a student. I think he really knew all about painting, a knowledge that is rare, has become very rare, and yet is so exciting.

His effort is magnificent in its continuity, and it ends in that radiant colour which we saw in the last works of his life. What admirable virtuosity is displayed in the incidental effects. What marvellous embroideries on faded and aged silk for the cushions for some old lady, dreaming of luxury, and with a spotless past marred only by eyes closed to poverty!

However, I remember something Moreau once said which will correct this impression. He confided to me his regret at not being a father, and added that the sight of a worker holding his child by the hand moved him profoundly. "Bachelorhood dries up one's sensibility", he added. "My solitude is detestable."

In fact, a bachelor, he produced the work of a refined bachelor, rigorously shut off from the buffeting of life; his work is the fruit of his life, it is art, nothing but art, but that is a great deal . . .

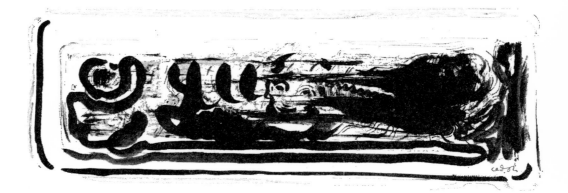

1885

ODILON REDON

36   Madame Redon   1885   D   (625)

37 Chimera 1888 L (M 90)

38　Vision　1879　L　(M 34)

38a　Making Eyes　1844　Lithograph by Isidore Grandville

39 White Woman's Body with Skull 1888 L (M 89)

40   My Irony Exceeds All Others   1889   L   (M 97)

41   False Friendliness   1879   L   (M 33)

42   Head of a Martyr   1877   D   (577)

43   The Fool   1877   D   (578)

44   Mephistopheles (Foolishness) (Madness)   c. 1877   D   (579)

45 Winged Head Flying over the Sea   before 1879   D   (584)

46   Emerging from the Larva   1897   L   (M 27)

47 Seeds Everywhere 1879 L (M 28)

48   A Mask Tolling the Hour of Death   1882   L   (M 40)

49   The Masque of the Red Death   1883   D   (609)

50   A Strange Juggler   L   (M 58)

51   Marsh Flower   1885   D   (614)

52 Light Profile 1886 L (M 61)

53   The Wall Splits Open and a Death's Head Appears   1886   L   (M 78)

Balloon Seller   1880   D   (744)

55   Monument in the Jardin du Luxembourg, Paris   Ph

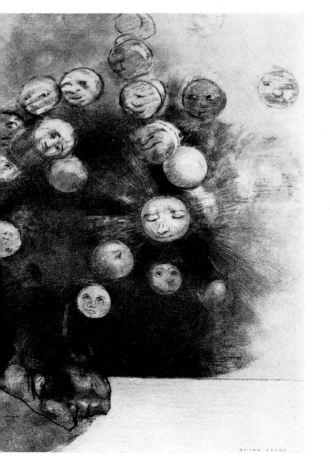

Must there not be an Invisible World?
1887   D   (654)

57   Must there not be an Invisible World?
1887   L   (M 79)

58   The Dream is Consummated in Death   1887   L   (M 81)

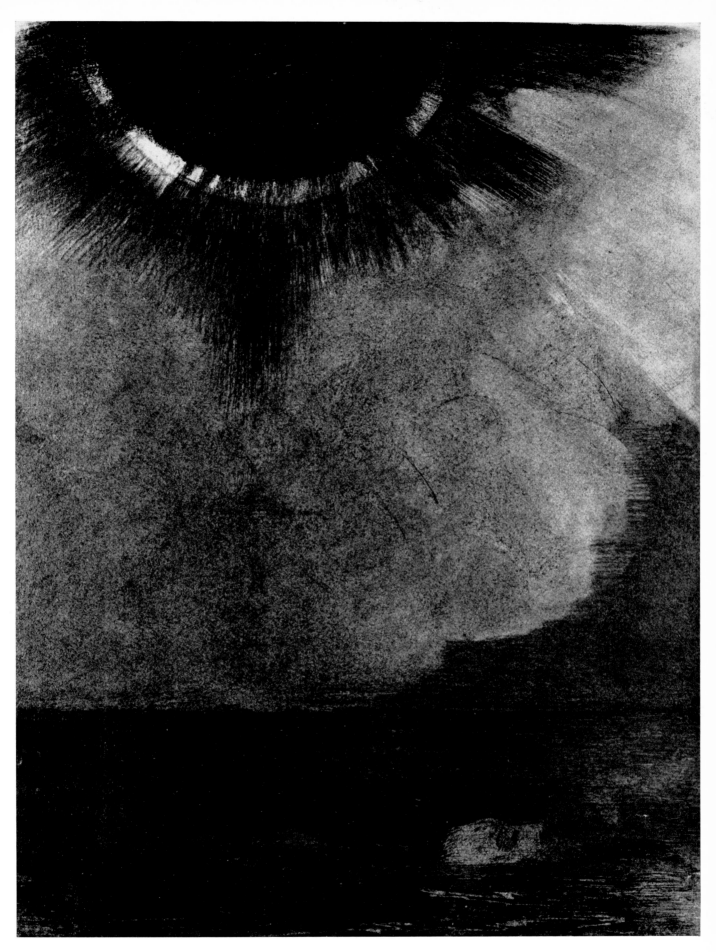

59   The Dream is Consummated in Death   1887   D   (655)

60 Bodies like Pictures 1889 L (M 98)

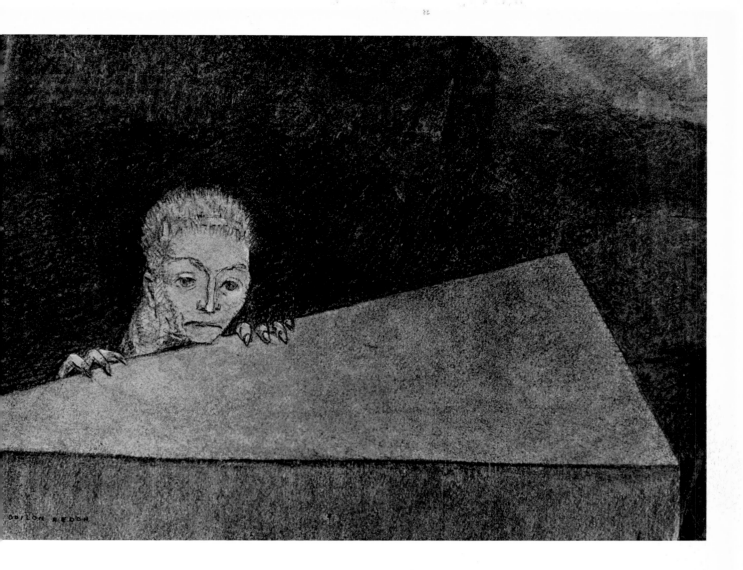

61 Ressurection of Lazarus c. 1885 D (624)

62   Tree Face   1885–90   D   (639)

63　Ghost　after 1895　D　(706)

64　From 'The Haunted House'　1896　L　(M 164)

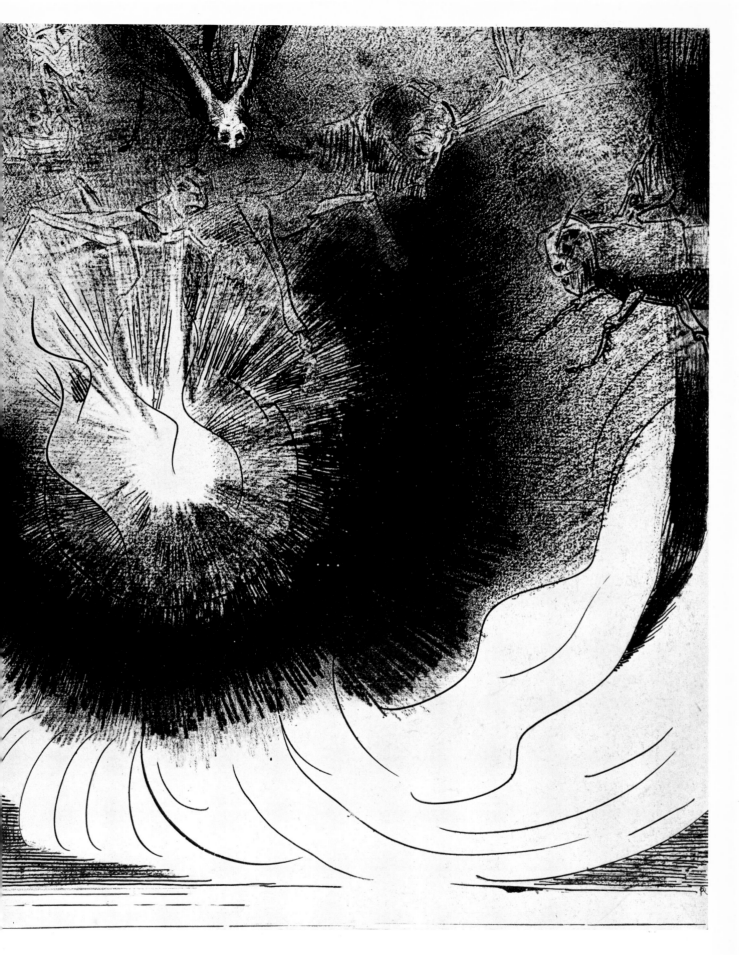

65 'Revelation'. From Heaven there fell an enormous Star   1899   L   (M 178)

66 Gustave Moreau, Oedipus
and the Sphinx 1864 O

67 Gustave Moreau, The Apparition O

68 Gustave Moreau, Alexander's Triumph O (detail)

69 Jean François Millet, The Fisherman c. 1870 D

70 Jean François Millet, The Bouquet of Marguerites c. 1865 P

71 Rodolphe Bresdin, Caesar and his Legions etching

72 Pierre Puvis de Chavannes, Summer 1891 O

Georges Seurat, The Black Bow   1882   D

74   Georges Seurat, La Grande Jatte   1886   O

75   Paul Gauguin, Vision after the Sermon   1888   O

76 Edvard Munch, The Cry   1893   O

77 Vincent van Gogh, Cypresses   1888–89   O

78 Henri de Toulouse-Lautrec, Jane Avril
    1893   Poster

Chronology

Born in Bordeaux on	20 April 1840	
Grows up in Peyrelebade until in the care of his uncle	1851	
In boarding school in Bordeaux	1851–57	
Studies drawing with Stanislas Gorin de Beaux	1855	
Studies architecture at his father's wish; fails to get accepted for the architecture class of the Ecole des Beaux-Arts in Paris. Takes part in an exhibition of pictures in Bordeaux	1860	
Makes the acquaintance of the botanist Armand Clavaud. Trip to the Pyrenees	1861	
Loses his father's fortune through a vine-louse crisis in Peyrelebade	1863	
Makes the acquaintance of the graphic artist Rodolphe Bresdin. Accepted in the painting class of the Ecole des Beaux-Arts in Paris; for some months an independent pupil of Jean-Léon Gérôme	1864	Gustave Moreau's *Oedipus and the Sphinx* exhibited in the Salon
Meeting with Corot		
Accepted for exhibition in the prints section of the Salon	1867	
Review of the Paris Salon exhibition in the Bordeaux newspaper *La Gironde*	1868	

Takes part in the war	1870–71	
	1873	Bresdin emigrates to Canada
In Madame de Rayssac's salon he meets Fantin-Latour, Chenavard and the composer Ernest Chausson. From now on he regularly spends the winter in Paris, and the summer until 1897 in Peyrelebade	1874	Death of Redon's father
Paints in Barbizon	1877	
First visit to Belgium and Holland. Study of Rembrandt; Fantin-Latour shows him the method of lithographic reproduction as a means of duplicating his charcoal drawings	1878	
First lithographic sequence: *Dans le rêve (In the Dream)*	1879	Puvis de Chavannes' wall paintings in the Paris Panthéon
Marriage to Camille Falte, a Creole whom he had met in the Rayssac circle. Landscape studies in Brittany	1880	
First exhibition of his charcoal drawings in the editorial offices of *La Vie Moderne;* little attention paid to it by the public	1881	Puvis de Chavannes' *The Poor Fisherman,* a model for the Symbolist movement
Exhibition in the hall of the newspaper *Le Gaulois* of 22 charcoal drawings. Second lithographic sequence, *For Edgar Poe.* Reviews by Emile Hennequin and Joris-Karl Huysmans appear in the press. Friendly relations develop with both	1882	
Third lithographic sequence, *Les Origines* (with Surrealistic elements)	1883	
President of the first Salon des Indépendants, exhibits alongside Schuffenecker, Cross, Signac and Seurat	1884	J.-K. Huysmans's novel *A rebours (Against the Grain)* describes Redon's art as 'monstrous'. Ensor exhibits with Les XX in Brussels
Fourth lithographic sequence, *Hommage à Goya.* First meeting with Mallarmé	1885	Seurat paints *La Grande Jatte.* Gauguin calls for a painting of 'suggestion' working directly through the media
Exhibits in Brussels at the invitation of Les XX (Further exhibitions there in 1887 and 1890) Takes part in the eighth and last Salon des Impressionistes. Fifth lithographic sequence, *La Nuit.* Birth and death of his first child. Begins to make a name for himself	1886	Moréas publishes the manifesto of Symbolism. Gauguin in Pont-Aven. Théodore de Wyzewa analyzes 'symphonic' painting in an article in the *Revue Wagnérienne.* Rimbaud's *Illuminations* published. Gustave Moreau exhibits his illustrations to La Fontaine's *Fables*

	1887	Edmond Picard publishes an essay in the magazine *L'Art Moderne* with the programmatic title 'L'Art nouveau'
Series of lithographs for E. Picard's *Le juré*		
First series of lithographs for *La tentation de Saint-Antoine*, after Flaubert, published by Deman in Brussels	1888	Death of Hennequin. Gauguin's first exhibition; his *Vision after the Sermon*. Genesis of 'Cloisonnisme' and 'Synthétisme': Bernard and Gauguin in Pont-Aven. Founding of the Nabi group: Van Gogh and Gauguin in Arles. The periodical *Le Japon Artistique* founded by the art dealer Siegfried Bing, appears till 1891
Continuation of the series *For Gustave Flaubert*. Birth of Redon's second son Ari. Participation in the exhibition of graphic artists at Durand-Ruel's. Makes the acquaintance of André Mellerio, his later biographer, Maurice Denis and Emile Bernard	1889	Huysmans's book on art criticism, entitled *Certains*, contains a chapter on Redon, who is described as 'Le Monstre'. Exhibition of Gauguin and the Synthetists in the Café Volpini. Gustave Moreau becomes a member of the Institut de France. Schuré's *Les grands initiés* and Bergson's *Données immédiates de la conscience* cast a new light on the potentialities of intuition. The Universal Exhibition in Paris
Makes the acquaintance of his future patron Andries Bonger through Emile Bernard. Graphic sequence for Baudelaire's *Fleurs du Mal*. Transition to colour: the first pastels	1890	Denis gives *Definition of Neo-Traditionalism* (Symbolism). Clavaud's death. Arthur Symons publishes in London a study, *A French Blake: Odilon Redon*
Lithographic sequence *Songes (Dreams)*. Destrée publishes the first catalogue of Redon's lithographs in Brussels. Redon becomes mentor of the Nabis in place of Gauguin	1891	Gauguin's first voyage to Tahiti, advised by Redon and his wife. Symbolist Manifesto by Aurier. First exhibition of the Nabi group in the gallery Le Barc de Boutteville. Death of Seurat. Toulouse-Lautrec designs the first modern poster. The Natanson brothers take over *La Revue Blanche*
L'Echo de Paris publishes Emile Bernard's interview with Redon. Acknowledged by Aurier as a forerunner of the Symbolists (article in *La Revue Encyclopédique*)	1892	Burne-Jones exhibition in Paris. First Salon of the Rosicrucians. Victor Horta's house for Tassel in Brussels heralds the appearance of Art Nouveau
The collector Andries Bonger in Holland, Baron Domecy in Burgundy and the dealer Vollard become Redon's patrons	1893	Bernard leaves for Italy and the East. Maurice Denis' illustrations for Gide's *Voyage d'Urien*, the first modern illustrated book. Gauguin, back from Tahiti, exhibits his South Seas pictures
Redon's first one-man show at Durand-Ruel's: 51 charcoal drawings, 9 paintings, 10 pastels and 22 lithos. Exhibition in the Kunstkring, The Hague, at the instigation of Andries Bonger.	1894	Outbreak of the Affaire Dreyfus. Thirty articles in French, Belgian, Dutch, German and Italian newspapers and magazines reflect Redon's triumph. The end of his

Exhibits in Brussels with La Libre Esthétique together with Gauguin, Ensor, Beardsley, Maillol, Denis, Chéret, Toorop and William Morris. Writes *Confidences d'artiste*		relations with Huysmans. Vuillard's decorations for Alexander Natanson
Visit to London, Religious period (to 1903)	1895	Banquet for Puvis de Chavannes. Cézanne exhibition at Vollard's. Strindberg criticizes Gauguin
Third series for Flaubert's *La tentation de Saint-Antoine*	1896	Maurice Denis's theory of religious painting. Mellerio's book *Le mouvement idéaliste en peinture* published. Siegfried Bing with the help of Henry van der Velde opens his workshops L'Art Nouveau, a meeting-place for artists of all nations supporting the idea of a decorative social art: Carrière, Denis, Beardsley, Signac, Zorn, Rodin, Bourdelle, Tiffany, Bonnard, Gallé, Toulouse-Lautrec, Valloton, Vuillard etc.
Loss of Peyrelebade. Colour lithograph for Vollard	1897	
Visit to Amsterdam for the Rembrandt exhibition. Exhibition of pastels and drawings at Vollard's	1898	Death of Mallarmé, Gustave Moreau and Puvis de Chavannes
Last lithographic sequence, *The Revelation of St John*. Takes part in the Symbolist exhibition at Durand-Ruel's	1899	Signac publishes *D'Eugène Delacroix au Néoimpressionisme*, a theory on the training of the eye for colour
Decoration of a room in the Château de Domecy, Burgundy. Beginning of the flower studies. Friendly relations with Francis Jammes. Exhibition at Durand-Ruel's: 14 pastels and 22 paintings. Spends this and the next eight summers at St Georges-de-Dionne near Royan, by the sea. First trip to Italy (Venice)	1900	
Exhibition at Vollard's. Visits Renoir at Cagnes	1901	Maurice Denis paints his picture *Hommage à Cézanne* with Redon in the place of honour. Van Gogh exhibition in Paris
Decoration of Mme Ernest Chausson's salon finished. *The World of the Chimeras*, a decorative folding-screen for the Princess Cystria. Meeting with Count Kessler	1902	Debussy's opera *Pelléas et Mélisande*
Receives the Légion d'honneur. Beginning of his friendship with Gabriel Frizeau. New exhibition at Durand-Ruel's: 15 pastels, 25 paintings	1903	Death of Gauguin

The French State buys the picture *With Closed Eyes*. The great nude studies. The Salon d'Automne shows a whole room full of Redon's pictures in colour, comprising 62 works; his graphic work is forgotten. Also took part in the Salon d'Automne of 1905, 1906 and 1907	1904	Controversy round Emile Bernard: his quarrel with Gauguin, his visit to Cézanne in Aix and his article on Redon in *L'Occident*
Decorative folding-screens: *Buddha* and *The Red Tree* (1905–08). The variations on *Apollo's Sun Chariot* and *Pegasus* (1905–10)	1905	The Villa Stoclet in Brussels by Joseph Hoffmann: the end of Jugendstil and Art Nouveau
Paintings and pastels exhibited at Durand-Ruel's	1906	Maurice Denis visits Cézanne and publishes his *Notes* (1907). Death of Cézanne. Gauguin memorial exhibition in the Paris Salon d'Automne. Separation of Church and State in France
Auction of part of the contents of Redon's studio (53 works). Break with Francis Jammes. Exhibition in Rotterdam. Visit to Switzerland	1907	Cézanne retrospective in the Salon d'Automne
Exhibition at Druet's. Decorative designs for the Gobelins factory. Second trip to Italy	1908	
Moves into a villa in Bièvres near Paris. Declares his admiration for Monticelli in a letter to Andries Bonger (12 March 1909)	1909	
Venus Anadyomene. Studies in the Musée des Tissus in Lyon. Participation in the Post-Impressionist exhibition at the Grafton Gallery, London	1910	
Decoration of the library of the former abbey of Fontfroide, commissioned by Gustave Fayet	1910/11	
Connexion with the Hahnlosers, his Swiss patrons. Participation in the exhibition *A Century of French Art* in Leningrad	1912	Special number of the periodical *La Vie* in Redon's honour: roundrobin sent to leading artists
Participation in the Armory Show in New York, Chicago and Boston with 40 works, also in the exhibition of French art at the Zürich Kunsthaus	1913	Mellerio's catalogue of the graphic work appears (206 works). Simultaneously a facsimile work independent of this appears in The Hague (192 works)
Participation in the international art exhibition in Berlin. Exhibition of 43 works at the Alfred Flechtheim Gallery, Düsseldorf	1914	
Dies at the age of 76 on 6 July 1916. With Jean Zoubaloff's gift to the Petit Palais des Beaux-Arts a whole group of his works become accessible to the public	1916	

Exhibition at Bernheim-Jeune's, *Odilon Redon, paysages d'après nature*, shows for the first time 25 intimate nature studies from his early years	1917	
Exhibition in the Kunstmuseum Winterthur. 100 graphic works exhibited in New York	1919	
Great retrospective exhibition, especially of the works in colour, at the Galerie Barbazanges, Paris (214 works)	1920	
Exhibitions at Amsterdam and Brussels art galleries	1921	
Retrospective exhibition at the Galerie Druet, Paris (300 works)	1923	Mellerio's richly illustrated monograph appears
	1925	Claude Roger-Marx's monograph published by *La Nouvelle Revue Française*
First public exhibition in the Musée des Arts Décoratifs, Paris (247 works)	1926	
	1929	Monograph by Charles Fegdal
Exhibition in the Petit Palais (231 works)	1934	
	1955	Sven Sandström publishes a study in Lund
Exhibition in the Orangerie (205 works)	1956/57	Roseline Bacou's book containing much new material appears in Lausanne
Exhibition in the Museum of Modern Art, New York, and The Chicago Art Institute: Odilon Redon, Gustave Moreau, Rodolphe Bresdin (173 works)	1961/62	

Exhibitions

Group exhibitions in which Redon participated with only a few works are not mentioned, particularly in the later years. The two letters in the left-hand column are used as a reference in the Catalogue

Pa	1881	Paris, *La Vie Moderne*. Charcoal drawings
Pb	1882	Paris, *Le Gaulois*. Prints and drawings
Pc	1883	Paris, Société des Artistes Français
Pd	1886	Paris, Artistes Indépendants (Impressionists). 15 drawings
Ba	1886	Brussels, Les XX
Pe	1889	Paris, Galerie Durand-Ruel
Bb	1890	Brussels, Les XX
Pf	1891	Paris, Ecole des Beaux-Arts, Lithographs
Pg	1894	Paris, Galerie Durand-Ruel. Charcoal drawings, paintings, pastels, prints, 124 Works
Ha	1894	The Hague, Kunstkring. 40 charcoal-drawings
Ph	1898	Paris, Galerie Ambroise Vollard. Pastels and drawings
Pi	1900	Paris, Exposition Universelle 1 drawing, 3 lithographs
Pj	1900	Paris, Galerie Durand-Ruel. 14 pastels, 20 paintings
Pk	1901	Paris, Galerie Ambroise Vollard
Ka	1903	Cracow, Art Association
Pl	1903	Paris, Galerie Durand-Ruel. 15 pastels, 25 paintings
Pm	1904	Paris, Salon d'Automne. A whole room containing 62 works
Pn	1906	Paris, Galerie Durand-Ruel. 23 pastels, 22 paintings
Po	1908	Paris, Galerie E. Druet. 52 works
Na	1913	New York, Chicago, Boston: Armory Show. 40 works
Da	1914	Düsseldorf, Alfred-Flechtheim-Galerie. 43 works
Bc	1917	Berlin, Galerie Paul Cassirer
Pp	1917	Paris, Galerie Bernheim-Jeune. 85 works
Nb	1919	New York, Ehrich Print Gallery. Prints
Wa	1919	Winterthur, Museum
Pq	1920	Paris, Galerie Barbazanges. 214 works
Bd	1920/21	Brussels, Galerie Georges Giroux. 46 oil paintings, 8 pastels, 26 watercolours, 5 decorative works, 37 drawings, 14 lithographs
Aa	1921	Amsterdam, Galerie de Vries. Toulouse-Lautrec and Odilon Redon
Nc	1922	New York, Museum of French Art
Pr	1923	Paris, Galerie E. Druet. 300 works
La	1926	London, Lefèvre Gallery
Ps	1926	Paris, Musée des Arts decoratifs. 247 works
Nd	1928	New York, Gallery César de Hauke. 57 works

Ca	1928/29	Chicago, Art Institute. Paintings, Pastels, Drawings, 48 works
Cb	1929	Chicago, Art Institute. 207 graphic works
Pt	1929	Paris, Galerie Dru. Lithographs
Nc	1931	New York, Museum of Modern Art. Lautrec-Redon. 39 works
Be	1932	Bern, Museum. Despiau, Matisse, Redon. Prints
Nf	1932	New York, Gallery Durand-Ruel. Cézanne, Gauguin, Odilon Redon
Pu	1934	Paris, Petit Palais. 231 works
Lb	1938	London, Wildenstein. 40 works, mostly paintings
Bf	1938	Bordeaux, Salon des Artistes Indépendants
Pv	1942	Paris, Galerie de France. Charcoal drawings
Pw	1947	Paris, Galerie Jacques Dubourg. 9 paintings 11 pastels
Ab	1948	Arnhem, Ver. van Beeldende Kunst
Px	1949	Paris, Bernheim-Jeune. Les Magiciens de la Peinture
Py	1949/50	Paris, Orangerie, Carrière et le Symbolisme. 50 works
Pz	1950	Paris, Galerie Berri-Argenson. 29 works
Ng	1951	New York, Gallery J. Seligmann, Cleveland Museum of Art, Minneapolis, Walker Art Center. 18 pastels, 17 drawings
Nh	1952	New York, Museum of Modern Art, Picasso-Redon. Prints and drawings
Lc	1952	Linz, Neue Galerie Wolfgang Gurlitt. Prints
Paa	1955	Palm Beach, Florida. Society of the Four Arts
Wb	1956	Washington, Corcoran Gallery. Visionaries and Dreamers
Pab	1956/57	Paris, Orangerie. 244 works, Catalogue by Roseline Bacou
Hb	1957	The Hague, Gemeentemuseum. 225 works
Hc	1957	Houston, Texas, Contemporary Arts Museum. The Magical World of Redon, Klee, Baziotes
Bg	1957	Brussels, Palais des Beaux-Arts. Le Mouvement Symboliste
Bh	1957	Bordeaux. Bosch, Goya et le Fantastique
Pac	1958	Paris, Galerie Stephen Higgons. 31 drawings, 44 prints, 5 paintings, 4 pastels
Bi	1958	Bern, Kunsthalle. 219 works
Ni	1958	New York, The New Gallery. 40 works
Nj	1959	New York, Paul Rosenberg. 13 paintings, 13 pastels
Ld	1959	London, Matthiesen Gallery 85 works
Le	1959	London, Arts Council of Great Britain, Lithographs
Nk	1961/62	New York, Museum of Modern Art, and Art Institute of Chicago. Odilon Redon-Gustave Moreau-Rodolphe Bresdin. 173 works. Essay by John Rewald

Selected Bibliography

A *Autobiography*

1   *A soi-même. Journal (1867–1915)*. Paris, H. Floury, 1922. 179 pp.
2   *Lettres d'Odilon Redon*. 1878–1916. Paris und Brussels, G. van Oest, 1923. 143 pp.
3   *Lettres de Vincent van Gogh, ... Odilon Redon à Emile Bernard*. Tonnerre, Editions de la Rénovation Esthétique, 1926. 196 pp.
4   *Lettres de Gauguin, Gide, Huysmans, Jammes, Mallarmé, Verhaeren à Odilon Redon*. Paris, José Corti, 1960. 317 Ill.
5   Westheim, Paul (Editor). *Künstlerbekenntnisse*. Berlin, Propyläen, (1924). pp. 69–89
6   Hess, Walter: *Dokumente zum Verständnis der modernen Malerei*. Rowohlts Deutsche Enzyklopädie. Hamburg, Rowohlt, 1956, pp. 114–115
    Further letters in 16, 17, 23

B *Monographs, Studies and Illustrated works*

7   Pach, Walter. *Odilon Redon*. New York, 1913, 16 pp.
8   Mellerio, André. *Odilon Redon* (The graphic work with Catalogue). Paris, Société pour l'Etude de la Gravure Française, 1913. 167 pp. Ill.
9   *L'Œuvre Graphique d'Odilon Redon*. 192 plates in facsimile. The Hague, M. M. Artz & De Bois, 1913

10 Mellerio, André. *Odilon Redon, Peintre, Dessinateur et Graveur*, Paris, H. Floury, 1923, 215 pp. Ill.
11 Roger-Marx, Claude. *Odilon Redon*. Les Peintres français nouveaux, Nr. 21. Paris, Nouvelle Revue Française (1925). 19 pp. Ill.
12 Miedema, R. *Odilon Redon en Albrecht Dürer*. Amsterdam, 1928
13 Fegdal, Charles, *Odilon Redon*. Maîtres de l'Art Moderne. Paris, Rieder, 1929. 64 pp. Ill.
14 Leblond, Marius et Ary. *Les Fusains d'Odilon Redon*, Paris, 1941
15 Roger-Marx, Claude. *Redon. Fusains*. Paris, Braun & Cie, (1950). 17 plates
16 Sandström, Sven. *Le Monde Imaginaire d'Odilon Redon*. Lund, Gleerup, 1955. 231 pp. Ill. and Bibliography
17 Bacou, Roseline. *Odilon Redon*. Two volumes. Geneva, Pierre Cailler, 1956. 290 and 59 pp. Ill. (123 pl.) and bibliography

C *Important Catalogues*

18 Destrée, Jules. *L'Œuvre lithographique d'Odilon Redon*. Brussels, Deman, 1891. 80 pp. Ill.
19 *Exposition Rétrospective*. Paris, Galerie Barbazanges, 1920
20 *O. R.* New York, De Hauke & Co., 1928

21 *Catalogue of Paintings, Pastels and Drawings by Odilon Redon.* Foreword by Daniel Catton Rich. Chicago, The Art Institute, 1929

22 *O. R. Pastels and Drawings.* Foreword by Ary Leblond, New York, Jacques Seligmann & Co, 1951–52

23 *O. R.* Foreword by J. Bouchot-Saupique and Claude Roger-Marx. Text by Roseline Bacou, Paris, Orangerie des Tuileries, 1956–57

24 *O. R.* Foreword by Vitale Bloch. The Hague, Gemeentemuseum, 1957

25 *O. R. Magician du Noir et Blanc.* Foreword by Claude Roger-Marx. Paris, Stephen Higgons, 1958

26 *O. R.* Foreword by Franz Meyer-Chagall. Bern, Kunsthalle, 1958

27 *An Exhibition of Painting and Pastels by O. R.* New York, Paul Rosenberg, 1959

28 *O. R.* London, The Matthiesen Gallery, 1959

29 *O. R. Gustave Moreau, Rodolphe Bresdin* Text by John Rewald, Harold Joachim and Dore Ashton, New York, Museum of Modern Art, and Chicago, The Art Institute, 1961–62

Further catalogues in 8 and 17

D   *General works*

30 Huysmans, J.-K. *A Rebours.* Paris, Charpentier, 1884

31 Huysmans, J.-K. *Certains.* Paris, Tresse & Stock, 1889

32 Jourdain, Frantz. *Les Décorés, ceux qui ne le sont pas.* Paris, Simonis Empis, 1895

33 de Gourmont, Rémy. *Le Problème du Style.* Paris, Mercure de France, 1896

34 Mellerio, André. *Le Mouvement Idéaliste en Peinture.* Paris, Floury, 1896

35 Meier-Graefe, Julius. *Entwicklungsgeschichte der modernen Kunst.* Stuttgart, 1904

36 Denis, Maurice. *Théories 1890–1910.* Paris, Rouart & Watelin, 1912

37 Salmon, André. *Propos d'Atelier.* Paris, Les Trente (1920)

38 Klingsor, Tristan. *La Peinture.* Paris, Rieder, 1921

39 Fontainas, André. *Histoire Générale de l'Art Français.* Paris, Librairie de France, 1922

40 Pach, Walter. *The Masters of Modern Art.* New York, 1924

41 Kröller-Müller, H. *Die Entwicklung der Modernen Malerei.* Leipzig, 1925

42 Focillon, Henri. *Du Réalisme à nos Jours.* Paris, H. Laurens, 1928

43 Roger-Marx, Claude. *La Gravure Originale en France, de Manet à nos Jours.* Paris, Hypérion, 1939

44 Girou, Jean. *Peintres de Midi.* Paris, Floury (1939)

45 Hauteceur, Louis. *Littérature et Peinture en France.* Paris, Armand Colin, 1942

46 Dorival, Bernard. *Les Etapes de la Peinture française contemporaine.* Paris, Gallimard, 1943

47 Francastel, Pierre. *Nouveau Dessin. Nouvelle Peinture.* Paris, Médicis (1946)

48 Bazin, Germain. *L'Epoque Impressioniste.* Paris, Tisné, 1947

49 Chassé, Charles. *Le Mouvement Symboliste dans l'Art du XIXᵉ Siècle.* Paris, Floury, 1947

50 Michaud, Guy. *Message Poétique du Symbolisme.* Paris, Nizet, 1947

51 Berger, Klaus. *French Master Drawings of the Nineteenth Century.* New York, Harper 1950

52 Schmidt, Georg. 'Die Entwicklung der Malerei von Ingres bis Bonnard' In: Raynal, Maurice: *Geschichte der Modernen Malerei II*, Geneva, Skira, 1950

53 Soffici, Ardengo. *Trenta Artisti Moderni.* Florence, Vallecchi, 1950

54 Humbert, Agnès. *Les Nabis et leur Epoque.* Geneva, Pierre Cailler, 1954

55 Rewald, John. *Post-Impressionism from Van Gogh to Gauguin.* New York, The Museum of Modern Art, 1956

56 Lethève, Jacques. *Impressionistes et Symbolistes devant la Presse.* Collection Kiosque. Paris, Armand Colin, 1959

57 Rookmaaker, H. R. *Synthetist Art Theories.* Amsterdam, Swets and Zeitlinger, 1959

E   *Articles in periodicals*

From the overwhelmingly copious literature only those articles are listed that are particularly important, that have been forgotten till now, or have only recently appeared. More complete lists are to be found in 8, 16, 17, 23, 55.

58 Symons, Arthur. 'A French Blake: O. R.' *The Art Review*, London, July 1890

59 Morice, Charles. 'O. R.' *Les Hommes d'Aujourd'hui.* Vol. 8, No. 386, 1890

60 Aurier, G.-A. 'Les Symbolistes' *La Revue Encyclopédique*, Paris, No. 32, 1892

61 Lorrain, Jean. 'Un Etrange Jongleur' *L'Echo de Paris*. 10 April 1894

62 Veth, J. C. 'Redons lithographische Serien.' *Kunst and Künstler*, Ill., Berlin, 1904

63 Bernard, Emile. 'O. R. *L'Occident*', Paris, May, 1904

64 Jammes, Francis. 'O. R. Botaniste' *Vers et Prose*, December 1906

65 Cohen-Gosschalk, Johanna. 'O. R.' *Zeitschrift für Bildende Kunst*, December 1910

66 'Hommage a O. R.' 21 contributions. *La Vie*. 30 XI and 7 XII 1912

67 Salmon, André. 'O. R.' *L'Art Décoratif*, Paris, January 1913

68 Doin, Jeanne. 'O. R.' *Mercure de France*, Paris, July 1914

69 Fontainas, André. 'O. R.' *Mercure de France*, Paris, August 1916

70 Hahnloser-Bühler, Hedy. 'O. R. als Graphiker.' *Das Graphische Kabinett*. Winterthur, 1919

71 Grohmann, Will. 'O. R.' *Thieme-Becker Künstlerlexikon*. Leipzig, no date

72 Gann, Louise C. 'The Metaphor of Redon.' *International Studio*, London, November, 1923

73 Biermann, Georg. 'O. R.' *Der Cicerone*, Leipzig, April 1924

74 Born, Wolfgang. 'Der Traum in der Graphik des O. R.' *Graphische Künste*. Vienna 1929

75 Morland, Jacques. 'O. R. et le Symbolisme.' *Mercure de France*, Paris, August 1936

76 De Graaf, D. A. 'O. R.' *Apollo*, The Hague, May 1946

77 Troendle, Hugo. 'Erinnerungen an O. R.' *Das Kunstwerk*, Baden-Baden, I, 6, 1947

78 Roger-Marx, Claude. 'O. R., Peintre et Mystique.' *L'Œil*, Paris, May 1956

79 Berger, Klaus. 'The Pastels of O. R.' *College Art Journal*, New York, Fall, 1956

80 Bacou, Roseline. 'Unité de l'Œuvre d'O. R.' *La Revue des Arts*, Paris, October 1956

81 Rewald, John. 'Odilon Redon et Emile Bernard.' *Gazette des Beaux-Arts*, Paris and New York, November, 1956

82 Roumeguère, Pierre. 'Le Mystère d' O. R.' *La Vie Médicale*. Paris, christmas 1956

83 Veronesi, Giulia. 'O. R.' *Emporium* v. d. 126, No. 747. March 1957

84 Bersier, J. E. 'O. R. et Nous.' *Etudes d'Art*, No. 13. Algier 1957

85 Berger, Klaus. 'The Reconversion of O. R.' *Art Quarterly*, Detroit, Summer 1958

Further articles in 18, 21, 22, 23, 24, 25, 26, 29

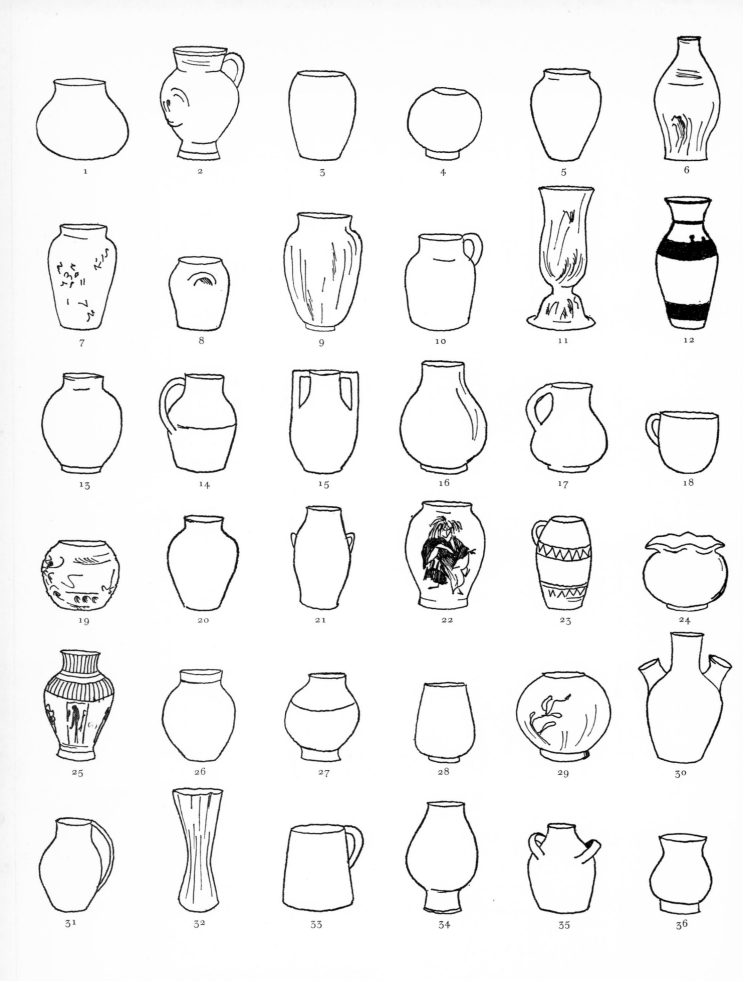

Diagrams of Vase shapes in Redon's paintings and pastels

Catalogue

The catalogue of Redon's graphic work was published by Mellerio in 1913 (Bibliography no. 8) and reprinted with additions in his monograph (Bibliography no. 10). All references to this work are marked with an M followed by the number. Better reproductions are to be found in the two portfolios (Bibliography no. 9).

The oil paintings and pastels are here catalogued for the first time. Completeness has been aimed at, but the author is aware that this goal can only be approached. The works are today scattered too widely over all the continents and the innumerable flower-pieces in particular are too difficult to distinguish. The catalogue is based upon 1) the author's own study of the originals in France, the U.S.A., Switzerland, Holland, Belgium, Great Britain and Germany, 2) all available exhibition catalogues, 3) preparatory works by Fegdal, Sandström and Roseline Bacou (Bibliography nos. 13, 16, 17,) 4) information kindly supplied by the directors of the National Museum for Western Art in Tokyo, by the late M. Georges Wildenstein, and by M. Ari Redon, the artist's son. The author would like to express his thanks to them; likewise to Messrs John Rewald, Germain Seligman and Victor Thaw in New York, and Harold Joachim in Chicago. Furthermore to all owners of Redon's works who have lent him photographs and given permission to reproduce them. His particular thanks are due to the American Council of Learned Societies and the General Research Fund of the University of Kansas, who made it possible for him to make prolonged trips for purposes of study, to take academic leave and to obtain the necessary secretarial assistance.—Drawings and watercolours are, of course, impossible to trace in their entirety.

Particular attention has been paid to dating. Redon himself only very rarely placed a date on his work. Occasional dates given in catalogues and the like often contradict one another or have proved to be impossible: for example, we find a certain date proposed, whereas it can be demonstrated that the picture was to be seen years before in an exhibition. My dating is based upon a stylistic analysis which is explained in the text. An iconographic analysis of the subject matter, biographical facts and arguments based on Redon's philosophical outlook have always been employed as a check. A precise dating, year by year, seems impossible, because many tendencies often overlap for a time. In relation to the paintings and pastels, in particular, the total *œuvre* has here been divided up into a number of groups determined on the one hand by the inspiration of the theme, on the other by the stylistic development. Within each group a chronological order has been attempted. In cases where my dating differs significantly from that of a previous publication the latter date is given in brackets.

For easier identification previous owners and references to the literature are given in every possible case. Exhibitions in which the work has been shown are generally indicated by two letters as explained in the table of *Exhibitions* (pp. 175–176).

Oil Paintings

1 SELF-PORTRAIT   1867
Oil on wood 35 × 25 cm
Coll.: Paris, A. Redon
Exhib.: Wa; Pr, No. 12; Ps, No. 82; Pu,
No. 11; Pab, No. 1, repr.; Ld, No. 51,
repr.; Nk, No. 2, repr.
Lit.: Robert Rey, Art et Décoration, Aug.
1920, p. 45, repr.; Fegdal, 1929, Pl. 1,
repr.; Bacou, 1956, No. XIV, repr.

2 SELF-PORTRAIT   1875–77
Oil
Coll.: Paris, Claude Roger-Marx
Exhib.: Etapes de l'Art contemporain, II,
Paris, Galerie des Beaux-Arts, 1934, No. 91;
Lb, No. 4
Lit.: Bacou, 1956, No. 1, repr.

3 SELF-PORTRAIT   1875 (C. 1880)
Oil on wood 42 × 32 cm
Coll.: Paris, A. Redon
Exhib.: Pu, No. 11; Hb, No. 154; Bi, No.
127

Intimate Nature Studies   1870-95

4 THE HEATH IN MÉDOC (CLOUDS). Before 1870
Oil 33 × 41 cm
Coll.: Paris, A. Redon
Exhib.: Bd, No. 34; Landscape in French
Art, London, 1949, No. 352
Lit.: Fegdal, 1929, No. 4, repr.

4.a STREET IN FONTARABIE
Oil 52 × 46 cm
Coll.: Tokyo, S. Fukushima; Tokyo, Nikko-
Shoken Co.

5 OUTSKIRTS OF THE TOWN WITH TWO RIDERS
C. 1870
Oil on cardboard 46 × 45 cm
Coll.: Basel, Beyeler
Exhib.: Maîtres de l'Art Moderne, Galerie
Beyeler, Basel, 1956, No. 7, repr.

6 STREET IN BARBIZON   1875
Oil
Exhib.: Pg, No. 60

7 LANDSCAPE NEAR FONTAINEBLEAU   C. 1875
Oil
Coll.: Béziers, Gustave Fayet

8 THE TREE
Oil 35 × 26 cm
Coll.: Winterthur, Jäggli-Hahnloser
Exhib.: Bi, No. 137

9 BRUSHWOOD IN SPRING   C. 1875 in Barbizon
Oil on cardboard 23 × 32.5 cm
Coll.: Paris, A. Redon
Exhib.: Pj, No. 11; Pr, No. 203; Ca, No. 15;
Mostra di Capolaveri della Pittura francesa
dell'ottocento, Rom, 1955, No. 89, repr.;
Pab, No. XXXI, repr.; Ld, No. 56, repr.;
Sources du XXe Siècle, Musée d'Art Mo-
derne, Paris, 1960, No. 577
Lit.: Bacou, 1956, No. 60, repr.

10 SEATED WOMAN IN THE FOREST   C. 1875
Oil 33 × 20 cm
Coll.: Paris, G. B.

11 TREES IN PEYRELEBADE   C. 1875
Oil 24 × 33 cm
Coll.: New York, John Hay Whitney
Exhib.: Nk, No. 4

12 VILLAGE STREET   C. 1875
Oil 24 × 30.5 cm
Coll.: Rotterdam, Van Valkenburg; Rotter-
dam, Boymans Museum
Exhib.: Pab, No. XXX, repr.; Hb, No. 157;
Bi, No. 133; repr.; Ld, No. 54, repr.

13 VILLAGE STREET   C. 1875
Oil 42 × 30 cm
Coll.: Aerdenhout, Gomperts
Exhib.: Hb, No. 160, repr.; Ld, No. 55,
repr.

14 BRITTANY. STREET IN DOUARNENEZ   1875
Oil on cardboard 33 × 25 cm
Coll.: Paris, A. Redon
Exhib.: Pp, No. 12; Pr, No. 179; Ps, No.
73; Bi, No. 130

15 ROCKS IN BRITTANY 1875(?)
Oil on wood 25×33.5 cm
Coll.: The Hague, Vitale Bloch
Exhib.: Hb, No. 156, repr.; Bi, No. 132,
repr.; Ld, No. 53, repr.

16 STREET IN QUIMPER, BRITTANY C. 1880
Oil on cardboard 31.5×23 cm
Coll.: Paris, A. Redon
Exhib.: Nk, No. 6, repr.

17 IN THE HARBOUR (BRITTANY) C. 1880
Oil 19×27 cm
Coll.: New York, Mrs. Richard J. Bernhard
Exhib.: Nk, No. 8, col. repr.

18 THE HEATH NEAR PEYRELEBADE
Oil on wood 25×35 cm
Coll.: The Hague, Vitale Bloch
Exhib.: Hb, No. 157a; Bi, No. 146

19 ENVIRONS OF PEYRELEBADE C. 1880
Oil on cardboard 33×25.5 cm
Coll.: New York, Stephen Hahn
Exhib.: Nk, No. 9

20 THE PATH 1880 (1895)
Oil 47×45 cm
Coll.: Paris, A. Redon
Exhib.: Ps, No. 77; Lb, No. 36; Bi, No. 134

21 LANDSCAPE NEAR PEYRELEBADE C. 1880
Oil on cardboard 46.5×44 cm
Coll.: Paris, A. Redon
Exhib.: Nk, No. 5, col. repr.

21a LANDSCAPE
Oil on wood 21×29.4 cm
Coll.: Kyoto, S. Takeuchi; Osaka,
K. Hori; Tokyo, K. Toyama
Exhib.: Redon, Tokyo, Kyuryudo Gallery,
1954

22 THE TREE 1880
Oil 33×25.5 cm
Coll.: Paris, A. Redon
Exhib.: Pu, No. 20; Bi, No. 135

23 AVENUE OF TREES IN AUTUMN
Oil 25.3×32 cm
Coll.: Tokyo, K. Nakagawa

Exhib.: Pq; Pr; Redon, Tokyo, Kyuryudo
Gallery, 1954; Masterpieces of European Art,
Kyoto, 1957

24 MARSH LANDSCAPE IN THE HEATH
Oil on wood 33×24 cm
Coll.: Wassenaar, B. Meijer
Exhib.: Hb, No. 162; Bi, No. 129

25 VILLAGE IN MÉDOC
Oil
Coll.: Abbaye de Fontfroide, Mme.
Fayet

26 HARBOUR IN BRITTANY C. 1880 (1885)
Oil on cardboard 26.5×41 cm
Coll.: Almen, Bonger
Exhib.: Ps, No. 75; Het Franse Landschap,
Amsterdam, 1951, No. 110; Pab, No. 125;
Hb, No. 159; Ld, No. 57, repr.
Lit.: Sandström, 1955, p. 154, repr.

27 SEACOAST IN BRITTANY C. 1880
Oil
Coll.: Almen, Bonger
Lit.: Sandström, 1955, Pl. 118, repr.

28 AT THE HARBOOR OF MORGAT 1882
Oil on cardboard 26.5×29.5 cm
Coll.: Paris, M. R. Gérard; Alkmaar
Holland, Dr. Prins; Emery Reves
Exhib.: Pp, No. 19

29 ROCKS 1880
Oil on cardboard 18.5×27.5 cm
Coll.: Paris, A. Redon
Exhib.: Pp, No. 18; Pu, No. 4; Hb, No. 163;
Bi, No. 136

30 CLIFFS AT EBBE 1880
or 1883
Oil on cardboard 23×33 cm
Coll.: Paris, S. Morin; London, Eliot
Hodgkins
Exhib.: Pab, No. 123

31 PINK ROCKS AT ORY 1880
Oil 22×34 cm
Coll.: Béziers, Gustave Fayet; New York,
New Gallery

32 PINK ROCKS C. 1880
Oil

Coll.: Paris, A. Leblond
Exhib.: Ps, No. 58

33 THE SEA AT MORGAT 1883 (1875)
Oil 42.5 × 69 cm
Coll.: Paris, A. Leblond
Exhib.: Pq, No. 62; Pr, No. 202; Ps, No.
57; Pu, No. 13; Pab, No. 127; Hb, No. 166;
Bi, No. 131; Ld, No. 58, repr.
Lit.: Mellerio, 1923, p. 69, repr.

33a THE SEA IN BRITTANY
Oil 36.5 × 42 cm
Coll.: Tokyo, R. Umehara
Exhib.: Redon, Tokyo, Kyuryudo Gallery,
1954

34 HOUSES IN MÉDOC C. 1890
Oil
Coll.: Paris, M. A. Leblond; New York,
Mrs. Diodata o'Toole
Exhib.: Ps, No. 59; Ne, No. 92, repr.

35 SEACOAST
Oil 19 × 34.5 cm
Coll.: Paris, Valentine Abdy
Exhib.: Hb, No. 158

36 SAILING-BOAT IN BRITTANY 1885 (?)
Oil 20.5 × 31.5 cm
Coll.: Paris, A. Redon
Exhib.: Pr, No. 220; Ps, No. 75; Pab, No.
XXXII, repr.; Nk, No. 7
Lit.: Bacou, 1956, No. 61, repr.; Klaus Berger, The Art Quarterly, Summer 1958,
p. 153, repr.

37 SMALL VILLAGE IN MÉDOC 1890
Oil on cardboard 28 × 34.5
Coll.: Paris, A. Redon
Exhib.: Hb, No. 164; Bi, No. 147

38 THE SACLAY POND (1910?)
Oil 34 × 24 cm
Coll.: Paris, Dr. Paul-Emile Weill;
Boulogne sur Seine, Mme Henry Kapferer
Exhib.: Pq, No. 21; Bd, No. 18; Pu, No. 58;
Hb, No. 161; Bi, No. 128

39 ROAD IN BIÈVRES 1890 or later (?)
Oil on wood 35 × 26.5 cm

Coll.: The Hague, P. Arntzenius
Exhib.: Pp, No. 5; Hb, No. 165, repr.; Bi,
No. 145

40 SEACOAST 1893/34 (?)
Oil 41 × 74 cm
Coll.: Baden, Switzerland, Sidney, W.
Brown
Exhib.: Bi, No. 152

41 POND 1895
Oil 25 × 33 cm
Coll.: Paris, A. Redon
Exhib.: Bi, No. 153; Paysages de France,
Bernheim, Paris, 1961

42 OAK IN MÉDOC 1895
Oil 39.5 × 32 cm
Coll.: London, Matthiesen Gallery
Exhib.: Wa

43 HERDS IN MÉDOC C. 1895 (?)
Coll.: Formerly: Paris, Parent
Exhib.: Pp, No. 21; Ps, No. 64
Lit.: Mellerio, 1923, p. 13, repr.

44 THE HOUSE AT PEYRELEBADE 1895–98
Oil 35 × 43 cm
Coll.: Paris, A. Redon
Exhib.: Pp, No. 1; Pr, No. 171; Ps, No. 78;
Pab, No. 136
Lit.: Fegdal, 1929, Tafel V, repr.; Bacou,
1956, No. 65, repr.

45 VILLAGE POND IN PEYRELEBADE 1895–98
Oil
Coll.: Paris, A. Redon

Visions and Allegories
I Fantasy 1860-1900

46 GREECE SURRENDERS ON THE RUINS OF
MISSOLONGHI (Copy after Delacroix).
C. 1859 (1875)
Oil
Coll.: Paris, A. Redon
Exhib.: Pq, No. 7; Pu, No. 9
Lit.: Sandström. 1955, No. 18

47　ROLAND IN THE VALLEY OF RONCEVAUX
1862
Oil 49×61 cm
Coll.: Paris, A. Redon
Exhib.: Pq, No. 14; Pr, No. 6, Ps, No. 71;
Pu, No. 2; Py, No. 123; see: Pencil Draw-
ing Collection (Coll. A. Leblond, 34×
25.8 cm) repr. Mellerio, 1923, p. 39, exh:
Hb, No. 204

48　CRUSADERS ON THE SEA　C. 1865
Oil 29×25.5 cm
Coll.: New York, Walter Pach
Exhib.: Ni, No. 1; Nk, No. 1, repr.
Lit.: Sandström, 1955, No. 16, repr.

49　LION HUNT　Copy after a lost painting by
Delacroix, Variations: Paris, private Collec-
tion. Before 1870
Oil 40×50 cm
Coll.: Bordeaux, Museum
Exhib.: Pj, No. 33; Bd, No. 46; Pq, No. 6;
Pr, No. 104; Ps, No. 83; Pu, No. 8; Lb,
No. 29; Pab, No. 120
Lit.: Fegdal, 1929, No. 10, repr.; Sand-
ström, 1955, No. 15, repr.

50　DISTRIBUTING WREATHES—THE VANITY OF
FAME　1870
Oil 42×50 cm
Coll.: Paris, Keller; Paris, Professor Lemée;
Paris, Stephen Higgons
Exhib.: Autour de Gustave Moreau, Galerie
Les Deux Iles, Paris, 1961; Nk, No. 3,
repr.

51　THE THOUGHT ON THE PINNACLE OF THE
WORLD　1880 or earlier
Oil 21×26 cm
Coll.: formerly Paris, M. A. Leblond
Exhib.: Ps, No. 56; Pu, No. 19; Py, No. 124;
Bi, No. 138
Lit.: Mellerio, 1923, p. 33, repr.

52　FALLEN ANGEL　1880
Oil on wood 35×245 cm
Coll.: The Hague, P. Arntzenius
Exhib.: Hb, No. 171, repr.; Bi, No. 141,
repr.

53　CAIN AND ABEL　(see M. 18) C. 1886
Oil

Coll.: Paris, A. Leblond
Exhib.: Pq, p. 59; Ps, No. 60; Pu, No. 23
Lit.: Mellerio, 1923, No. 114, repr.

54　WITH CLOSED EYES　1890　(see M. 107)
Oil on canvas mounted on cardboard
38×30 cm
Coll.: Paris, Luxembourg, 1904; Paris,
Louvre, 1929
Exhib.: Ps, No. 1; Pu, No. 25; Cinquante-
naire du Symbolisme, Bibliothèque Natio-
nale, Paris, 1936, No. 1062; Les Impres-
sionistes, Jeu de Paume, Paris, 1947, No. 218;
Pab, No. XXI, repr.
Lit.: Mellerio, 1923, p. 161, repr.; Sand-
ström, 1955, Abb. 127, repr.; Bacou, 1956,
Nr. 44, repr.

55　WITH CLOSED EYES　1890
Oil on wood 51×41 cm
Coll.: Almen, Bonger
Exhib.: Hb, No. 172
Lit.: Johanna Cohen-Gosschalk, Zeitschrift
für bildende Kunst, December 1910, Pl. 10
repr.

56　WITH CLOSED EYES　C. 1895
Oil 65.5×51 cm
Coll.: Mannerdorf, Switzerland, Staub-
Terlinden; Northampton, Smith College
Museum
Exhib.: La Peinture française du XIXe
siècle en Suisse, Gazette des Beaux-Arts,
Paris, 1938, XXX, repr.; Nj, No. 1. repr.;
Magic of Flowers in Painting, Wildenstein,
New York, 1954, No. 57
Lit.: Gazette des Beaux-Arts, 1938, No. 91,
Tafel XXX, repr.

57　WITH CLOSED EYES (Second Version). After
1900
Oil
Coll.: New York, Wildenstein

57a　WITH CLOSED EYES　C. 1905
Oil 62×58 cm
Coll.: Paris, A. Vollard; Paris, W. Goetz;
New York, New Gallery

58　WOMAN WITH CORSAGE OF FLOWERS
C. 1890 (Before 1900) (1875)
Oil 64×38 cm

Coll.: Paris, A. Leblond; New York, Paul Rosenberg
Exhib.: Pq, 60; Pu, 14; Py, 125; Nk, 20, col. repr.
Lit.: Bacou, 1956, 63, repr.

59 MONKS C. 1890
Oil 104×42 cm
Coll.: Paris, Claude Roger-Marx
Exhib.: Cinquantenaire du Symbolisme, Paris, Bibl. Nat., 1936, No. 1064; Pz, No. 5; Bh, No. 335

60 HEAD WITH OWLS
Oil on wood 39×31.5 cm
Coll.: The Hague, H. P. Bremmer, heirs
Exhib.: Hb, No. 170; Bi, No. 140

61 ARAB GUITARIST 1893
(1875)
Oil 50×44 cm
Coll.: Paris, Jacques Zoubaloff; Paris, Petit Palais, 1916
Exhib.: Pu, No. 10; Chefs-d'œuvre du Petit Palais, Zürich, 1947, No. 277; Les origines de l'art contemporain, Rennes, 1951, No. 47; Maîtres français de la collection du Petit Palais, Rotterdam, 1952, No. 103; Art Francais, Tokyo, 1955, No. 42; Pab, No. 130; Bi, No. 151

62 PRAYER C. 1893 (see M. 124)
Oil on wood 32×29 cm
Coll.: Paris, Mme. Albert Marquet
Exhib.: Bh, No. 340

63 CALIBAN'S DREAM 1895 (Bacou: 1900, Sandström: 1880–85)
Oil on wood 44.5×39 cm
Coll.: Paris, A. Redon
Exhib.: Pq, No. 18; Pr, No. 8; Ps, No. 79; Pu, No. 28; Les Origines de l'Art Moderne, Strasbourg, Besançon, Nancy, 1947; Px; Landscape in French Art, London, 1949, No. 350; Pz, No. 7; Pab, No. XVII, repr.
Lit.: Sandström, 1955, p. 104, repr. Novotny Painting and Sculpture in Europe, 1780–1880; The Pelican History of Art, 1960, No. 151b, repr.

64 MAN'S HEAD C. 1895
Oil on cardboard 51×18 cm

Coll.: Paris, P. Bacou, 1910
Exhib.: Pab, No. 133; Bi, No. 139; Ld, No. 62, repr.
Lit.: Bacou, 1956, No. 55, repr.

65 THE CYCLOPS 1895–1900 (1898)
Oil on wood 64×51 cm
Coll.: Otterlo, Kröller-Müller, 1922, No. 567
Exhib.: Py, No. 139; Ld, No. 63, repr.; Nk, No. 19, col. repr.
Lit.: Raynal, History of modern painting, Geneva, 1949, Vol. 1, p. 79, col. repr. Sandström, 1955, p. 68, repr.; Rewald, Post-Impressionism, 1956, p. 171, col. repr.; Bacou, 1956, p. 66 and 155, Nr. 56, repr.

66 DESPAIR
Oil on wood
Coll.: Formerly Sermizelles, Yonne, de Domecy
Lit.: Mellerio, 1923, p. 70, repr.

67 WINGED DEMON BRINGING THE HEAD OF A BEHEADED MAN 1897–99. After an earlier charcoal drawing
Oil
Coll.: Le Vésinet, Maurice Denis

67a THE MONSTER
Oil on canvas mounted on cardboard 47.7×22.5 cm
Coll.: Tokyo, private ownership

68 THE FIRST GLANCE 1897–1900
Oil 27×15.5 cm
Coll.: Paris, Jean Paulhan
Exhib.: Bi, No. 159

69 THE PRISONER (EVE?) 1910 or earlier
(see 169)
Oil 50×65.5 cm
Coll.: Cologne, Wallraf-Richartz-Museum

70 THE SECRET 1898–99
Oil 74×54.5 cm
Coll.: Washington, Phillips Gallery
Exhib.: Wb, No. 29, repr.; Nj, No. 3, repr. Nk, No. 43

71 THE APPEARANCE OF WOMAN Before 1900
Oil on wood 52×37 cm

Coll.: Amsterdam, C. Hoogendijk;
Otterlo, Kröller-Müller Museum, No. 573,
1912
Exhib.: Ab; Pab, No. 134, Tafel XXIII,
repr.; Bh, No. 336
Lit.: Bacou, 1956, No. 58, repr.

72 APPARITION OF A NAKED WOMAN Before
1900
Oil 39×32 cm
Coll.: Detroit, W. R. Valentiner
Exhib.: Nd, No. 5; Ca, No. 20; Nc, No. 76,
repr.

73 APPARITION
Oil 55×33.5 cm
Coll.: Winterthur, Jäggli-Hahnloser
Exhib.: Hb, No. 184

74 APPARITION
Oil 129×72.5 cm
Coll.: Paris, André Schoeller
Exhib.: Bi, No. 192

75 APPARITION C. 1900
Oil on wood 22×18 cm
Coll.: Paris, Bernheim-Jeune, 1909; Prague,
private ownership, 1910; Chicago, Dr. Robert C. Levy
Exhib.: Société Manes, Prag, 1910

75a THE DREAM (WOMAN UNDER A TREE)
C. 1900
Tempera 26×35 cm
Coll.: Moskau, Schtschukin; Leningrad,
Hermitage

76 OANNES Before 1900
Oil 64×49 cm
Coll.: Otterlo, Kröller-Müller Museum,
1916, No. 569
Exhib.: Py, No. 137; Het Fantastiche in de
Kunst, Museum Ostende, 1953, No. 20;
Pab, No. 176; Bi, No. 188
Lit.: Sandström, 1955, p. 131

77 OANNES C. 1900 (see M. 147)
Oil 65×54 cm
Coll.: Winterthur, Hedy Hahnloser-Bühler;
Bern, Hans. R. Hahnloser
Exhib.: Pq, No. 47; Bi, No. 165

78 OANNES C. 1905–06
Oil 65×54 cm
Coll.: The Hague, Gemeentemuseum
Exhib.: Hb, No. 195; Bi, No. 190; Ld, No.
85, repr.

79 FLIGHT
Oil 65.5×51 cm
Coll.: Bern, E. Vatter
Exhib.: Bi, No. 189

80 SIREN C. 1900
Oil 27×21.5 cm
Coll.: Geneva, Charles Im Obersteg
Exhib.: Bi, No. 160

81 READING C. 1900
Oil with pastel 47×47 cm
Coll.: Paris, Bourgeat; Paris, Jacques
Zoubaloff; Paris, Petit Palais, 1916
Exhib.: Pu, No. 36; Huysmans, Bibliothèque
Nationale, Paris, 1948; Pab, No. 132
Lit.: Jean Cassou, Etat de l'Art décoratif,
Beaux-Arts, 1932, p. 5, repr.; Bacou, 1956,
No. 54, repr.

81a WOMAN READING
Oil on cardboard 51×45 cm
Coll.: Tokyo, M. Hosokawa; Kurashiki,
Ohara Art Gallery; Osaka-fu, private
ownership
Exhib.: Pq, Masterpieces from all over the
world, Osaka, 1955; Masterpieces of European Art, Kyoto, 1957

82 HEAD OF A MYTHOLOGICAL FIGURE
After 1900
Oil 53.5×39 cm
Coll.: Cleveland, Mrs. John B.
Exhib.: The Logic of Modern Art, Kansas
City, 1961; Nk, No. 11, repr.

Visions und Allegories
II Colour 1901 - 14

83 FANTASTIC MAGIC
Oil on cardboard 22×28 cm
Coll.: Paris, Mme. Albert Marquet
Exhib.: Bh, No. 341

84　THE FATES　　After 1900 (see lithograph
M. 118)
Oil 33×25 cm
Coll.: Amsterdam, C. M. van Gogh;
Otterlo, Kröller-Müller Museum, 570
Exhib.: Ab, No. 33; Bi, No. 185

85　MYSTIC DIALOGUE　　After 1900
Oil 52×31.5 cm
Coll.: Paris, Philippe Fontaine
Exhib.: Bi, No. 170

86　MYSTIC DIALOGUE
Oil
Coll.: Paris, Marquis de Gonet

87　MYSTIC DIALOGUE
Oil
Coll.: Béziers, d'Andoque

88　SILENCE　　1902 (1895?)
Oil 34×26 cm
Coll.: Paris, A. Redon
Exhib.: Pu, No. 33; Bi, No. 163

89　THE THOUGHT　　1905 (see Pastel 421)
Oil on cardboard 29×26 cm
Coll.: De Steeg, van Deventer
Exhib.: Hb, No. 187, repr. in the catalogue

90　THE FALLEN ANGEL　　C. 1905
Oil 81×100 cm
Coll.: New York, E. and A. Silberman
Exhib.: Nk, No. 13, col. repr.

91　INITIATION INTO STUDY: TWO YOUNG GIRLS
C. 1905 (see M. 118)
Oil 90×74 cm
Coll.: Paris, Wilhelm Uhde; New York,
John Quinn; Amsterdam, Dr. W. Sieger;
New York, Wildenstein
Exhib.: Pn, No. 18; Na, No. 289; Hb, No.
189; Wildenstein, London, 1959, No. 36
Lit.: The John Quinn Collection, New York
1926, p. 103, repr.; Vente John Quinn,
Hotel Drouot, Paris, 28. X. 1926, No. 66,
repr.

92　EMERGING FROM THE LARVA　　C. 1905
Oil 36.5×29 cm

Coll.: Hilversum, Koster von Schwartzen-
berg
Exhib.: Hb, No. 192

93　SCENE WITH TWO WHITE GIRLS　　C. 1905
Oil 64.5×47.5 cm
Coll.: Princeton University Art Museum
Exhib.: The Two Sides of the Medal, De-
troit, 1954, No. 133, repr.; Nk, No. 53, col.
repr.

94　WAITING PRIESTESSES　　C. 1905 (see M. 66,
1886)
Oil 24×19.5 cm
Coll.: Paris, Katia Granoff; Cincinnati,
Thomas C. Adler, 1933
Exhib.: Art Museum, Cincinnati

95　CAT
Oil
Coll.: Paris, J. Hessel; Chicago, Martin
A. Ryerson
Exhib.: Wa, No. 1; Pq, No. 57; Nd, No. 6;
Ca, No. 16; Ne, No. 73

96　RED TREE NOT REDDENED BY THE SUN　　1905
Oil 44.5×34.5 cm
Coll.: New York, Mrs. Mabel Garrison
Siemonn
Exhib.: Ni, No. 6, repr.; Nk, No. 14
Lit.: Florent Fels, L'Art Vivant, Geneva,
1950, p. 112, repr.

97　RED TREE WITH FIGURE IN FLIGHT　　1906(?)
Oil on cardhoard 52×28.5 cm
Coll.: Béziers, Gustave Fayet; Paris,
P. Bacou
Exhib.: Ps, No. 18; Delacroix et les Maîtres
de la couleur, Atelier Delacroix, Paris, 1952,
No. 24; Pab, No. 166; Bi, No. 181; Ld, No.
73, repr.

98　DEATH　　After 1905 (see M 97, 1889)
Oil 58×48 cm
Coll.: Béziers, Gustave Fayet, 1909, Arles,
Léon Fayet; New York, Louise R. Smith
Exhib.: Ps, No. 19; Pab, No. XLIV, repr.;
Bi, No. 177; Nk, No. 41, col. repr.

98a　THE BELLRINGER (for a wall panel?)
Oil 142.3×61 cm
Coll.: Kurashiki, Ohara Art Gallery

Exhib.: with other works from the Ohara Collection in Kyoto, 1927 and 1928, in Osaka, 1943, in Tokyo, 1944, in Nagoya, 1960

99   ALSACE   After 1905, perhaps 1909
Oil 65 × 53 cm
Coll.: Winterthur, Museum
Exhib.: Bi, No. 197, repr.; Französische Malerei von Delacroix bis Picasso, Stadthalle, Wolfsburg, 1961, No. 124

100   QUEEN OF SHEBA   (After Flaubert). 1910
Oil 23.5 × 15 cm
Coll.: New York, New Gallery
Exhib.: Ni, No. 7, repr.

101   THE LOOK   C. 1910 (?)
Oil 73 × 73 cm
Coll.: Paris, Jacques Dubourg; London, Denys Sutton
Exhib.: Pw, No. 7; Ld, No. 76, repr.
Lit.: A. Salmon, L'Art Décoratif, 1913, p. 13, repr.; Bacou, 1956, No. 87, repr.

102   SAPPHO   After 1910
Oil
Coll.: London, Denys Sutton

103   SILENCE   1911
Oil 56 × 55.5 cm
Coll.: The Hague, D'Audretsch; The Hague, G. Oudshoorn; Los Angeles, Donald Winston
Exhib.: Hb, No. 200; Ni, No. 11, repr.

104   SILENCE (Variation on the decoration in Fontfroide, No. 330)   C. 1911
Oil on paper 54 × 54.6 cm
Coll.: New York, Lillie P. Bliss, 1913; New York, Museum of Modern Art, 1931
Exhib.: Na, No. 300; Nd, No. 15; Ca, No. 3; Ne, No. 99; Literature and Poetry in Painting, Wadsworth Atheneum, Hartford, 1933; Fantastic Art, Dada and Surrealism, Museum of Modern Art, New York, 1936, No. 69; Paintings and Sculptures from the Armory Show, Cincinnati, 1944; Pab, No. LXIV, repr.; Nk, No. 54, repr.
Lit.: Mellerio, 1923, p. 28, repr. Louise Gebhard Cann: The Metaphor of Redon, International Studio, LXXVIII, 1923, p. 106; A. H. Barr Jr., Fantastic Art, Dada and Surrealism, 1936, p. 107, repr.; Trico-

lor, II, No. 2, 1945, p. 73, repr.; Paintings and Sculpture in the Museum of Modern Art, New York, 1948, p. 36

105   DREAM   1908 (?)
Oil 73.5 × 54 cm
Coll.: Winterthur, L. Jäggli-Hahnloser
Exhib.: Pq, No. 48; La Peinture Française du XIXᵉ siècle en Suisse, Paris, Gazette des Beaux-Arts, 1938, No. 90; Py, No. 136; Pab, No. 161; Hb, No. 191; Bi, No. 202

106   DREAM
Oil 56 × 44 cm
Coll.: Paris, Robert Ellissen; Fribourg, Claude Blancpain
Exhib.: Lb; Bi, No. 205

107   THE POET'S DREAM
Oil on wood 52 × 26.5 cm
Coll.: The Hague, A. S. J. Loudon; New York, New Gallery
Exhib.: Hb, No. 194

108   SALOME   1910 (1880)
Oil 73 × 60.5 cm
Coll.: Le Vésinet, Maurice Denis; Paris, Robert Ellissen; Basel, Beyeler
Exhib.: Ps, No. 17; Pu, No. 21; Lb, No. 14; Py, No. 132; Bi, No. 171; Galerie Beyeler, Basel, 1958, No. 4, col. repr.

109   BLACK SUN (SILENCE)
Oil
Coll.: Béziers, Gustave Fayet
Lit.: Bacou, 1956, No. 53, repr.

110   THE RED SPHINX   1912–13 (1900?)
Oil 61 × 50 cm
Coll.: Winterthur, Hedy Hahnloser-Bühler, 1913; Bern, Prof. Hahnloser
Exhib.: Hauptwerke der Sammlung Hahnloser, Lucerne, 1940, No. 90a; Pab, No. 173; Bi, No. 186
Lit.: L'Histoire de la Peinture Moderne, Geneva, Skira, Vol. I, p. 78, repr.

111   DANTE AND BEATRICE   C. 1914
Oil
Coll.: Detroit, W. R. Valentiner
Exhib.: Nd, No. 4; Ps, No. 13; Ca, No. 19; Ne, No. 78

Religious Mood
1895 - 1905 (1910)

112 THE MADONNA AT DAWN   C. 1895
Oil 53.5×37 cm
Coll.: Paris, Ernest Chausson; New York,
James W. Barney; Detroit, Isidore Levin
Exhib.: Pg, No. 52; Pq, No. 39; Bd. No. 15;
Nd, No. 12; Ca, No. 1; Ne, No. 104, repr.;
The Two Sides of the Medal, Detroit, 1954,
No. 132; Nk, No. 12
Lit.: Mellerio, 1923, p. 152, repr.

113 CHRIST AND THE SERPENT   1895–1900 (?)
Oil 65×50 cm
Coll.: Paris, Marcel Kapferer; Paris, Georges
Renand
Exhib.: Pq, No. 119; Py, No. 141;
Pab, No. 165; Bh, No. 338; Bi, No. 179
Lit.: Bacou, 1956, Vol. I, p. 127

114 FLIGHT INTO EGYPT   1900
Oil 45×38 cm
Coll.: Paris, A. Redon
Exhib.: Pu, No. 45; Bi, No. 161

115 CHRIST AND THE SAMARITAN WOMAN
After 1900 (?)
Oil 64.5×50 cm
Coll.: New York, John Quinn; Wassenaar,
I. S. van den Bergh; Haarlem, J. H. de Bois;
Basel, Dr. Raeber
Exhib.: Bi, No. 191; Ld, No. 81, repr.
Lit.: Mellerio, 1923, p. 25, repr.

116 CHRIST AND THE SAMARITAN WOMAN
Oil
Coll.: Paris, Ullern
Exhib.: Pq, No. 84
Lit.: Roger-Marx, 1925, p. 45, repr.

117 THE HEAD OF CHRIST APPEARS OVER THE SEA
Before 1905
Oil 61×46.5 cm
Coll.: Männerdorf, Switzerland, Emile
Staub-Terlinden; New York, Wildenstein
Exhib.: La Peinture française en Suisse,
Gazette des Beaux-Arts, Paris, 1938, No. 89;
Wb, No. 26, repr.

118 VISION IN THE CLOUDS   C. 1905
Oil 81.5×66 cm

Coll.: Cannes, Mme. Gorodiche
Exhib.: Bi, No. 206, repr.

119 CHRIST WITH CLOSED EYES   1905 (?)
Oil 55×46 cm
Coll.: Paris, Armand Parent; Paris, S. Morin
Exhib.: Pq, No. 89, Pr. No. 42; Ps, No. 67;
Lb, No. 17; Pab, No. XLIX, repr.
Lit.: Fegdal, 1929, Pl. XXII, repr.

120 THE RED THORN BUSH
Oil
Coll.: Le Vésinet, Maurice Denis
Exhib.: Pq, No. 41

121 JACOB WRESTLING WITH THE ANGEL
C. 1905
Oil on wood 47×41.5 cm
Coll.: New York, Matthew H. Futter
Exhib.: Nk, No. 37, col. repr.

122 JACOB WRESTLING WITH THE ANGEL (for a
wall panel?)   Before 1909
Oil 143.5×62 cm
Coll.: Paris, J. Hessel; Paris, Marcel
Kapferer; New York, Alexander M. Bing;
New York, The Brooklyn Museum, 1960
Exhib.: Ps, No. 50; Pw, No. 9; Variation on
34; see Paris Catalogue 1956, on No. 168

123 JACOB WRESTLING WITH THE ANGEL
1909–10 (?)
Oil 26.5×12 cm
Coll.: Paris, A. Redon
Exhib.: Pq, No. 3; Bd, No. 14; Pr. No. 25;
Pab, No. 168

124 CHRIST ON THE CROSS   1910
or earlier (see No. 354.a and 355)
Oil
Coll.: Paris, A. Redon
Exhib.: Ps, No. 81; Pu, No. 59; Lb, No. 3;

Myth: Orpheus, Angelica, Phaeton
1905 - 1910

125 ORPHEUS WITH CLOSED EYES
Oil
Coll.: Paris, A. Redon
Exhib.: Bd, No. 38

126 ORPHEUS WITH CLOSED EYES
Oil
Coll.: Béziers, d'Andoque

127 ORPHEUS'S DEATH   C. 1904
Oil 29×75.5 cm
Coll.: Béziers, Gustave Fayet; Paris,
Marcel Kapferer; Cambridge, USA, Fogg
Art Museum
Exhib.: Lb, No. 40; Wb, No. 27, repr.
Lit.: André Salmon, L'Art Décoratif, Paris,
1913, No. 1, repr.

128 ANGELICA ON A ROCK   C. 1904
Oil 29×23 cm
Coll.: Winterthur, L. Jäggli-Hahnloser
Exhib.: Bi, No. 174

129 ROGER AND ANGELICA   1904/05
Oil 46×33.5 cm
Coll.: Winterthur, H. Hahnloser-Bühler;
Bern, Prof. Hahnloser
Exhib.: Bd, No. 29; Pq, No. 1; Bi, No. 178,
repr.; Hauptwerke der Sammlung Hahn-
loser, Lucerne 1940, No. 86

130 RESCUE OF ANDROMEDA   1908
Oil 50×32.5 cm
Coll.: Paris, Galerie Druet; Paris, Galerie
Europe; Neuss, Clemens-Sels Museum
Exhib.: Po, No. 16; Centenaire de l'art
français, St. Petersburg, 1912, No. 517
Lit.: Fegdal, 1929, No. 55, repr. als 'St
George'

131 PERSEUS AND ANDROMEDA   C. 1908 (see 170)
Oil on cardboard 32.5×28.5 cm
Coll.: Winterthur, Mme. Hedy Hahnloser-
Bühler; Winterthur, Mme. Jäggli-Hahn-
loser
Exhib.: Wa, No. 7; Pab, No. 170; Bi,
No. 183

132 ANDROMEDA   After 1908 (see 171)
Oil 57×73 cm
Coll.: Paris, J. Hessel; Paris, Chambaudet;
Chicago, Martin A. Ryerson; Chicago, Art
Institute
Exhib.: Wa; Ca, No. 11; Ne; Nk, No. 33

133 ROGER AND ANGELICA   1909–10 (1905?)
Oil 30×29 cm

Coll.: Otterlo, Kröller-Müller, No. 568
Exhib.: Ab, No. 34; Py, No. 138; Bi,
No. 184; Ld, No. 84, repr.
Lit.: Sandström, 1955, p. 105; Bacou, 1956,
p. 158

134 SAINT GEORGE AND THE DRAGON   C. 1907
(c. 1910)
Oil 29.5×27 cm
Coll.: Cologne, Wallraf-Richartz-Museum

135 SAINT GEORGE AND THE DRAGON   After 1907
(c. 1910)
Oil
Coll.: Paris, M. Desjardins
Exhib.: Pq, No. 40; Ps, No. 10

136 SAINT GEORGE AND THE DRAGON   1909–10
Oil 48×38.5 cm
Coll.: Paris, Marquise de Gonet, 1910
Exhib.: Pab, No. L, repr.; Sources du XXe
Siècle, Musée d'Art Moderne, Paris, 1960,
No. 580

137 BATTLE OF THE CENTAURS   C. 1905
Oil 50×65 cm
Coll.: Paris, Jacques Dubourg
Exhib.: Bi, No. 173; Ld, No. 65, repr.

138 CENTAUR AND DRAGON   C. 1908
Oil on cardboard 25×18 cm
Coll.: Paris, Jacques Zoubaloff; Otterlo,
Kröller-Müller, 1927
Exhib.: Ab, No. 32; Pab, No. XXVI, repr.;
Bg, Nr. XI, repr.; Bh, No. 339
Lit.: Sandström, 1955, p. 81; Bacou, 1956,
p. 156

139 PEGASUS AND BELLEROPHON   After 1900
(before 1900)
Oil 47×47 cm
Coll.: Paris, André Mellerio; Melbourne,
National Gallery, 1950
Exhib.: Ps, No. 53
Lit.: Mellerio, 1923, p. 52, repr.; Bacou,
1956, No. 57, repr.

140 RIDER ON THE BEACH WITH TWO SHIPS
(first appearance of the motif of the rearing
horse). 1905 (1907)
Oil on cardboard 38.5×40 cm

Coll.: Paris, Jacques Zoubaloff; Paris, private ownership
Exhib.: Pab, No. 155

141 PEGASUS AND THE DRAGON C. 1907
(Bacou: 1905–07, 1956 Cat.: 1907–1910)
Oil on cardboard 46.5×62.5 cm
Coll.: Paris, Marcel Kapferer; Paris, Baudoin, 1928; Otterlo, Kröller-Müller, 1920, No. 572
Exhib.: Wa; Pq, No. 64; Bd, No. 6, repr.; Pr, No. 49; Ps, No. 54; Py, No. 140; Pab, No. XLIII, repr.; Bg, No. 772, repr.; Hb, No. 190; Bi, No. 182
Lit.: Sandström, 1955, p. 33; Bacou, 1956, No. 79, repr.

142 REARING HORSE ON RED PEAK C. 1907
Oil 45×35 cm
Coll.: Paris, A. Redon
Exhib.: Pq, No. 91, repr.; Pr, No. 3; Pu, No. 55
Lit.: Fegdal, 1929, No. 3, repr.; Bacou, 1956, No. 78, repr.

143 THE SILVER PEGASUS ON A PEAK C. 1907
Oil on wood 60×50 cm
Coll.: Paris, Raoul de Ricci
Exhib.: Ps, No. 83 bis; Pab, No. 159

144 THE WHITE PEGASUS 1908
Oil 50×65 cm
Coll.: Paris, A. Leblond
Exhib.: Pu, No. 57; Py, No. 143
Lit.: Mellerio, 1923, p. 129, repr.

145 THE WHITE PEGASUS C. 1908
Oil
Coll.: Paris, Paul Istel

146 PEGASUS (Preliminary drawing in the Prentenkabinet, Amsterdam)
Oil
Coll.: Paris, A. Redon

147 PEGASUS GALLOPING WITH THE MUSE THROUGH THE AIR 1907–10 (1900)
Oil
Coll.: Paris, Marcel Kapferer
Exhib.: Na, No. 285; Pq, No. 65; Bd, No. 5; Ps, No. 52; Pu, No. 35; Lb, No. 10

Lit.: A. Fontainas und L. Vauxelles, L'Art Français de la Révolution à nos Jours, 1922, p. 220, repr. in colour

148 BLACK PEGASUS 1909–10
Oil 52×60 cm
Coll.: Paris, Marquise de Gonet
Exhib.: Pq, No. 44; Pab, No. LIV, repr.
Lit.: Match, No. 398, 24 November 1956, repr. in colour

149 PHAETON'S FALL. (TWO HORSES) 1905–06
Oil 53×21 cm
Coll.: New York, Sidney Simon
Exhib.: Nj, No. 11, repr.; Nk, No. 49, repr.

150 PHAETON'S FALL 1905–06
Oil 73×54 cm
Coll.: Amsterdam, Huinck; New York, Werner E. Josten
Exhib.: Nj, No. 10, repr.; Nk, No. 21, col. repr.

151 PHAETON'S FALL. (THREE HORSES) C. 1910
Oil on paper 36×45 cm
Coll.: Paris, J. Zoubaloff; Amsterdam, Van Gelder; Zürich, Emil Bührle
Exhib.: Marlborough Gallery, London, 1956

152 AURORA C. 1910
Oil 65×81 cm
Coll.: Paris, Maxime de Thomas; New York, private ownership

153 APOLLO'S SUN CHARIOT WITH FOUR HORSES (study for 154). 1905 (1900)
Oil 66×81 cm, horizontal format
Coll.: New York, Metropolitan Museum of Art, 1927
Exhib.: Paa, No. 32; Wb, No. 9, repr.; Nk, No. 46
Lit.: Sandström, 1955, No. 26, repr.

154 APOLLO'S SUN CHARIOT WITH FOUR HORSES 1905, dated
Oil 89×162 cm, horizontal format
Coll.: Paris, Jacques Zoubaloff; Paris, Petit Palais, 1916
Exhib.: Pu, No. 41; De David à Cézanne, Brussels, 1947, No. 132; Py, No. 127, repr.; Bi, No. 207, repr.

155 APOLLO'S SUN CHARIOT WITH FOUR HORSES
(Replica of 154) C. 1907
Oil, horizontal format
Coll.: Park Forest, USA, Mary Malone

156 APOLLO'S SUN CHARIOT
Oil
Coll.: New York, Adelaide Milton de Groot

157 APOLLO'S SUN CHARIOT WITH FOUR HORSES
1907
Oil 45×28.5 cm, vertical format
Coll.: Cambridge, England, Captain S. W.
Sykes
Exhib.: La, No. 11; Maxwell Art Gallery,
Peterborough, 1953, No. 15; Ld, No. 83,
repr.

158 APOLLO'S SUN CHARIOT WITH FOUR HORSES
1907–08
Oil with Pastel 100×83 cm, vertical format
Coll.: Paris, Marquise de Gonet, 1908
Exhib.: Pq, No. 43; Chefs-d'œuvre de l'Art
Français, 1937, No. 389; Pab, No. LIII, repr.
Lit.: Mellerio, 1923, p. 136, col. repr.;
Chefs-d'œuvre de l'Art Français du Moyen-
Age au XXe Siècle, Paris, 1937, Pl. 115,
repr.

159 APOLLO'S SUN CHARIOT WITH FOUR HORSES
(Variation of 158) 1907–10 (Carrière-
Catalog: 1915, Sandström: 1895)
Oil 100×80 cm, vertical format
Coll.: Bordeaux, Gabriel Frizeau; Bordeaux,
Musée des Beaux-Arts, 1953
Exhib.: Ps, No. 33; Py, No. 134
Lit.: Sandström, 1955, p. 30; Bacou, 1956,
No. 93, repr.

160 APOLLO'S SUN CHARIOT WITH BLACK AND
WITHE HORSE 1907–10
Oil 72×53 cm, vertical format. Worked
over with pastel
Coll.: New York, John Quinn; New York,
Phillip L. Godwin, 1926; New Haven, Yale
University Museum, 1958
Exhib.: Na, No. 287; Wadsworth Athene-
um, Hartford; Impressionist and Post-
impressionist paintings, Metropolitan Mu-
seum, New York, 1921, No. 91, repr.;
Cleveland Museum, 1936, No. 340; Nine-
teenth Century French Painting, Yale

University Museum, 1950, No. 14; Nj,
No. 15, repr.
Lit.: John Quinn collection catalogue, 1926,
p. 14, No. 105, repr.

161 APOLLO'S SUN CHARIOT WITH FOUR WHITE
HORSES 1908 (1907–10)
Oil 40×78 cm, horizontal format
Coll.: Béziers, Gustave Fayet; Paris, Paul
Bacou
Exhib.: Ps, No. 29; Lb, No. 21; Ld,
No. 82, repr.

162 APOLLO'S SUN CHARIOT WITH MUSE AND FOUR
PALE HORSES 1908 (1907–10)
Oil 49.5×66 cm, horizontal format
Coll.: Paris, J. Hessel; New York, Alexander
M. Bing
Exhib.: Nj, No. 16, repr.

163 APOLLO'S SUN CHARIOT IN FLOWERS WITH
FOUR HORSES C. 1909
Oil 78.5×105 cm, horizontal format
Coll.: Béziers, Gustave Fayet, 1910; Font-
froide, Mme. Fayet
Exhib.: Pq, No. 51; Ps, No. 29; Pz, No. 2
Lit.: André Salmon, ›L'Art décoratif‹, 1913,
p. 14, repr.; Claude Roger-Marx, 1925,
p. 53, repr.; Fegdal, 1929, pl. 57, repr.;
Bacou, 1956, Vol. II. Frontispiece, col.
repr.

164 APOLLO'S SUN CHARIOT WITH FOUR HORSES
AND DRAGON C. 1910
Oil heightened with pastel 75×60 cm,
vertical format
Coll.: Paris, Prinz Antoine Bibesco; Paris,
C. Roger-Marx
Exhib.: Ps, No. 4; Pu, No. 93; Pz, No. 6;
Pab, No. 157 (col. repr. on the exhibition
poster)
Lit.: Claude Roger-Marx, ›Maîtres du XIXe
et du XXe siècle‹, Geneva, 1954, col. repr.;
Bacou, 1956, No. V, col. repr.

Bodies, Faces, Profiles
(1882) 1900 - 12

165 BATHING GIRLS
Oil 21.5×16 cm
Coll.: Winterthur, L. Jäggli-Hahnloser

Exhib.: Bi, No. 180
Lit.: Claude Roger-Marx, 1925, p. 39, repr.

166 BATHING GIRLS
Oil 51.5×45.5 cm
Coll.: Basel, Raeber
Exhib.: Bi, No. 167

167 BATHING GIRLS
Oil
Coll.: Paris, M. Kapferer
Exhib.: Pq, No. 66; Bd, No. 12; Ps, No. 53

168 EVE 1904 (1895)
Oil 61×46 cm
Coll.: Paris, A. Leblond
Exhib.: Pq, No. 61; Ps, No. 61; Pu, No. 30;
Pab, No. 145; Hb, No. 181, repr.; Nk,
No. 32, repr.
Lit.: Mellerio, 1923, p. 20, repr.

169 EVE 1904
Oil
Coll.: Paris, Marquise de Gonet

170 PERSEUS AND ANDROMEDA C. 1908
Oil
Coll.: Paris and New York, Bignou; Los
Angeles, Dalzell Hatfield
Exhib.: Ps, No. 6

171 ANDROMEDA After 1908 (1912)
Oil 175×91.5 cm
Coll.: New York, David Rockefeller
Exhib.: Nk, No. 58, col. repr.

172 PANDORA 1909–10 (for a wall panel?)
Oil 143×62.2 cm
Coll.: New York, John Quinn; New York,
Alexander M. Bing, 1926; New York,
Metropolitan Museum, 1959
Exhib.: Nc, No. 1; The John Quinn Collec-
tion, Art Center, New York, 1926, No. 28;
Nd, No. 9; Ne, No. 94; Masterpiedes of Art,
World's Fair, New York, 1940, No. 350;
Nj, No. 18, repr.; Nk, No. 45, repr.

173 NUDE WITH FLOWERS (PANDORA?)
Oil 103×62 cm
Coll.: Zürich-Zollikerberg, Mme. Hegi;
Basel, Beyeler
Exhib.: Bi, No. 200

174 BIRTH OF VENUS 1908
Oil
Coll.: Paris, Galerie Druet
Exhib.: Pr, No. 15
Lit.: Fegdal, Paris, 1929, No. 53, repr.

175 BIRTH OF VENUS 1912 (1905)
Oil
Coll.: Paris, M. Kapferer; Paris, Professor
Gosset; Paris, Bourgeat
Exhib.: Pq, No. 69; Bd, No. 8; Ps, No. 37;
Pu, No. 44

176 SEA GODDESS (1909–10)
Oil 50×65 cm
Coll.: Paris, B. Débrise
Exhib.: Pab, No. 174

177 BIRTH OF VENUS 1912
Oil
Coll.: J. B. van Gelder
Exhib.: Ps, No. 92; Lb, No. 23

178 BIRTH OF VENUS (Seated on a cloud, seen
from the back)
Oil 22×15 cm
Coll.: Crafton, Pennsylvania, Dr. Saklat-
walla
Exhib.: Ca, No. 17; Nd, No. 20; Ne,
No. 70, repr.

179 BIRTH OF VENUS 1912
wall panel, Oil 141×61 cm
Coll.: Paris, Dr. Sabouraud; Paris, R.
Hauert; Paris, Stephen Higgons
Exhib.: Pq, No. 2; Pr, No. 54; Ps, No. 90;
Pu, No. 53; Lb, No. 30; Py, No. 142, repr.;
Pab, No. LI, repr.; Bi, No. 199, repr.;
Sources du XXᵉ Siècle, Paris, 1960, No. 581;
Nk, No. 55, repr.
Lit.: Charles Chassé, Le Mouvement Sym-
boliste, 1947, p. 48, repr.

180 SAINT SEBASTIAN 1909/10 (1900)
Oil on wood 27.5×18.5 cm
Coll.: Paris, A. Redon
Exhib.: Bd, No. 21; Pq, No. 52; Pr, No. 24;
Py, No. 131; Pab, No. 169

181 SAINT SEBASTIAN 1910 Preliminary study
as watercolour 24.6×17.7 cm; ibid.
Oil 92×59.5 cm

Coll.: Paris, A. Leblond; Brussels, Dosbourg; Basel, Museum
Exhib.: Pq, No. 63; Bd, No. 30, repr. as 'Ariane enchained'; Ps, No. 12; Bi, No. 198
Exhib.: Py, No. 154; Bi, No. 214, repr.

182 MADAME REDON, PORTRAIT 1880
Oil on cardboard 35.5×26.5 cm
Coll.: Tokyo, Nikko-Shoken

183 MADAME REDON, PORTRAIT 1882
Oil 45.5×37 cm
Coll.: Paris, Mme. Goedhoop-de Jong; Paris, Louvre, 1926
Exhib.: Bi, No. 143; Nk, No. 10, repr.
Lit.: Mellerio, 1923, p. 51, repr.

184 ARI REDON IN RED 1896, dated
Oil on wood 38×29.8 cm
Coll.: Paris, A. Redon
Exhib.: Pu, No. 27; Pab, No. 131
Lit.: Claude Roger-Marx, l'Œil, 1956, p. 25, repr.

185 ARI IN A SAILOR SUIT 1897
Oil on cardboard 42×21 cm
Coll.: Paris, A. Redon
Exhib.: Pu, No. 27; Bonnard, Vuillard et les Nabis, Paris, Musée d'Art Moderne, 1955, No. 60; Pab, No. XXXV, repr.; Bi, No. 156, repr. Sources du XXᵉ Siècle, Musée d'Art Moderne, Paris, 1960, No. 578; Nk, No. 17
Lit.: Bacou, 1956, No. 69, repr.

186 CHILD'S FACE
Oil
Coll.: Béziers, Gustave Fayet

187 MADAME GABRIEL FRIZEAU, PORTRAIT
After 1900
Oil
Coll.: Bordeaux, Jean Frizeau

188 GAUGUIN, PORTRAIT 1903
Oil 66×44 cm
Coll.: Paris, Hessel, 1912; Paris, Henry Kapferer; Paris, Louvre, 1950
Exhib.: Na, No. 280; Pq, No. 68; Bd, No. 3; Pr, No. 37; Ps, No. 45; Lb, No. 7; Py, No. 126; Pab, No. 144; Hb, No. 180
Lit.: Henri Dorra, Gazette des Beaux-Arts, 1953, p. 192–203; Rewald, Post-Impressionism, New York, 1956, p. 450, repr.

189 MADAME A. BONGER-VAN DER LINDEN, PORTRAIT 1905
Oil 63×60 cm
Coll.: Amsterdam, Municipal Museum
Exhib.: Hb, No. 185; Ld, No. 66, repr.

190 VIOLETTE HEYMANN, PORTRAIT 1909
Coll.: New York, New Gallery
Exihb.: Ni, No. 4, repr.

191 EVOCATION OF THE PAINTER K. X. ROUSSEL 1912
Oil 73×54 cm
Coll.: Paris, Raoul Pellequer; New York, Chester Dale
Exhib.: Nd, No. 14; Ca, No. 6; French Art, Pennsylvania Museum of Art, Philadelphia, 1937; Chester Dale Collection, National Gallery of Art, Washington, 1942, p. 28, repr. in catalog

192 YOUNG GIRL WITH SHINING FLOWER
C. 1900
Oil on wood 26.5×15 cm
Coll.: Paris, Prince Bibesco; Paris, G. B.

193 OPHELIA WITH CLOSED EYES 1901–02
Oil 74×63 cm
Coll.: Almen, Bonger
Exhib.: Pn, No. 4; Hb, No. 179

194 OPHELIA WITH CLOSED EYES 1905–06
Oil on cardboard 58×46 cm
Coll.: Paris, M. Kapferer; New York, Ian Woodner
Exhib.: Pn, No. 16; Pq, No. 70 (as 'Profile'); Bd, No. 7 (as 'Profile'); Pr, No. 47; Py, No. 129; Pab, No. 149; Nk, No. 40, col. repr.

195 OPHELIA 1908–09
Oil on paper 67×48.5 cm
Coll.: Béziers, Gustave Fayet, 1909; Paris, Paul Bacou
Exhib.: Pab, No. 160; Bi, No. 196

196 THE CHOSEN GIRL 1904–05
Oil
Coll.: Paris, Durand-Ruel; Paris, A. Leblond
Lit.: Mellerio, 1923, No. 152, repr.; Besson, La Peinture française au XIXᵉ Siècle, Vol. 3 (Les Maîtres), 1938, No. 51, repr.

197 PARISIENNE
Oil 100 × 80 cm
Coll.: Brussels, Baron René Boel
Exhib.: Bg, No. 775

198 HEAD WITH FLOWERS: BUDDHA
C. 1905 (1906–08) (1895)
Oil 52 × 47 cm
Coll.: Paris, Marcel Kapferer; New York,
Mrs. Arthur Lehman
Exhib.: Ps, No. 48; Paa, No. 12, repr.; Nj,
No. 13, repr.; Nk, No. 15, col. repr.

198a THE YOUNG BUDDHA
Oil 64.5 × 49 cm
Coll.: Kyoto, B. Tsuchida; Ashiya, private
ownership
Exhib.: Masterpieces of European Art,
Tokyo, 1947; Redon, Tokyo, Kyuryudo
Gallery, 1954; Masterpieces of European
Art, Kyoto, 1957

199 HEAD BENT FORWARD   C. 1905
Oil 49 × 49 cm
Coll.: London, Lady Hulton
Exhib.: The Collection of Sir Edward and
Lady Hulton, Tate Gallery, London, 1957,
No. 26; Ld, No. 79, repr.

200 SPRING   1906–08
Oil 54.5 × 73 cm
Coll.: New York, Ehrich Gallery; Worcester
Art Museum, 1919
Exhib.: Nc; Women's City Club, Boston,
1925; Fogg Art Museum, Cambridge, 1929;
Ne, No. 100, repr.; Addison Gallery of
American Art, Andover, 1945; Paa, No. 15;
The 1913 Armory Show in Retrospect,
Amherst College, 1958
Lit.: Catalogue of Paintings and Drawings,
Worcester Art Museum, 1922, p. 150, 151,
197, repr.

201 APPARITION OF A WOMAN IN A POINTED ARCH
Oil
Coll.: Almen, Bonger

202 WOMAN'S PROFILE IN A POINTED ARCH
Oil 54 × 50 cm
Coll.: Paris, private ownership

203 WOMAN IN PROFILE WITH FLOWER VASE
Oil 65.5 × 50.5 cm

Coll.: London, Sir Robert Mayer
Exhib.: Ld, No. 78, repr.

204 YOUNG GIRL WITH POPPIES
Oil 52 × 37 cm
Coll.: Zürich, Mme. R. Hahnloser-Gass-
mann
Exhib.: Bi, No. 204

204a WOMAN'S PROFILE
Oil 46 × 19 cm
Coll.: Nishinomiya-shi, Y. Fukui; Osaka,
Y. Koike; Tokyo, A. Fujiyama
Exhib.: Osaka, Municipal Museum, 1936;
Fujiyama, Collection, Yokohama and Osaka
1963

205 FLOWERS WITH TWO WOMENS PROFILES
1912
Oil 61 × 50 cm
Coll.: Paris, M. Kapferer; Basel, Beyeler;
Paris, S. Higgons; Cambridge, Mass.,
private ownership
Exhib.: Na, No. 283; Pr. No. 45; Bi, No.
194; Nk, No. 38, col. repr.
Lit.: Claude Roger-Marx, 1925, p. 41,
repr.

206 GIRL'S PROFILE BENT OVER A BOWL OF
FLOWERS   1912
Oil
Coll.: Béziers, A. d'Andoque

207 YOUNG GIRL IN PROFILE ON BLUE GROUND
1912
Oil on Cardboard 54 × 52.5 cm
Coll.: Winterthur, Hedy Hahnloser-Bühler;
Bern, Hans Hahnloser
Exhib.: Pab, No. 183; Bi, No. 153; Nk,
No. 59, repr.
Lit.: Sandström, 1955, No. 131, repr.

207a GIRL'S PROFILE WITH FLOWERS   1912
Oil on Cardboard 39.9 × 39 cm
Coll.: Kyoto, S. Takeuchi; Osaka-fu, Shuzo
Fukui
Exhib.: Pp

208 CHURCH WINDOW WITH RED TREE   1906–08
Oil 73.5 × 51 cm
Coll.: Almen, Bonger, 1905
Exhib.: Pab, No. 146; Hb, No. 183

209 CHURCH WINDOW   C. 1908
Oil 65×50 cm
Coll.: Paris, A. Redon; Laren, P. A. Regnault
Exhib.: Po, No. 12; Ps, No. 80; Hb, No. 182

210 CHURCH WINDOW
Oil 64×55 cm
Coll.: Paris, Etienne Bignou; New York, M. B. Sanders, 1931; New York, Mrs. H. J. Heinz II; Montreal, Lazarus Phillips, 1958
Exhib.: Ne, No. 91; Nk, No. 24
Lit.: Fegdal, Pl. 49, repr.

211 THE CATHEDRAL   1912
(Preliminary drawing No. 703)
Oil 92.5×73.5 cm
Coll.: Paris, P. Bacou; Paris, S. Higgons; Winterthur, Willy Dünner; Munich, Pinakothek, 1960
Exhib.: Bi, No. 176; Pac, No. 80; Sources du XXe Siècle, Musée d'Art Moderne, Paris, 1960, No. 583

Poetry of the Sea   1900 - 13

212 THE BARKS IN A COASTAL LANDSCAPE
Before 1900
Oil 73×100 cm
Coll.: Laren, N. H. Regnault
Exhib.: Musée de Batavia, Djakarta, 1936; Stedelijk Museum, Eindhoven, 1947, No. 69; Hb, No. 188
Lit.: Collection de P-A Regnault, Catalogue de vente, Amsterdam, 22.10.1958, No. 101, repr.

213 RED BARK   1900
Oil
Coll.: Paris, Henri Kapferer
Exhib.: Pq, No. 73; Bd, No. 13; Ps, No. 46; Lb, No. 2

214 THE BARK WITH THREE OARS   After 1900
Oil on wood 29.5×48 cm
Coll.: Zürich, Werner Herold; Paris, Mme. Paul Istel; New York, Wildenstein

Exhib.: La Peinture française dans les Collections suisses, Gazette des Beaux-Arts, Paris, 1938, No. 84; Paa, No. 13

215 THE BARK (WITHOUT SAIL) WITH TWO PEOPLE   1901 (After 1900)
Oil 55×46 cm
Coll.: Paris, Armand Parent; Paris, Albert Sarraut
Exhib.: Pq, No. 79; Ps, No. 66; Lb, No. 24; Pz; Het Franse Landschap, Amsterdam, 1951, No. 108; Ld, No. 71, repr.

216 SAILING BOAT WITH TWO WHITE WOMEN   1900
Oil 33×41 cm
Coll.: Paris, Théo van Gogh; Amsterdam, Madame J. van Gogh-Bonger; New York, David Rockefeller
Exhib.: Nj, No. 5, repr.; Nk, No. 39

217 THE RED BARK   1905 (After 1900)
Oil on wood 32×40 cm
Coll.: Paris, A. Redon
Exhib.: Pr; Ps; Pu; Landscape in French Art, London, 1949, No. 353

218 RED TWO-MASTER WITH NIMBUS   1906
Oil 27×40 cm
Coll.: Almen, Bonger
Exhib.: Po, No. 9; Ps; Het Franse Landscap, Amsterdam, 1951, No. 109; Ld, No. 72, repr.

219 SUNSET   Before 1907
Oil on wood 28.5×45.5 cm
Coll.: Paris, M. Kapferer
Exhib.: Po, No. 11; Pp, No. 20; Pab, No. 153; Bi, No. 175

220 RED BOAT WITH BLUE SAIL   1906–07
Oil 54×73 cm
Coll.: Winterthur, Hedy Hahnloser-Bühler; Winterthur, L. Jäggli-Hahnloser
Exhib.: Pq, No. 46; Bi, No. 166; Reproduced as a Schroll print in colour

221 THE GRAY SAIL WITH NIMBUS, FOUR PEOPLE IN THE BOAT   C. 1908 (after 1900)
Oil 35×38 cm
Coll.: Béziers, Gustave Fayet; Béziers, A. d'Andoque
Exhib.: Ps, No. 30
Lit.: Bacou, 1956, No. 92, repr.

222 SAILING BOAT
Oil 47×50.5 cm
Coll.: Winterthur, Hedy Hahnloser-Bühler;
Bern, Prof. Hans Hahnloser
Exhib.: Bi, No. 168

223 BARKS IN VENICE 1908
Oil on Cardboard 32×84 cm
Coll.: Paris, Jean-Arthur Fontaine, 1910;
Paris, Dr. Weill; Basel, Galerie Beyeler
Exhib.: Po, No. 8; Pq, No. 88; Ps, No. 159;
Pu, No. 51; Lb, No. 5; Pab, No. 154; Bi,
No. 169
Lit.: Fegdal, 1929, No. 27, repr.

224 VIEW OF VENICE 1908
Oil
Coll.: Paris, A. Fontaine; Paris, Dr. Paul-
Emile Weill
Exhib.: Po, No. 7; Pq, No. 9; Ps, No. 31;
Pu, No. 51
Lit.: Fegdal, 1929, No. XXVII, repr.

225 THE BARKS 1908 (1910)
Oil 63×80 cm
Coll.: Paris, Robert Ellissen
Exhib.: Ps, No. 16; Lb, No. 9; Py, No. 133

226 ON THE BOTTOM OF THE SEA C. 1905
Oil 58.5×48 cm
Coll.: New York, Charles Goldman
Exhib.: Nk, No. 34, col. repr.

227 UNDERSEA VISION C. 1908 (1910)
Oil 35.5×24 cm
Coll.: Bordeaux, Gabriel Frizeau; New York,
Irving W. Schwartz
Exhib.: Pl, No. 13; Nk, No. 52, col. repr.

228 UNDERSEA VISION 1908
Oil 54×65 cm
Coll.: Paris, Madame Albert Marquet
Exhib.: Pp; Py, No. 130

229 UNDERWATER LANDSCAPE C. 1908
Oil
Coll.: Solothurn, Josef Müller

230 STRANGE FLOWERS IN SURREALIST LANDSCAPE
C. 1910
Oil 50×26 cm

Coll.: Paris, A. Redon
Exhib.: Ld, No. 80, repr.

231 UNDERSEA VISION 1913
Oil 51.5×43.5 cm
Coll.: Béziers, A. d'Andoque; Paris, S.
Higgons; New York, New Gallery
Exhib.: Bi, No. 187; Nk, No. 57, col. repr.

Still-Lifes 1900 - 15

232 STILL-LIFE WITH POMEGRANATE 1901
Oil 24.5×24.5 cm
Coll.: New York, Dr. R. A. Kling
Exhib.: Nk, No. 27

233 LEMON AND PAPRIKA 1901
Oil 27.5×47 cm
Coll.: Almen, Bonger
Exhib.: Pl, No. 3; Pab, No. XXXIII, repr.;
Hb, No. 177
Lit.: Bacou, 1956, No. 68, repr.

234 STILL-LIFE WITH JUG AND LEMON
(Rostrup 1900, Bacou 1915)
Oil 50×73 cm
Coll.: Ordrupgaard, Denmark, Art Gallery
Exhib.: Französische Malerei, Zürich, 1917,
No. 61; Pq, No. 11

235 PEACH 1902
Oil
Coll.: Almen, Bonger
Exhib.: Pl, No. 9

236 QUINCE
Oil
Coll.: Paris, Mme. H. Gouin

237 STILL LIFE WITH PEARS AND PEACH
Before 1903
Oil
Coll.: Paris, A. Redon
Exhib.: Pl, No. 8; Pn, No. 17

238 STILL-LIFE WITH PEAR
Oil
Coll.: Algier, Musée des Arts

239 STILL-LIFE WITH TWO PAPRIKAS
C. 1905
Oil 38 × 26 cm
Coll.: Paris, Mme. H. Gouin
Exhib.: Pab, No. 181

240 STILL-LIFE. FRUIT ON A GREEN PLATE 1915
Oil 21 × 38 cm
Coll.: Paris, Jacques Dupont, 1931
Exhib.: Pab, No. 182; Bi, No. 150

Flower Pieces
I Early Works   before 1900

241 BINDWEED AND MARGUERITES IN A GRAY VASE
1867
Oil on wood 33 × 25 cm
Coll.: Almen, Bonger
Exhib.: Pab, No. 121; Hb, No. 155

241a FLOWER STILL-LIFE 1866–68
Signed: »à mon ami Alfred Maître
ODILON REDON«
Oil on canvas 33.7 × 24.5 cm
Coll.: London, Marlborough Fine Art Ltd;
Karlsruhe, Staatl. Kunsthalle

242 TWO HANDLED JUG WITH ROSE AND OTHER
FLOWERS (VASE 15)
Oil 33 × 28 cm
Coll.: Winterthur, R. Bühler; Paris, Bern-
heim-Jeune
Exhib.: Vier Eeuwen Stilleven in Frankrijk,
Boymans, Rotterdam, 1954, No. 106
Lit.: Mellerio, 1923, No. 70, repr.

243 TULIPS (VASE 24)
Oil 16 × 10.4 cm
Coll.: Formerly Paris, Durand-Ruel
Lit.: Bacou, 1956, No. 64, repr.

244 THREE BINDWEEDS AND FIVE MARGUERITES
Oil
Coll.: Almen, Bonger

245 THREE BINDWEEDS AND FIVE MARGUERITES
Oil on wood
Coll.: Rotterdam, D. G. van Beuningen;
No. 147

246 FLOWERS. LILIES AND NARCISSI C. 1880
(1870)
Oil 18 × 30 cm
Coll.: Holland, private ownership
Exhib.: Ld, No. 59, repr.

247 WHITE AND RED CARNATIONS IN A WHITE
PORCELAIN CUP (VASE 18) 1884
Oil on wood 25 × 15 cm
Coll.: Almen, Bonger 1902
Exhib.: Pab, No. 128; Hb, No. 169, repr.;
Ld, No. 61, repr.
Lit.: Sandström, 1955, p. 155, No. 119,
repr.; Bacou, 1956, No. 62, repr.

248 FLOWERS Before 1900
Oil 48 × 65 cm
Coll.: Basel, Magdalena Hutton-Rudolph
Exhib.: Bi, No. 149

Flower Pieces
II Objective Portrayal of Space
1900 - 04/05

249 JUG WITH FLOWERS (VASE 17)   C. 1900
Oil 46.5 × 38.5 cm
Coll.: The Hague, Gemeentemuseum
Exhib.: Hb, No. 168; Bi, No. 144; Ld,
No. 60, repr.

250 BUNCH OF FLOWERS IN A VASE (VASE 16)
C. 1900
Oil 46 × 35.5 cm
Coll.: Amsterdam, Madame J. van Gogh-
Bonger; Laren, V. W. van Gogh; New
York, Wildenstein
Exhib.: Magic of Flowers in Painting, Wil-
denstein, New York, 1954, No. 56

251 FLOWERS IN A BLUE BOWL (VASE 4)   1900
Oil 36 × 44 cm
Coll.: Paris, private ownership
Exhib.: Trente ans d'Art Indépendant,
Paris, 1926, No. 3163; Pab, Nr. XXXVI, repr.

252 VASE WITH ROSES ON A TABLE 1900
Oil 38 × 36 cm
Coll.: Almen, Bonger
Exhib.: Bi, No. 196; Ld, No. 64, repr.

253 VASE WITH ROSES AND CARNATIONS ON A RED
TABLECLOTH (VASE 21) 1900–01
Oil 65×49.5 cm
Coll.: Amsterdam, Madame J. van Gogh-
Bonger; Laren, V. W. van Gogh; New
York, Wildenstein
Exhib.: Magic of Flowers in Painting, Wil-
denstein, New York, 1954, No. 55, repr.

254 FLOWERS IN VASE (VASE 1) C. 1900
Oil 51×65 cm
Coll.: New York, Albert D. Lasker
Exhib.: Nj, No. 4, repr.

255 VASE WITH PEONIES (VASE 27) After 1900
Oil 51.5×45 cm
Coll.: Luzerne, Rosengart; Baltimore, Dr.
Claribel and Etta Cone; Baltimore, Museum
of Art (Cone Collection)
Exhib.: Pn, No. 12; French Nineteenth
Century Paintings owned in Maryland
Baltimore, 1951, No. 152; The Cone Collect-
ion, Knoedler, New York, 1955

256 BIG BOUQUET OF WILD FLOWERS IN PATTERNED
VASE (VASE 9) 1900–01
Oil 75×63 cm
Coll.: Almen, Bonger, 1901
Exhib.: Pl, No. 2; Pab, No. XXXIX, repr.;
Hb, No. 175, repr.; Sources du XXᵉ Siècle,
Musée d'Art Moderne, Paris, 1960, No. 579
Lit.: Bacou, 1956, No. X, col. repr.

257 BEGONIA IN POT After 1900
Oil 65×49.5 cm
Coll.: Winterthur, Hedy Hahnloser-Bühler
Bern, Hans R. Hahnloser
Exhib.: Die Hauptwerke der Sammlung
Hahnloser, Lucerne, 1940, No. 98; Pab,
No. 137; Hb, No. 174

258 BEGONIAS IN POT C. 1901
Oil 56×46 cm
Coll.: New York, G. David Thompson
Exhib.: Nj, No. 6, repr.

259 BEGONIAS IN A POT RED GROUND
Before 1905
Oil 55×46.5 cm
Coll.: Paris, Bernheim-Jeune; New York,
Wendell T. Bush; New York, Museum of
Modern Art

Exhib.: Na, No. 273
Lit.: Alfred H. Barr, Painting and Sculpture
in the Museum of Modern Art, New York,
1948, No. 673

260 STILL-LIFE WITH FLOWERS (Copy after Cé-
zanne, V. 358). 1901 (Rewald: 1895)
Oil 46.5×55 cm
Coll.: Paris, A. Leblond
Exhib.: Pu, No. 32; Hb, No. 178

261 SMALL BUNCH OF FLOWERS WITH FOUR
ANEMONES (VASE 1) 1900–02
Oil 24.5×20 cm
Coll.: Almen, Bonger, 1902
Exhib.: Pab, No. 141; Hb, No. 176
Lit.: Bacou, 1956, No. 73, repr.

262 GERANIUM IN A VASE WITH A BLUE PATTERN
(VASE 2) After 1900
Oil
Coll.: St. Louis, Steinberg

263 GERANIUM IN A POT C. 1900–05
Oil 65×50.5 cm
Coll.: Paris, Vaquez, 1905; Paris, R. Pac-
quement
Exhib.: Pn, No. 20; Collections Parisiennes,
Paris, Galerie Beaux-Arts, 1955, No. 92;
Pab, No. 147

264 FLOWERPOT WITH GERANIUMS C. 1903
Oil 65×49 cm
Coll.: Cleveland, Ralph M. Coe
Exhib.: Nd, No. 7; Ca, No. 5; Ne, No. 96;
Pictures collected by Yale alumni, New
Haven, 1956, No. 103, repr.

265 FLOWER VASE (VASE 19) C. 1904
Oil 38.5×31.5 cm
Coll.: Paris, J. Zoubaloff; Otterlo, Kröller-
Müller. 1927
Exhib.: Hb, No. 196, repr.; Ld, No. 68, repr.

266 ANEMONES IN A DARK VASE IN A ROCOCO
FRAME (VASE 31) Before 1905
Oil 73×55 cm
Coll.: Paris, Claude Roger-Marx; New York,
Germain Seligman
Exhib.: Pn, No. 21; Cinquante ans de Pein-
ture Française, Pavillon de Marsan, Paris,

1925, No. 62; Ps, No. 84; Ca, No. 13;
French Art, London, 1932, No. 478
Lit.: Claude Roger-Marx, 1925, p. 49, repr.;
Fosca, Amour de l'Art, 1929, p. 320, repr.

267   BUNCH OF FLOWERS Before 1905
Oil 32.5 × 21.5 cm
Coll.: Rheinfelden, Switzerland, Adolf Ro-
niger-Hürlimann
Exhib.: Bi, No. 164

Flower-Pieces
III Decorative Phase 1905 - 09/10

268   FLOWERS IN A BROWN JUG (VASE 33) 1905
Oil 81 × 65 cm
Coll.: Paris, Prince Bibesco
Exhib.: Ps, No. 5; French Art, London,
1932, Nr. 477; Py, No. 128

269   BUNCH OF WILD FLOWERS IN A VASE WITH A
HANDLE (VASE 10) 1905
Oil 51.5 × 40 cm
Coll.: New York, Wildenstein; Washington,
private ownership

270   TWO-HANDLED VASE WITH GERANIUM (VASE
35) Cl 1905
Oil 27 × 22 cm
Coll.: Paris, Bernheim-Jeune, 1910; Paris,
Marcel Kapferer; Paris, G. Martin; New
York, Carstairs

271   BUNCH OF FLOWERS (VASE 4) 1905
Oil 63 × 48 cm
Coll.: New York, Sam A. Lewisohn; New
York, Dr. Ernest Kahn
Exhib.: Nj, No. 9, repr.

272   VASE WITH BLACK POPPY (VASE 26) C. 1905
(1895)
Oil 72 × 53 cm
Coll.: Paris, Prince Bibesco
Exhib.: Pu, No. 29
Lit.: Bacou, 1956, No. 84, repr.

273   POPPIES After 1905
Oil 54.5 × 65.5 cm
Coll.: Holland, private ownership
Exhib.: Hb, No. 197

274   POPPIES After 1905
Oil on wood 33 × 23 cm
Coll.: Holland private ownership
Exhib.: Hb, No. 167

275   BUNCH OF FLOWERS IN A BLUE VASE (VASE 37)
After 1905
Oil 55 × 46 cm
Coll.: New York, Wildenstein; New York;
private ownership

276   FLOWERPOT WITH APPLE-BLOSSOM TWIG AND
OTHER FLOWERS C. 1905–06
Oil 130 × 67.5 cm
Coll.: Paris, Marcel Kapferer; New York,
Wildenstein

277   FLOWERS IN GREEN-PATTERNED VASE
(VASE 9) in the colours of the Fauves
C. 1907 (Bacou: 1900–03, Paris Catalogue:
1910)
Oil on wood 60 × 38 cm
Coll.: Paris, A. Redon
Exhib.: Pr, No. 14; London, 1932, No. 12;
Pab, No. XLV, repr.
Lit.: Bacou, 1956, No. 75, repr.

278   FLOWERS IN GREEN VASE 1905–06
Oil
Coll.: Philadelphia, Pennsylvania Museum
of Art

279   FLOWERS IN GREEN VASE WITH HANDLES
(VASE 15) 1905–06
Oil 27.5 × 21.5 cm
Coll.: Pittsburgh, Dr. Beram D. Saklat-
walla; Pittsburgh, Carnegie Institute, 1946
Exhib.: Nd, No. 19; Ca, No. 18, repr. as
frontispiece; Ne, No. 87

280   FLOWERS IN GREEN VASE (VASE 5) 1905–06
Oil 55 × 74.5 cm
Coll.: Amsterdam, W. Sieger; New York,
Wildenstein

281   FLOWERS IN GREEN VASE (VASE 5) 1905–08
Oil 73 × 54 cm
Coll.: New York, Kraushaar; Hartford,
Anne Parrish Titzell; Hartford, Atheneum
Exhib.: Nj, No. 12, repr.

282   WILD FLOWERS 1905–08
Oil 65 × 50 cm

Coll.: Winterthur, Dr. Hahnloser; Winterthur, Museum
Exhib.: Pab, No. 148; Hb, No. 186; Französische Malerei von Delacroix bis Picasso Stadthalle, Wolfsburg, 1961, No. 125

283 GREEN VASE WITH BUTTERFLY (VASE 5)
After 1905
Oil 65 × 50 cm
Coll.: Paris, P. Bacou
Exhib.: Lb, No. 35; De David à Cézanne, Brussels, 1947, No. 134; Pz, No. 10
Lit.: Bacou, 1956, No. 83, repr.

284 JAPANESE VASE WITH BUTTERFLY (VASE 22)
1905–08
Oil 90 × 63.5 cm
Coll.: Paris, M. Kapferer; Paris, E. Bignou; Scotland, private ownership
Exhib.: Pq, No. 74; Bd, No. 1, repr.; Ld, No. 77, repr.
Lit.: Fegdal, 1929, No. 52, repr.

285 BIG BUNCH OF WILD FLOWERS IN GRAY VASE (VASE 2) After 1905; (Rosenberg: 1902–04; Rewald: 1890)
Oil 64 × 50 cm
Coll.: New York, Cornelius J. Sullivan; New York, Henry C. Southam; New York, Donald S. Stralem
Exhib.: Brooklyn Museum, New York, 1926; Nd, No. 23; Museum of Fine Arts, Springfield, Mass., 1933, No. 129; The Magic of Flowers, Wildenstein, New York, 1954; Inaugural Exhibition, Fort Worth, Texas, 1954; Paa; Hc; Nj, No. 7, col. repr.; Nk, No. 36
Lit.: Rewald, Post-Impressionism, 1956, p. 167, col. repr.

285a BIG BUNCH OF WILD FLOWERS IN PATTERNED VASE (VASE 4) After 1905
Oil 47 × 63.5 cm
Coll.: Paris, Jos. Hessel; Paris, Marcel Guérin; Emery Reves
Exhib.: La; Ca 23

286 STILL-LIFE WITH BLUE JUG C. 1905
Oil 38 × 35 cm
Coll.: Paris, Dr. Sabouraud; Paris, David-Weill
Exhib.: Ps, No. 87; Pu, No. 34; Pab, No. 143

287 RED POPPY 1906
Oil 27 × 19 cm
Coll.: Paris, Paul Jamot, 1907; Paris, Louvre, 1941
Exhib.: Pm, No. 1450; Pu, No. 48; Donation Paul Jamot, Orangerie, Paris, 1941, No. 90; Nouvelles Acquisitions, 1939–45, Louvre, Paris, 1945, No. 105; Pab, No. 151
Lit.: P. Jamot: Le Salon d'Automne, Gazette des Beaux-Arts, 1906, II, p. 482

288 PEONIES, LILIES AND LEAVES IN PATTERNED VASE (VASE 9) 1907
Oil on cardboard 72 × 60 cm
Coll.: Béziers, Gustave Fayet; Béziers, A. d'Andoque
Exhib.: Ps, No. 25; Pab, No. 152

289 WILD FLOWERS WITH BUTTERFLY AND THE PATTERNED VASE (VASE 9) 1907
Oil 67 × 51 cm
Coll.: Béziers, Gustave Fayet; Paris, P. Bacou
Exhib.: Ps, No. 28; Lb, No. 25; De David à Cézanne, Brussels, 1947, No. 133; Pz, No. 10; Pab, No. 162
Lit.: Claude Roger-Marx, 1925, p. 55, repr.; Bacou, 1956, No. 80, repr.

290 PATTERNED VASE WITH FLOWERS (VASE 9)
1907/08 (C. 1910)
Oil on cardboard 69 × 53 cm
Coll.: Chicago, Art Institute, Louis L. Coburn Memorial Collection
Exhib.: Cb, No. 4; Nj, No. 21; Nk, No. 42, repr.

291 FLOWER VASE WITH THREE BUTTERFLIES
C. 1908
Oil on wood 35 × 27 cm
Coll.: Paris, Georges Bernheim; Paris, Follot; New York, Wildenstein

292 BUNCH OF FLOWERS WITH RED LEAVES
Oil 55 × 32.7 cm
Coll.: Kyoto, S. Takeuchi; Tokyo, T. Yamaguchi
Exhib.: Redon, Tokyo, Kyuryudo Gallery, 1954; Masterpieces of European Art, Kyoto, 1957

293 FLOWER VASE (VASE 8) 1908–10
Oil 61 × 46.5 cm
Coll.: New York, Aaron W. Davis
Exhib.: Nj, No. 20, repr.

294 GARDEN FLOWERS IN GREEN VASE (VASE 26)
C. 1910
Oil 55×75 cm
Coll.: New York, John Hay Whitney
Exhib.: Nk, No. 47, col. repr.

295 FLOWERS IN A GLASS 1910
Oil 46×52 cm
Coll.: Paris, Jos. Hessel, 1910; Paris,
G. Renand
Exhib.: Pq, No. 54; Pab, No. 175; Bi, No. 172

296 THREE BLUE VASES C. 1910
Oil 73×54 cm
Coll.: Ascona, Von der Heydt; Wuppertal,
Städtisches Museum
Exhib.: Die Farbe, Kunstgewerbemuseum,
Zürich, 1944; Ld, No. 67, repr.; Franzö-
sische Malerei von Delacroix bis Picasso,
Stadthalle, Wolfsburg, 1961, No. 123, col.
repr.
Lit.: Charles Sterling, La Nature Morte,
Paris 1952, p. 107, Pl. 198, repr. in Colour

297 FLOWERS IN A TEAPOT C. 1910
Oil 41×33 cm
Coll. Boston, Montgommery Sears

298 INDIAN WOMAN WITH WHITE BUTTERFLY
1910 (1916)
Oil 65×50 cm
Coll.: Paris, Hessel; Paris, M.-A. Leblond;
New York, Ian Woodner
Exhib.: Pr, No. 64; Py, No. 135; Galerie
Charpentier, Paris; Nk, No. 44, repr.
Lit.: Mellerio, 1923, p. 15, repr.

299 BUTTERFLIES 1910
Oil 34×26.5 cm
Coll.: New York, Paul M. Hirschland
Exhib.: Ni, No. 8

300 BUTTERFLIES After 1910
Oil 73×54 cm
Coll.: Paris, G. Renand
Exhib.: Chefs-d'œuvre de l'art français, Pa-
ris, 1937, No. 370; Pab, No. 179
Lit.: Match No. 398, 24 November 1956,
repr. in Colour

301 DREAM OF BUTTERFLIES After 1910
Oil
Coll.: Winterthur, Dr. A. Hahnloser;
Detroit, Institute of Arts; New York, E. und
A. Silbermann
Exhib.: Wa, No. 4; Nd, No. 3; Ca, No. 8;
Ne, No. 81, repr.

302 BUTTERFLIES C. 1910-12
Oil
Coll.: Paris, J. Hessel; Greenwich, Conn.,
I. Ethelyn McKinney
Exhib.: Pu, No. 60
Lit.: College Art Journal, Fall 1959, repr.

303 BUTTERFLIES 1910-12
Oil 55×41.5 cm
Coll.: Detroit, Institute of Art
Exhib.: Nd, No. 2; Ca, No. 9; Ne, No. 85;
Art from Ingres to Pollock, University of
California, Berkeley, 1960, p. 55, repr.; Nk,
No. 51
Lit.: David, M. Robb, The Harper History
of Painting, 1951, No. 435, repr.

304 ANEMONES WITH BUTTERFLIES 1912-14
Oil
Coll.: Paris, Armand Parent; New York,
Mrs. C. N. Bliss, Jr.; Paris, private owner-
ship
Exhib.: Pq, No. 80; Pr, No. 43; Ps, No. 70;
Nd, No. 18

305 FOOTED VASE WITH FLOWERS AND FIVE
BUTTERFLIES (VASE 11) 1912-14
Oil 73×54 cm
Coll.: France, private ownership; New
York Wildenstein; Dallas, Texas, private
ownership
Exhib.: Nk, No. 60, col. repr.

306 WILTED FLOWERS C. 1912
Oil
Coll.: Paris, M. Kapferer

307 WHITE CHINESISE VASE WITH FLOWERS
(VASE 7) C. 1912 (1902-05)
Oil 74×55 cm
Coll.: Cleveland, Roberta Holden Boble;
Cleveland, Museum of Art, 1935
Exhib.: French Painting from the XVth
Century to the Present Day, San Francisco,

1934, No. 137, repr.; Autumn Flower Show, Cleveland Museum of Art, 1935; Survey of French Painting, Baltimore, 1934; Survey of French Painting, Carnegie Institute, Pittsburgh, 1936, No. 36; Nj, No. 8, repr.
Lit.: Decorative Arts, December, 1934, repr.; Art News, January 1936, p. 16

308 BUNCH OF FLOWERS WITH POPPIES IN CHINESISE VASE ON PINK BACKGROUND (VASE 7)
C. 1912
Oil 72.7 × 54 cm
Coll.: Paris, Marcel Kapferer; New York, Caroll Galleries, 1915; New York, John Quinn, 1920; Boston, Mrs J. Montgommery Sears, 1925; New York, Mabel Choate; New York, Metropolitan Museum, 1958
Exhib.: Na, No. 273; Fiftieth Anniversary Exhibition, Metropolitan Museum, New York, 1920; Impressionist and Post Impressionist Paintings, Museum of Modern Art, New York, 1921, No. 94
Lit.: House and Garden, September 1944, col. repr.

309 CHINESISE FLOWER VASE WITH ANEMONES
C. 1912
Oil 73 × 54 cm
Coll.: Paris, Marcel Kapferer; New York, Paul Wyler
Exhib.: Wiesbaden, 1921; Lb

310 TURQUOISE VASE (VASE 5) 1912
Oil 65 × 50 cm
Coll.: Winterthur, Hedy Hahnloser-Bühler; Bern, Hans R. Hahnloser
Exhib.: Wa; Pq, No. 45; Bd, No. 9; La Peinture française du XIXe siècle en Suisse, Paris, Gazette des Beaux-Arts, 1938, Nr. 87; Die Hauptwerke der Sammlung Hahnloser, Lucerne, 1940, No. 90, repr.; Pab, No. 178; Hb, No. 198; Bi, No. 203
Lit.: Doris Wild, Moderne Malerei, Zürich, 1950, repr.

311 ETRUSCAN VASE (VASE 25) C. or after 1912
Tempera on Canvas 81.3 × 59.1 cm
Coll.: New York, John Quinn, 1915; New York, Lillie P. Bliss, 1925; New York Museum of Modern Art, 1931; New York, Metropolitan Museum, 1951

Exhib.: Impressionist and post-impressionist paintings, New York, Metropolitan Museum, 1921, No. 92, repr.; Nd, No. 16; Ca, No. 2; Ne, No. 84; The Lillie P. Bliss Collection, Museum of Modern Art, New York, 1934, No. 50; Paintings and Sculpture in the Museum of Modern Art, New York, 1942, No. 511; Pab, No. LXII, repr.; Nk, No. 26, repr.
Lit.: R. Shoolman and Charles E. Slatkin, The Enjoyment of Art in America, Philadelphia, 1942, No. 574, repr.; Sandström, 1955, p. 168, No. 132, repr.

312 ANEMONES IN VASE WITH FOOT (VASE 11)
1912–14
Oil 74 × 76 cm
Coll.: Philadelphia, Irving S. Vogel; New York, Mrs. A. L. Spitzer
Exhib.: Nj, No. 23, repr.
Lit.: Rewald, Post-Impressionism, 1956, p. 175, col. repr.

313 A ROSE, TWO MARGUERITES AND A CORNFLOWER IN A SMALL GREEN VASE
(VASE 16) 1912–14
Oil 46 × 34 cm
Coll.: Paris, J. Hessel; Paris, Leroux-Haudebert; Algiers, Museum, 1954
Exhib.: Pu, No. 43; Pab, No. 180; Hb, No. 199

314 ANEMONES AND POPPY IN A VASE (VASE 13)
1914–15
Oil 73 × 57 cm
Coll.: New York, Frank Altschul
Exhib.: Nj, No. 25, repr.

Decorative Folding-Screens and Wall Panels

315 FANTASTIC FLOWERS AND ANIMALS FOR THE CHÂTEAU DOMECY IN BURGUNDY 1900–1903
18 panels, tempera, oil and pastel, each Screen 250 × 160 cm

316 PLANTS 1901–02
Five-section screen, tempera, height 244 cm, Width 183, 40.5, 28, 74, 30.5 cm
Coll.: Paris, Madame Ernest Chausson; New York, Kraushaar Gallery; Chicago,

Mrs. Rue Winterbotham Carpenter; Charlotte, Vermont, Mrs. Geneviève Carpenter Hill
Exhib.: Nk, No. 28, repr.

317   SCREEN FOR OLIVIER SAINSÈRE   PARIS
1902–03
Exhib.: Ps, No. 176

318   THE WORLD OF CHIMERAS. FANTASTIC PEGASUS
Centrepiece of a three-section screen for Princess Cystria, Paris; two sidepieces disappeared in Paris during the last war. November 1903
Tempera 240×80 cm
Coll.: Paris, Princess Cystria; Paris, Ch. A. Girard; Paris, Madame Gustave Coquiot; New York, Gallery Silbermann; Pleasantville, New York, Reader's Digest
Exhib.: Wb, No. 28, repr.; Pab, No. 185

319   BUDDHA   1904–05
Screen, Tempera 160×120 cm
Coll.: Almen, Bonger, 1905
Exhib.: Pab, No. 186; Hb, No. 202
Lit.: Bacou, 1956, No. 85, repr.

320   FLOWERING TREE   1904–05
Screen, tempera on canvas 174.5×89 cm
Coll.: Almen, Bonger, 1905
Exhib.: Pab, No. 187; Hb, No. 201

321   RED SCREEN   1905
Eoll.: Paris, Prince Bibesco
Exhib.: Ps, No. 168

322   FLOWERING BRANCH   1906
Screen, tempera 156×104 cm
Coll.: Paris, private ownership
Exhib.: Pab, No. 188

323   LANDSCAPE WITH RED TREES   1906
Screen, tempera 79×53 cm
Coll.: Paris, A. Vollard, 1906; Paris Jacques Ulmann
Exhib.: Pab, No. 187 bis; Sources du XXᵉ siècle, Paris, 1960, No. 582; Ld, No. 74, repr.

324   THE RED SCREEN   1906–08
Three almost abstract compositions in tempera, each 168×74 cm

Coll.: Almen, Bonger
Exhib.: Pab, No. 189; Hb, No. 1203
Lit.: Bacou, 1956, No. 100, repr.

325   ORIENTAL CARPET FANTASY (Flowers and semi-abstract forms) 1906–08
Screen, oil and tempera
Coll.: Solothurn, Josef Müller

326   UNDERSEA WORLD.   STUDY IN BLUE AND GRAY 1906–08
Screen, tempera
Coll.: Paris, Madame de Polès
Exhib.: Po. No. 2

327   FLOWERS   1906–08
Screen, tempera
Coll.: Béziers, A. d'Andoque
Exhib.: Ps, No. 169

328   SPRING   1908
Screen, tempera:
Coll.: Moskow, Shchukin; Moskow, Museum for Western Art
Exhib.: Po, No. 1

329   DAY   1910–11
Screen, tempera 200×650 cm
Coll.: Abbaye de Fontfroide, Gustave Fayet
Lit.: Bacou, 1956, No. 97, repr.

330   NIGHT   1910–11
Screen, tempera: 200×650 cm
Coll.: Abbaye de Fontfroide, Gustave Fayet
Lit.: Bacou, 1956, No. 98, 99

331   SPRING AND FLOWER GODDESS   1912
Screen, tempera
Coll.: Winterthur, Richard Bühler

Pastels

Early Landscapes   before 1900

332   WINDMILL   1890 or earlier
Pastel 30×37 cm
Coll.: The Hague, Dr. H. P. Bremmer heirs, Floris Bremmer
Exhib.: Pq, No. 25; Bd, No 19; Hb, No. 131; Bi, No. 142

333   LANDSCAPE   1890 or earlier
      Pastel
      Coll.: Winterthur, Richard Bühler
      Lit.: Mellerio, 1923, p. 10, repr.

Visions and Allegories
1890-1900

334   TIME   C. or before 1890
      Pastel and charcoal 34×25 cm
      Coll.: Otterlo, Kröller-Müller, No. 787,
      Exhib.: Py, No. 151

335   WITH CLOSED EYES   1890
      (see M. 107)
      Pastel 60×53.5 cm
      Coll.: Paris, Jos. Hessel; New York, de
      Hauke; Cleveland, Powell Jones; Gates
      Mills, Ohio, Frank Griesinger
      Exhib.: Pq, No. 115; Nd, No. 29; Ca, No.
      28; Ng, No. 18; Les Deux Ecritures,
      Galerie Marcel Guiot, Paris, 1953, No. 76

336   SUFFERING   C. 1890
      Pastel
      Coll.: Domecy, Sermizelles, Robert de Do-
      mecy
      Lit.: Mellerio, 1923, p. 17, repr.

337   MYSTIC RIDER   Charcoal drawing, 1869
      1890 worked over with pastel after
      Coll.: Paris, Antoine de La Rochefoucauld;
      Bordeaux, Museum
      Exhib.: Pg, No. 8
      Lit.: Sandström, 1955, No. 36, repr.; Melle-
      rio, 1923, (as 'Sphinx'), p. 167, repr.

338   AN OLD ANGEL. (SPHINX WITH WINGS)
      1892–95
      Pastel 51×36 cm with charcoal
      Coll.: Paris, Maurice Fabre, 1902;
      Paris, Jacques Zoubaloff; Paris, Petit Palais,
      1916
      Exhib.: Pu, No. 77; Pab, No. XXII, repr.

339   SALOME   Before 1894 (Inspired by Gustave
      Moreau)
      Pastel 50 × 35 cm
      Coll.: Paris private ownership
      Exhib.: Pg, No. 69; Pab, Nr. 72

340   THREE COLOURS. MYSTIC DIALOGUE
      C. 1895
      Pastel 44×31 cm with charcoal
      Coll.: Otterlo, Kröller-Müller, No. 786
      Exhib.: Düsseldorf, 1928, No. 396

341   THE YELLOW CAPE   C. 1895
      Pastel 47.5×35 cm
      Coll.: Almen, Bonger
      Lit.: Sandström, 1955, No. 129, repr.

342   BLOOD-FLOWER   1895 (Genesis of the motif
      of a Girl's head with flowers)
      Pastel 29.5×42.5 cm
      Coll.: Paris, A. Redon
      Exhib.: Retrospective d'Art Indépendant,
      Paris, 1926, No. 3165; Pab, No. XIII, repr.

343   MONSTER UNDER SEA WITH HUMAN HEAD
      C. 1895
      Pastel 52.5×44.5 cm
      Coll.: Almen, Bonger; The Hague, Galerie
      G. J. Nieuwenhuizen Segaar; London, pri-
      vate ownership; Chicago, Gallery Findlay
      Exhib.: Bd, No. 51; Pq, No. 34; Stedelijk
      Museum de Lakenhal, Leiden, 1950, No.
      129; Hb, No. 136; Ld, No. 43, repr.

344   CENTAUR   C. 1895 (1910)
      Pastel 72×59 cm
      Coll.: Béziers, Gustave Fayet; Paris, P.
      Bacou
      Exhib.: Ps, No. 110; Lb, No. 33, (as a
      painting); Pw, No. 16; Py, No. 144

345   LADY MACBETH   C. 1900 (1885)
      Pastel
      Coll.: Formerly Paris, Armand Parent
      Exhib.: Pu, No. 64
      Lit.: Fegdal, 1929, No. 17, repr.

346   THE BOOK   C. 1900
      Pastel 50×36 cm
      Coll.: Aerdenhout, H. C. Gomperts
      Exhib.: Bd, No. 54; Hb, No. 152

Religious Mood
1893-1905 (1910)

347   MEDITATION (CHRIST)   C. 1893
      Pastel 45×36 cm

Coll.: Almen, Bonger; New York, Wildenstein
Exhib.: Bi, No. 155

348   THE RED CROWN OF THORNS   1895
Pastel with charcoal 50 × 40 cm
Coll.: Béziers, Gustave Fayet; Paris, Paul Bacou
Exhib.: Ps, No. 109; Pab, No. 77
Lit.: Bacou, 1956, No. 47, repr.

349   THE RED CROWN OF THORNS   1895
Pastel 64.5 × 48.5 cm
Coll.: Laren, P. A. Regnault; Amsterdam, Gemeentemuseum; Antwerpen, Museum voor Schone Kunsten
Exhib.: Delft, 1948; Stedelijk Museum, Eindhoven, 1951; Hb, No. 134
Lit.: Collection P. A. Regnault, Catalogue de vente, Amsterdam, 22. 10. 1958, No. 100, repr.

350   CROWN OF THORNS   C. 1895
Black chalk
Coll.: London, British Museum
Lit.: Sandström, 1955, No. 79, repr.

351   CROWN OF THORNS   1897–99
Pastel and charcoal 51.5 × 37 cm
Coll.: Paris, Maurice Fabre, 1899; Béziers, Gustave Fayet, 1911; Arles, L. Fayet; London, private ownership
Exhib.: Pl, No. 25; Pm, No. 28; Ps, No. 109; Pab, No. 81; Bi, No. 157, repr.; Ld, No. 44, repr.

352   THE HEART OF JESUS   1895
Pastel 60 × 45 cm
Coll.: Paris, Paul Jamot; Paris, Louvre, 1939
Exhib.: Pu, No. 68; La donation Paul Jamot, Orangerie, Paris, 1941, No. 139; Les Impressionistes, Jeu de Paume, Paris, 1947, No. 217; Pastels, Orangerie, Paris, 1949, No. 109; Pastels de 19ème Siècle, Cabinet des Dessins, Paris, 1956; Pab, No. 78
Lit.: Luc Benoît, La Collection Paul Jamot. L'Amour de l'Art, 1926, p. 171, repr.; Bacou, 1956, No. IX, repr. in colour; Klaus Berger, College Art Journal, Fall 1956, p. 32, repr.

353   THE HEART OF JESUS   1895
Pastel 65 × 50 cm
Coll.: Otterlo, Kröller-Müller, No. 785
Exhib.: Düsseldorf, 1928, No. 409
Lit.: Bacou, 1956, p. 127

354   CHRIST IN SILENCE   1895
Pastel 58 × 45 cm
Coll.: Paris, J. Zoubaloff; Paris, Petit Palais, 1916
Exhib.: Pu, No. 78; Pab, No. 79
Lit.: André Salmon, L'Art Décoratif, 1913, p. 11, repr.; La donation J. Zoubaloff aux Musées de France, Paris, Ed. Morance, p. 36; Claude Roger-Marx, 1925, p. 37, repr.; Bacou, 1956, No. 46, repr.

354a   CHRIST ON THE CROSS
Pastel 48.5 × 36.5 cm
Coll.: Tokyo, K. Nakagawa
Exhib.: Redon, Tokyo, Kyuryudo Gallery, 1954; Masterpieces of European Art, Kyoto, 1957

355   MOUNT CALVARY   1895 or later
Pastel with pencil 67 × 50 cm
Coll.: Almen, Bonger; Zürich, Bührle
Exhib.: Ng, No. 10, repr.
Lit.: Mellerio, 1923, p. 40, repr.; Bacou, 1956, No. 50, repr.

356   VIRGIN MARY IN VEIL   Before 1898
Pastel 42 × 28 cm
Coll.: Amsterdam, S. de Swarte, 1898; Almen, Bonger
Exhib.: Ng, No. 8, repr.; Pab, No. 76
Lit.: Sandström, 1955, No. 128, repr.

357   HEAD OF JOHN THE BAPTIST   C. 1900
Pastel 50 × 37 cm
Coll.: Paris, Arthur Fontaine; Amsterdam, Prentenkabinet
Exhib.: Pq, No. 101; Hb, No. 140

358   HEAD OF CHRIST   C. 1900
Pastel 20 × 12.5 cm
Coll.: Paris, Armand Parent; Pittsburgh, Dr. B. D. Saklatwalla
Exhib.: Ps; Nd, No. 47; Ca, No. 42; Ne, No. 90; Ng, No. 35
Lit.: Fegdal, 1929, No. 22, repr.

359 SAINT SEBASTIAN IN THE AURA (with arms in the air) After 1900
Pastel
Coll.: Paris, Gobin; New York, C. M. de Hauke
Exhib.: Cb, No. 32
Lit.: Mellerio, 1923, p. 52, repr.

360 SAINT SEBASTIAN (with arms crossed over his head) Before 1910
Pastel
Coll.: Paris, Galerie Druet; Paris, Georges Bénard; Paris, de Hauke
Exhib.: Ps, No. 96; Ca, No. 33; Galerie J. Dubourg, Paris, 1948, No. 14
Lit.: Fegdal, 1929, No. 54, repr.; see 182

361 SAINT SEBASTIAN (with arms crossed behind his back) C. 1910
Pastel 66.5 × 53.5 cm
Coll.: Paris, Leblond; Kingspoint, N. Y., Norbert Schimmel
Exhib.: Ps, No. 139; Pu, No. 89; Ng, No. 14, repr.; Wb, No. 33; Ni, No. 10, repr.; Nk, No. 23
Lit.: Germain Seligman, Oh! Fickle Taste, 1952, p. 53, repr.

362 THE FLIGHT INTO EGYPT C. 1902
Pastel and gouache 50 × 61 cm
Coll.: Paris, Armand Parent, 1904; London, Leicester Galleries; New York, Mrs. John D. Rockefeller
Exhib.: Pl, No. 31; Pq, No. 131; Pr, No. 90; Ps, No. 143; Pu, No. 90; Ld, No. 47, repr.; Nk, No. 29
Lit.: Fegdal, 1929, pl. 19, repr.; Bacou, 1956, No. 77, repr.

363 SAINT GEORGE Before 1910
Pastel 54 × 39 cm
Coll.: Almen, Bonger; New York, Seligman; New York, George Murphy
Exhib.: Ng, No. 12, repr.; Wb, No. 32; Bh, No. 337

Myth (Orpheus, Buddha, Phaeton)
1903 - 10

364 ORPHEUS UNDER THE SPOTLIGHT 1903
Pastel 59 × 46.5 cm

Coll.: Paris, Ambroise Vollard; Ernest Hepburn; New York, Wildenstein
Exhib.: Pl, No. 34

365 ORPHEUS After 1903
Pastel 70 × 56.5 cm
Coll.: Paris, Wilhelm Uhde; New York, John Quinn; Cleveland, J. H. Wade; Cleveland Museum of Art, 1926
Exhib.: Na, No. 307; Impressionist and Post-Impressionist Paintings, Metropolitan Museum, New York, 1921, No. 96, repr.
Lit.: W. Pach, The Masters of Modern Art, 1924, p. 107, repr.; John Quinn Collection of Paintings, Watercolors, etc., 1926, repr.; Cleveland Museum of Art Bulletin, June 1926, repr.; R. H. Wilenski, French Painting, 1931, p. 332, repr.; Klaus Berger, College Art Journal, Fall 1956, p. 33, repr.; J. Rewald, Gazette des Beaux-Arts, November 1956, No. 13, repr.

366 BUDDHA'S ENLIGHTENMENT (IDOL)
C. or before 1900
Pastel
Coll.: Paris, Marcel Kapferer
Lit.: Claude Roger-Marx, 1925, p. 35, repr.; Germain Bazin, L'Epoque Impressioniste, 1947, p. 93, repr.

367 BUDDHA'S DEATH C. 1900
Pastel
Coll.: Nice, Henri Matisse
Exhib.: Pj, No. 4; Pq, No. 128

368 THE LIVING BUDDHA 1903/04
Pastel
Coll.: Paris, J. A. Fontaine; Paris, Arthur Fontaine
Lit.: Fegdal, 1929, No. 26, repr.

369 BUDDHA WANDERING AMONG FLOWERS
1905
Pastel and oil, perhaps a decorative screen
Coll.: Paris, Mme. Fernand Halphen
Exhib.: Pu, No. 46; Lb, No. 37
Lit.: Sandström, 1955, No. 114, repr.; Klaus Berger, Art Quarterly, Summer 1958, No. 5, repr.

370 BUDDHA Before 1906
Pastel 90 × 73 cm

Coll.: Paris, Marcel Kapferer, 1906
Exhib.: Pm; Pq, No. 117; Ps, No. 49; Pu, No. 86; Py, No. 146; Pab, No. 100, repr.
Lit.: A. Salmon: Art Décoratif, 1913, p. 15, repr.; Claude Roger-Marx: L'Amour de l'Art, 1920, p. 40, repr.; R. Rey: Art et Décoration, August 1920, p. 41, repr.; Claude Roger-Marx, 1925, p. 43, repr.; Fegdal, 1929, No. LIX, repr.; Bacou, 1956, No. II, repr. in colour; Claude Roger-Marx, L'Œil, May 1956, p. 28, repr.

371 RIDER WITH SPEAR. ST GEORGE AND THE DRAGON (?) C. 1904
Pastel
Coll.: Paris, Galerie Druet
Lit.: Fegdal, 1929, No. 58, repr.

372 THE GREEN RIDER C. 1904
Pastel 67 × 60 cm
Coll.: Winterthur, R. Bühler; New York, Wildenstein
Exhib.: Wa; Meisterwerke aus Privatsammlungen, Winterthur, Museum, 1922, No. 72; Vente Richard Bühler, Hotel National, Luzern, 2/IX/1935 No. 7, repr.; La Peinture française du 19ème Siècle en Suisse, Gazette des Beaux-Arts, 1938, No. 91a

373 PEGASUS C. or before 1905
Pastel
Coll.: Béziers, Gustave Fayet; New York, New Gallery
Exhib.: Ps, No. 111; Ni, No. 3, repr.

374 BRÜNHILDE ON A HORSE C. 1905
Pastel
Coll.: Paris, Marcel Bernheim
Lit.: Fegdal, 1929, No. 45, repr.

375 APOLLO'S SUN CHARIOT WITH TWO WHITE HORSES C. 1910
Pastel 47 × 57.5 cm
Coll.: Amsterdam, Cleyndert
Exhib.: Teekeningen van Fransche Meesters, Stedelijk Museum, Amsterdam, 1946, No. 159; Hb, No. 150

376 APOLLO'S SUN CHARIOT (PHAETON'S DOWNFALL) (see 153/164) C. 1910
Pastel

Coll.: Paris, Mme. Pierre Goujon
Exhib.: Musée de l'Art Moderne: Dessins des Collections Particulières, 1958
Lit.: Claude Roger-Marx, 1925, p. 61, repr.

377 THE WREATH. A MAN STANDING UPRIGHT WITH OUTSPREAD ARMS HOLDS A SHEAF OF LEAVES 1910
Pastel 66 × 54 cm
Coll.: Minneapolis, Mrs. Charles J. Martin
Exhib.: Nd, No. 34; Ca, No. 38; Ne, No. 77, repr.

378 ROGER AND ANGELICA 1910 (C. 1905)
Pastel 91.5 × 71 cm
Preliminary drawing in the Petit Palais, Paris, repr. in Mellerio, 1923, p. 135
Coll.: Paris, Wilhelm Uhde; New York, Lillie P. Bliss; New York, Museum of Modern Art
Exhib.: Na, No. 306; Nd, No. 27; Ne, No. 98; Illustrations from Tasso and Ariosto, Smith College Museum of Art, Northampton USA, 1946; Nk, No. 50, col. repr.
Lit.: Sandström, 1955, p. 84, repr.

Heads, Faces, Profiles
(1880) 1900 - 12

379 NAKED MAN 1893/94
Pastel
Coll.: Lyon, Prof. Jullian

380 FIGURE
Pastel
Coll.: Cleveland, Mrs. Peter Lloyd

381 EVE 1910–12
Pastel 65 × 43 cm
Coll.: Paris, Albert Sarraut
Exhib.: Le Nu dans la Peinture Française, Charpentier, Paris, 1953, No. 169; Ld, No. 49, repr.; XIX and XX Century Drawings, Marlborough Gallery, London, 1960, No. 67, repr.
Lit.: Bacou, 1956, No. XIII, repr.

381a NUDE   C. 1911
Pastel and pencil on tinted paper 60 × 68 cm
Coll.: Paris, Armand Parent; Tokyo, Bridge-
stone Gallery
Exhib.: Pq.; European Watercolours and
Drawings, Kamakura, 1953, and Tokyo,
1954; Jubilee Exhibition of the Ishibashi
Museums, Kurume, 1956; Masterpieces of
Drawing from the Whole World, Tokyo,
1957

382   BIRTH OF VENUS   1912 (1910)
Pastel 83 × 64 cm
Coll.: Paris, J. Zoubaloff; Paris, Petit Palais,
1916
Exhib.: Pu, No. 96; Pab, No. LX, repr.
Lit.: La donation J. Zoubaloff aux Musées
de France, Paris, Ed. Morancé, p. 37, repr.;
A. Alexandre, Renaissance de l'Art, 1919,
p. 420, repr.; Claude Escholier: Exposition
Redon, Bulletin des Musées de France,
1934, p. 67, repr.; Claude Roger-Marx
L'Œil, May, 1956, p. 28, repr. in colour;
Bacou, 1956, No. IV, repr. in colour; Klaus
Berger, The Art Quarterly, Summer 1958,
p. 154, repr.

383   THE HUNTER   1915–16
Coloured chalk on coloured paper 56 × 42 cm
Coll.: Otterlo, Kröller-Müller, 1923, No. 788
Exhib.: Pab, No. LXIII, repr.; Hb, No. 153,
repr.
Lit.: Bacou, 1956, No. 107, repr.

384   MADAME REDON DOING HANDWORK   1880,
dated
Pastel 50 × 35 cm
Coll.: Paris, A. Redon
Exhib.: Pg, No. 68; Pq, No. 97; Pr, No. 71;
Ps, No. 145; Ingres à Picasso, Galerie La
Renaissance, Paris, 1928; Pu, No. 63; Pab,
No. 70
Lit.: Bacou, 1956, Nr. VII, repr. in colour

385   THE VEIL   1895
Pastel 47.5 × 32 cm
Coll.: Amsterdam, Eisenlöffel; Otterlo,
Kröller-Müller, 1920, No. 790
Exhib.: Pab, No. 80, repr.; Hb, No. 135,
repr.
Lit.: Bacou, 1956, Nr. VIII, repr. in colour

386   ARI REDON   1897 (1894)
Pastel 45.5 × 31.5 cm
Coll.: Paris, Bignou; Chicago, Kate L.
Brewster; Chicago, Art Institute
Exhib.: Ps, No. 97; Ca, No. 21; Nk, No. 18,
col. repr.

387   ARI REDON AS A CHILD   1897
Pastel 45 × 30 cm
Coll.: Almen, Bonger
Exhib.: Pq, No. 96; Ng, No. 11; Pab,
Nr. XXVII, regr.; Hb, Nr. 137
Lit.: Bacou, 1956, No. 86, repr.

388   MADAME REDON WITH ARI   1898
Pastel 58 × 44 cm
Coll.: Almen, Bonger
Exhib.: Hb, No. 139, repr.
Lit.: Bacou, 1956, No. 88, repr.

389   MADAME REDON (THE YELLOW SCARF)
Before 1900
Pastel 66 × 50 cm
Coll.: Paris, Maurice Fabre; Otterlo, Kröl-
ler-Müller, 1912, No. 784
Exhib.: Pn, No. 45
Lit.: H. Kröller-Müller: Die Entwicklung
der Modernen Malerei, Leipzig, repr.,
p. 121; Bacou, 1956, No. I, repr. in colour

390   THE GRAPHIC ARTIST   Before 1900 (1905)
Pastel 47 × 47 cm
Coll.: Paris, Petit Palais
Exhib.: Pu, No. 83

391   PAULE GOBILLARD   1900, dated
Pastel 52 × 46 cm
Coll.: Paris, Mme. Paul Valéry
Exhib.: Pl, No. 18; Pm, No. 27; Pr, No. 96;
Pu, No. 76; Py, No. 153; Pab, No. XXXVIII,
repr.
Lit.: Bacou, 1956, No. 72, repr.

392   THE ASTRAKHAN COAT. MARIE BOTKIN,
PORTRAIT   1900
Pastel 57 × 48 cm
Coll.: Paris, A. Redon; The Hague, H. P.
Bremmer, heirs
Exhib.: The Collection of H. P. Bremmer,
Gemeentemuseum, Haag, 1950; Hb,
No. 141, repr.; Bi, No. 162; Ld, No. 46,
repr.

393 MADAME ARTHUR FONTAINE NÉE MARIE
DESJARDIN 1901, dated
Pastel 72 × 56 cm
Coll.: Paris, Dr. Abel Desjardin; Paris,
J. A. Fontaine; New York, Metropolitan
Museum, 1961
Exhib.: Pl, No. 17; Pm, No. 26; Pq,
No. 98; Ps, No. 104; Etapes de l'Art
Contemporain, II, Paris, Gazette des
Beaux-Arts, 1934, No. 84; La Femme, Paris,
Galerie Bernheim, 1948, No. 70; Py,
No. 147; Cinquante ans de peinture fran-
çaise dans les collections particulières, Paris,
1952, No. 133; Pab, No. 89, repr.
Lit.: Daulte, Le Dessin français de Manet à
Cézanne, Lausanne (1954), No. 28, repr.
in colour; Bacou, 1956, No. 76; Klaus
Berger, College Art Journal, Fall 1956,
p. 29, repr.

394 HOMAGE TO SCHUMANN Before 1903
Pastel 50 × 40 cm
Coll.: Almen, Bonger
Exhib.: Pl, No. 33; Ng, No. 7; Hb, No. 133,
repr.
Lit.: Bacou, 1956, No. XI, repr. in colour

395 JEANNE CHAIRE 1903, dated
Pastel 79.5 × 69 cm
Coll.: Basel, Museum
Exhib.: Pl, No. 19; Pr, No. 97; Galerie
Beyeler, Basel, 1955, No. 41, repr.

396 HOMAGE TO GAUGUIN 1904, dated
Pastel 62 × 51 cm
Coll.: Paris, A. Leblond
Exhib.: Pr, No. 101; Pu, No. 79; Py,
No. 152

397 MADAME REDON IN PROFILE 1905
Pastel with red chalk 55 × 44.5 cm
Coll.: Paris, Armand Parent; Paris, Louvre,
1951
Exhib.: Po, No. 28; Pu, No. 66; Pab,
No. XLVII, repr.; Il Disegno Francese,
Rome, 1960, No. 189
Lit.: Fegdal, 1929, No. 21, repr.; Bacou,
No. 82, repr.

398 SIMONE FAYET WITH DOLL 1906
Pastel
Coll.: Béziers, Gaston Fayet

399 PORTRAIT OF A YOUNG GIRL 1907, dated
Pastel
Coll.: Paris, G. B.

399a PORTRAIT OF A LADY
Pastel 48 × 36 cm
Coll.: Tokyo, private ownership
Exhib.: Redon, Tokyo, Kyuryudo Gallery,
1954; Masterpieces of European Art, Kyoto,
1957

400 GENEVIÈVE DE GONET AS A CHILD 1907,
dated
Pastel 45 × 30 cm
Coll.: Paris, Marquise de Gonet
Exhib.: Pab, No. XLVI, repr.

401 MADAME SABOURAUD 1907
Pastel
Coll.: Paris, Sabouraud
Exhib.: Po, No. 26; Ps, No. 153; Pu,
No. 80

402 MADAME GUSTAVE FAYET 1907
Pastel
Coll.: Abbaye de Fontfroide, Mme. G.
Fayet
Exhib.: Po, No. 23

403 YSEULT FAYET 1908, dated
Pastel 65 × 80 cm
Coll.: Béziers, Gustave Fayet; Béziers,
Mme. d'Andoque
Exhib.: Po, No 25; Ps, No. 118; Pab,
No. 105
Lit.: Bacou, 1956, No. XII, repr. in colour

404 SIMONE FAYET AT HER FIRST COMMUNION
1908, dated
Pastel 75 × 45 cm
Coll.: Béziers, Gustave Fayet; Paris, Mme.
P. Bacou
Exhib.: Po, No. 24; Ps, No. 117; Pab,
No. LII, repr.
Lit.: J. Doin, Mercure de France, July 1914,
p. 21; Bacou, 1956, No. 94, repr.; Match
No. 398, 24 Nov. 1956, repr. in colour

405 HOMAGE TO LEONARDO DA VINCI C. 1908
(c. 1900)
Pastel 150 × 50 cm

Coll.: Laren, Regnault; Amsterdam, Gemeentje Museum
Exhib.: Hb, No. 142, repr.

406 VIOLETTE HEYMAN 1909–10
Pastel 72 × 92.5 cm
Coll.: Paris, Marcel Kapferer; New York, C. W. Kraushaar Galleries; Cleveland, Hinman B. Hurlbut; Cleveland Museum of Art, 1926
Exhib.: Pq, No. 124; Ps, No. 137; Fifty Years of French Art, Cleveland, 1926; Ng, No. 16, repr.
Lit.: Mellerio, 1923, p. 88, repr. in colour; Cleveland Museum of Art Bulletin, March 1927; Germain Seligman, Oh! Fickle Taste, 1952, p. 51, repr.; Rewald, Post-Impressionism, 1956, p. 179, repr.

407 HEAD OF A YOUNG WOMAN Before 1910
Pastel 52.5 × 37.5 cm
Coll.: Paris, André Mellerio; New York, Grenville L. Winthrop; Cambridge, Fogg Museum, 1943
Exhib.: Pq, No. 125; Ps

408 MADAME REDON ILL 1912
Pastel
Coll.: Paris, A. Redon

409 THE WREATH. MALE HALF-LENGTH PORTRAIT 1910
Pastel with charcoal 45 × 35 cm
Coll.: Paris, A. Redon
Exhib.: Internationale Kunstausstellung, Berlin, 1914, No. 109; Pr, No. 67; Ps, No. 147; Pu, No. 92; Pab, No. 110
Lit.: Mellerio, 1923, p. 13, col. repr.; Bacou, 1956, No. 104, repr.

410 PARSIFAL C. 1900 (Bacou: 1912)
Probably an earlier charcoal drawing worked over
Pastel 64 × 49 cm
Coll.: Paris, A. Redon
Exhib.: Internationale Ausstellung Moderner Kunst, Berlin, 1914; Pr, No. 65; Ps, No. 148; Pab, No. 112

411 CHILD BEFORE THE NORTHERN LIGHTS C. 1893
Pastel 26.7 × 26.8 cm

Coll.: Paris, Stéphane Mallarmé; Paris, Pierre Granville
Exhib.: Pg, No. 61; Hb, No. 138; Bi, No. 154; Ld, No. 41, repr.
Lit.: John Rewald, Post-Impressionism, New York, 1956, p. 173, repr.

412 HALF-LENGTH PORTRAIT OF A WOMAN WITH DOWNCAST EYES C. 1895
Pastel 58 × 46 cm
Coll.: Paris, Petit Palais

413 RED-HAIRED WOMAN C. 1895
Pastel 29 × 32 cm
Coll.: Otterlo, Kröller-Müller, No. 789
Exhib.: Py, No. 150

414 HEAD OF A YOUNG WOMAN C. 1895
Pastel 42 × 29 cm
Coll.: London, private ownership
Exhib.: Ld, No. 42, repr.

415 YOUNG GIRL IN BROWN CAPE C. 1895
Pastel
Coll.: Paris, A. Redon

416 REVERIE 1900 (1890)
Pastel 54 × 36 cm
Coll.: Paris, Jos. Hessel; New York, Alexander M. Bing; New York, John D. Rockefeller jr.; New York, Museum of Modern Art
Exhib.: Ne; Pu, No. 65; Paa; Ni, No. 5
Lit.: Rewald, Post-Impressionism, 1956, p. 179, repr.; J. Canaday, Mainstreams of Modern Art, 1959, p. 389, repr.

417 THE CHILD IN A SPHERE OF LIGHT C. 1900 (1912)
Pastel 63.5 × 48.5 cm
Coll.: Paris, Jos. Hessel; Chicago, Martin A. Ryerson; Chicago, Art Institute
Exhib.: Pq, No. 109; Ne, No. 74
Lit.: Sandström, 1955, No. 130, repr.

418 CHURCH WINDOW (ANGEL WITH DEATH'S HEAD) C. 1900
Pastel with charcoal 87 × 68 cm
Coll.: Paris, Ricardo Vinès, 1904; Paris, private ownership
Exhib.: Pm, No. 29; Pq, No. 135; Ps, No. 154; Pab, No. 74; Pac, No. 84, repr.
Lit.: Claude Roger-Marx, L'Œil, May 1956, p. 27

418a CHURCH WINDOW   Before 1903
Pastel with charcoal 60×40 cm
Coll.: Paris, private ownership; New York,
New Gallery

419   CHURCH WINDOW, FRAGMENT   1903 or
earlier
Pastel with charcoal 52×36 cm
Coll.: Paris, Arthur Fontaine; Paris, Phi-
lippe Fontaine
Exhib.: Pl; Pq, No. 100

420   THE MAID OF ORLEANS   After 1900 (1905)
Pastel 52×27.5 cm
Coll.: Paris, A. Redon
Exhib.: Wa, No. 123; Pq, No. 94; Pr,
No. 68; Ps, No. 146; Pu, No. 82, Pab,
No. XXVIII, repr.
Lit.: G. Jean Aubry: ›Odilon Redon‹, La
Renaissance de l'Art Français, August 1920,
p. 333, repr.

421   THE THOUGHT   C. 1905
Pastel 59×48 cm
Coll.: Liège, Grandorge; Paris, Goldet;
New York, Wildenstein
Exhib.: De l'Impressionisme à nos Jours,
Musée National d'Art Moderne, Paris,
1958, No. 169

422   THE THOUGHT   After 1905
Pastel 71×41 cm
Coll.: Amsterdam, Cleyndert; Amsterdam,
Municipal Museum
Exhib.: Hb, No. 151
Lit.: Wylie Sypher, Rococo to Cubism in
Art and Literature, New York, 1960,
Pl. 19

423   WOMAN'S PROFILE IN A CIRCLE OF LIGHT
C. 1905
Pastel 52×36 cm
Coll.: Chicago, Joseph Winterbotham; Chi-
cago, Art Institute
Exhib.: Nk, No. 35

424   FACE IN A POINTED ARCH   C. 1905
Pastel
Coll.: Paris, Mme. Albert Marquet

425   FACE IN A POINTED ARCH   C. 1905
Pastel
Coll.: Paris, Mme. Henri Simon

426   DAY AND NIGHT (LEFT PROFILE OF A GIRL)
C. 1908
Pastel 47×61.3 cm
Coll.: Moscow, Pushkin Museum

Poetry of the Sea   1900 - 1910

427   HOLY WOMEN   Before 1900
Pastel 56×65 cm
Coll.: Paris, Armand Parent; New York,
Knoedler
Exhib.: Pq, No. 130; La Peinture Fran-
çaise, Galerie Wisselingh, Amsterdam,
1931, No. 43; Expressionism and Related
Movements, Cleveland, 1939, Nr. 59;
French Painting from David to Cézanne,
West Palm Beach, 1953, Nr. 12
Lit.: G. Jean Aubry, La Renaissance de
l'Art Français, August 1920, p. 133, repr.;
William M. Milliken, Art News, 11. Febr.
1931, p. 8

428   TWO HOLY WOMEN IN THE BARK   Before 1900
Pastel 61×51 cm
Coll.: Paris, Arthur Fontaine, before 1903;
Paris, H. Gouin, 1932; London, Reid und
Lefèvre
Exhib.: Pl, No. 30; Pm, No. 30; Pq,
No. 102; Ps, No. 119; Pab, No. 83; Gallery
Lefèvre, London, 1957
Lit.: Robert Rey: ›Odilon Redon‹, Art et
Décoration, August 1920, p. 39, repr.

429   HOLY WOMAN IN THE BARK   After 1900
Pastel 52×46 cm
Coll.: Paris, Ch. Waltner; Amsterdam,
Cleyndert
Exhib.: Pl, No. 37; Pn, No. 27; Hb,
No. 149

430   HOLY WOMAN IN THE BARK (WITH SAIL,
IN PLUNGING VIEW)   1900–03 (c. 1897)
Pastel 61.5×48 cm
Coll.: Almen, Bonger
Exhib.: Pl, No. 28; Ng, No. 2, repr.; Pab,
No. 82; Hb, No. 136a
Lit.: Bacou, 1956, No. 51 repr.

431 SAILING BOATS AT ROYAN   After 1903
Pastel 45×65 cm
Coll.: Paris, Ary Leblond
Exhib.: Pr, No. 102; Ps, No. 138; Pu,
No. 73
Lit.: Bacou, 1956, No. 70, repr.

432 CARRIED AWAY FROM THE SHORE: BOAT WITH
YELLOW SAIL   1906
Pastel 51×66.5 cm
Coll.: Paris, M. Kapferer; Zürich, E. Bührle
Exhib.: Pn, No. 23; Po, No. 33; Pq,
No. 122; Ps, No. 134; Pu, No. 91; Lb,
No. 34; Ng, No. 13, repr.; Französische
Malerei von Delacroix bis Picasso, Stadt-
halle, Wolfsburg, 1961, No. 126
Lit.: Germain Seligman, Oh! Fickle Taste,
1952, p. 54, repr.

433 SAILING BOATS AT VENICE   1908
Pastel
Coll.: Paris, Galerie Druet
Exhib.: Po, No. 35

434 FLOWERS IN SURREALIST LANDSCAPE
C. 1904
Pastel 57×39 cm
Coll.: Paris, M. Kapferer; Basel, Beyeler;
Paris, Higgons
Exhib.: Pq, No. 121; Pr, No. 77; Pac,
No. 81

435 ON THE SEABED. SHELLS WITH FANTASTIC
FLOWERS   1904
Pastel 61×51 cm
Coll.: Paris, Arthur Fontaine, 1904; Paris,
Philippe Fontaine
Exhib.: Pm, No. 38; Pq, No. 103; Pr,
No. 98; Ps, No. 120; Py, No. 148; Cin-
quante ans de peinture française dans les
collections parisiennes, Paris, 1952, No. 134;
Pab, No. XL, repr.
Lit.: Bacou, 1956, No. 105, repr.

436 VISION UNDER SEA   1904
Pastel
Coll.: Paris, G. B.

437 UNDERSEA LANDSCAPE   C. 1905
Pastel
Coll.: Paris, Jos. Hessel; Paris, Higgons
Exhib.: Pu, No. 72; Pac, No. 83

438 SEAHORSE IN AN UNDERSEA LANDSCAPE
Before 1909
Pastel 49×49 cm
Coll.: Paris, M. Kapferer; Paris, Higgons;
New York, New Gallery
Exhib.: Pac, No. 82; Nk, No. 16

439 MEMORY OF THE RAVENNA MOSAICS
After 1908 (1910)
Almost abstract decorative work
Pastel 60×47 cm
Coll.: Paris, Marcel Kapferer
Exhib.: Pu, No. 88; Pw, No. 17; Py,
No. 149; Pab, No. 109

440 PLAY OF COLOURS. ALMOST ABSTRACT
UNDERSEA LANDSCAPE   Before 1910
Pastel
Coll.: private ownership
Lit.: Bacou, 1956, No. 95, repr.

441 THE SHELL   1912
Pastel 48×56 cm
Coll.: Paris, A. Redon
Exhib.: Pq, No. 95; Pr, No. 72; Ps, No. 149;
Pu, No. 97; Pz, No. 18; Pab, No. LXI, repr.
Lit.: Claude Roger-Marx, ›Odilon Redon‹,
L'Œil, May 1956, repr. in colour; Bacou,
1956, No. VI, repr. in colour

Flower-Pieces
I   Early Works   before 1900

442 SHADOWED DREAM   1895–1900
Pastel 47×60.5 cm
Coll.: New York, Sam Adolph Lewisohn;
New York, Sidney Simon
Exhib.: Nd, No. 28; Ca, No. 37; Nj, No. 2,
repr.; Nk, No. 26
Lit.: Stéphane Bourgeois, The Adolph Lewi-
sohn Collection of Modern French Paint-
ings and Sculptures, New York, 1928,
p. 145, repr.

443 RADIANT FLOWERS   Before 1900
Pastel
Coll.: Nice, Henri Matisse
Exhib.: Pj, No. 2

Flower-Pieces
II Objective Portrayal of Space
1900 - 04/05

444 GERANIUMS IN A POT   C. 1900
Pastel 58 × 46 cm
Coll.: The Hague, Gemeentje Museum
Exhib.: Hb, No. 145; Ld, No. 45, repr.

445 FLOWERS   C. 1900
Pastel
Coll.: Chicago, Mrs. Robert R. McCormick
Exhib.: Ca, No. 39

446 GREEN VASE WITH PEDESTAL ON BLUE
GROUND (VASE 34)   The upper part of the
bouquet is missing   C. 1900
Pastel 33 × 46 cm
Coll.: Almen, Bonger, 1905
Exhib.: Ng, No. 1; Pab, No. 97; Hb, No. 146
repr.

447 ANEMONES AND TULIPS IN DARK VASE
(VASE 28)   C. 1902/03
Pastel 54 × 47.5 cm
Coll.: Paris, Bernheim-Jeune, 1907;
Brooklyn, Museum of Art, 1942

448 GERANIUMS, CORNFLOWERS AND MIMOSA IN
BLACK POT   1903–04
Pastel 57 × 47 cm
Coll.: Paris, Dr. Abel Dujardin; Paris,
Arthur Fontaine, 1904; Paris, Jean Arthur
Fontaine
Exhib.: Etapes d l'Art Contemporain, II,
Paris, Gazette des Beaux-Arts, 1934, No. 83;
Pab, No. 92

449 POPPIES AND MARGUERITES IN SMALL BLUE
VASE WITH HANDLE   1903–05
Pastel 56 × 45.5 cm
Coll.: Paris, A. Redon
Exhib.: Pab, No. 93

450 ROSES, PEONIES AND CORNFLOWERS IN SMALL
GREEN VASE   1903–05
Pastel 56 × 45.5 cm
Coll.: Paris, A. Redon
Exhib.: Pab, No. 94

451 GERANIUMS AND CORNFLOWERS IN BROWN
JUG   Before 1905
Pastel 62 × 49 cm
Coll.: Almen, Bonger, 1905
Exhib.: Ng, No. 5; Pab, No. 95; Hb, No. 143

452 SUNFLOWERS, GERANIUMS, AND CORNFLO-
WERS IN BROWN VASE   Before 1905
Pastel 61 × 48.5 cm
Coll.: Almen, Bonger, 1905
Exhib.: Ng, No. 4; Pab, No. 96; Hb, No. 144

453 BUNCH OF FLOWERS IN ROTUND VASE WITH
FLOWER PATTERN (VASE 29)   C. 1905
Pastel 48.5 × 65 cm
Coll.: Paris, Dr. Sabouraud; Paris,
C. de Hauke; Emery Reves
Exhib.: Ca, No. 23

454 PATTERNED VASE WITH ANEMONES (VASE 9)
C. 1905
Pastel 80,4 × 64.2 cm
Coll.: Paris, Jacques Seligmann; New York,
George P. Post; New York, Metropolitan
Museum, 1956

455 BLACK VASE WITH ANEMONES IN DECORATIVE
FRAME (VASE 31)   C. 1905
Pastel 66 × 58.5 cm
Coll.: Paris, Georges Benard; New York,
Germain Seligman
Lit.: Roger-Marx, 1925, p. 49, repr.

456 BLACK VASE WITH MARGUERITES (VASE 28)
C. 1905
Pastel 34 × 26.5 cm
Coll.: New York, John D. Rockefeller;
Princeton, Lambert, 1944

457 FLOWERS IN BLUE VASE   C. 1905
Pastel
Coll.: New York, C. de Hauke; Chicago,
Martin Ryerson; Palm Beach, Florida, Mrs.
Hugh Kirkland
Exhib.: Bd, No. 49; Pr, No. 84; Nd, No. 37;
Ca, No. 27
Lit.: Parnassus Magazine, 1931, p. 17

458 BLUE VASE WITH FLOWERS   C. 1905
Pastel
Coll.: Munich, Bienert

459   BOUQUET ON BLACK GROUND. IMAGINARY
FLOWERS (VASE 24)   1905
Pastel 38.5×32 cm
Coll.: Paris, Dr. P. E. Weill; Paris, private
ownership
Exhib.: Salon d'Automne, Paris, 1905, No.
13073; Pn, No. 40; Ps, No. 158; Pu, No. 71;
Pab, Nr. 98
Lit.: R. Rey: Art et Décoration, August
1920, p. 38, repr.; Bacou, 1956, Nr. III,
repr. in Colour

460   LARGE BUNCH OF WILD FLOWERS. LILIES,
NASTURTIUMS, GERANIUMS IN BLACK POT
1905–06
Pastel 36×27 cm
Coll.: Paris, M. Kapferer, 1906
Exhib.: Na, No. 305; Pq, No. 123; Pu, No.
47, as painting; Pab, No. 101
Lit.: Jacques Rivière-Alain Fournier, Cor-
respondance, Paris, 1926, II, p. 65–66

461   BUNCH OF WILD FLOWERS IN BLUE VASE
1905–08
Pastel 63.5×49.5 cm
Coll.: New York, Carstairs; New York,
private ownership

462   LARGE BUNCH OF WILD FLOWERS (VASE 37)
1905–08
Pastel 60.5×47.5 cm
Coll.: Almen, Bonger
Exhib.: Ng, No. 9, repr.

463   LARGE BUNCH OF WILD FLOWERS   1905–08
Pastel 63×52 cm
Coll.: Utrecht, Warren
Exhib.: Hb, No. 147

464   LARGE BUNCH OF WILD FLOWERS (VASE 9)
1905–08
Pastel 70×53.5 cm
Coll.: England, private ownership
Exhib.: Ld, No. 48, repr.

465   LARGE BUNCH OF WILD FLOWERS   1905–08
Pastel
Coll.: Paris, Mme. Paul Valéry

466   LARGE BUNCH OF WILD FLOWERS   1905–08
Pastel
Coll.: Béziers, d'Andoque

467   LARGE BUNCH OF WILD FLOWERS IN BLUE
TWO-HANDLED VASE (VASE 38)   1905–08
Pastel 82.5×63.5 cm
Coll.: Paris, Ambroise Vollard; Paris,
Richard Sussman; New York, Durlacher
Brothers; New York, Joseph Verner Reed
Exhib.: Pictures by Yale Alumni, Yale Uni-
versity Art Gallery, New Haven, 1956,
No. 227, repr.

468   VASE WITH JAPANESE WARRIOR, TWO OTHER
VASES IN THE BACKGROUND (VASE 22)
1905–08 (1910)
Pastel 91×72 cm
Coll.: Paris, F. Javal
Exhib.: Po, No. 40; Ps, Nr. 43; La Nature
Morte, Orangerie, Paris, 1952, No. 99;
Pab, No. LVI, repr.
Lit.: Sterling, Catalogue: La Nature Morte,
Paris, 1952, p. 123–4; Bacou, 1956, No. 91,
repr.

469   FLOWER FANTASY   1906–08
Pastel 43×48 cm
Coll.: Paris, private ownership; Scotland,
private ownership; New York, Charles
E. Slatkin; Rye, N. Y., William Doniger
Exhib.: Marlborough Gallery, London

470   FLOWERS AND BUTTERFLIES   1908–09
(1913)
Pastel 28×24 cm
Coll.: New York, New Gallery
Exhib.: Ni, No. 13, repr.

471   BLACK VASE WITH ANEMONES (VASE 5)
C. 1909–10
Pastel 87.9×68.5 cm
Coll.: Paris, Madame Robert André; Lon-
don, private ownership; Emery Reves
Exhib.: Bi, No. 211; Ld, No. 50, repr.

472   GREEN VASE WITH RED FLOWERS (VASE 27)
Before 1910
Pastel 47.5×40 cm
Coll.: Paris, Marcel Kapferer; Chicago,
Leigh B. Block; Great Neck, N. Y., Paul
M. Hirschland

Exhib.: Pq, No. 118; Pr, No. 92; Pu, No. 94; Ni, No. 9, repr.

473 ANEMONES IN TWO-HANDLED VASE (VASE 15)
Before 1910
Pastel
Coll.: New York, Charles E. Slatkin

Flower-Pieces
IV Crystalline Synthesis 1908 - 16

474 BOUQUET WITH LILIES (VASE 9) C. 1908
Pastel 63 × 48 cm
Coll.: Béziers, Gustave Fayet; Béziers, A. d'Andoque
Lit.: Bacou, 1956, No. 81, repr.

475 THREE FLOWER VASES C. 1908–10
Pastel
Coll.: Paris, Armand Parent; Paris, César de Hauke; London, Soho Gallery
Lit.: Fegdal, 1929, No. 20, repr.

476 TWO-HANDLED BROWN JUG WITH GERANIUMS (VASE 35) C. 1909
Pastel
Coll.: New York, César de Hauke
Exhib.: Pr, No. 82; Nd, No. 33; Ca, No. 26
Lit.: Claude Roger-Marx, 1925, p. 59, repr.

477 BLACK VASE WITH FLOWERS C. 1909
Pastel 40 × 32 cm
Coll.: Paris, Madame Olivier Sainsère; New York, Wildenstein

478 ANEMONES IN A BLUE VASE (VASE 23)
1909–10 (Bacou: 1912)
Pastel 62 × 62 cm
Coll.: Paris, J. Zoubaloff; Paris, Petit Palais, 1916
Exhib.: Pu, No. 95; Pab, No. LIX, repr.
Lit.: Mellerio, 1923, p. 32, repr. in colour; Claude Roger-Marx, L'Œil, May 1956, p. 24, repr.; Klaus Berger, College Art Journal, Fall 1956, p. 28, repr.

479 POPPY IN A GREEN VASE ON A RED GROUND (VASE 16) 1909–10
Pastel 80 × 60 cm
Coll.: Winterthur, Richard Bühler; Paris, J. Laroche

Exhib.: Chefs d'œuvre de l'art français, Paris, 1937, No. 391; Pab, No. 103
Lit.: Mellerio, 1923, p. 73, repr.

480 BOUQUET ON BLACK GROUND. ORANGE COLOURED-FLOWERS Before 1910
Pastel
Coll.: Princess Faucigny-Lucinge
Exhib.: Vente Galerie Charpentier, Paris, 3. December 1952, No. 51, repr.

481 PLUM BRANCH C. 1910
Pastel
Coll.: Paris, E. Bignou
Lit.: Fegdal, 1929, No. 48, repr.

482 LARGE BOUQUET IN WHITE FIGURED VASE ON BLACK GROUND (VASE 13) 1910
Pastel 52 × 45 cm
Coll.: Paris, Dr. Desjardin; Paris, Arthur Fontaine; Paris, Philippe Fontaine; New York, Wildenstein
Exhib.: Ps, Nr. 105; Pab, No. 99

483 FLOWERS IN A JUG (VASE 33) C. 1910
Pastel
Coll.: New York, Kraushaar; Cambridge, USA, Prof. Charles Kuhn

484 FLOWER STILL-LIFE WITH POPPY IN BLUE VASE
C. or after 1910
Pastel 64.1 × 49.8 cm
Coll.: Cincinnati, Mary Hanna; Cincinnati Art Museum, 1956
Exhib.: Cincinnati Print and Drawing Circle, 1933

485 EXOTIC FLOWERS
Pastel 62.5 × 49.5 cm
Coll.: Amsterdam, E. J. van Wisselingh; Ottawa, National Gallery of Canada, 1951

486 THE BIG 'GREEN VASE' (VASE 10) 1910–12
Pastel 54 × 62.5 cm
Coll.: Boston, Museum of Fine Arts
Exhib.: Nj, No. 22, repr.

487 BIG BUNCH OF WILD FLOWERS (VASE 9)
1912 (1905–10)
Pastel 82 × 61 cm
Coll.: Bern, Prof. Hans R. Hahnloser
Exhib.: Bi, Nr. 201

Lit.: Hans R. Hahnloser: Werke aus der Sammlung Hahnloser, Du, November 1956, p. 24, col. repr.

488 RED FLOWER   C. 1912
Pastel 64×48 cm
Coll.: Paris, Jacques Morland; Paris, private ownership
Exhib.: Ps, No. 141; Pab, No. 117

489 ORCHIDS   C. 1912
Pastel
Coll.: Previously Paris, E. Bignou
Exhib.: Ps, No. 99
Lit.: Fegdal, 1929, No. 51, repr.

490 YELLOW FLOWERS   1912
Pastel 65×49.5 cm
Coll.: New York, Museum of Modern Art
Exhib.: Ni, No. 12, repr.; Nk, No. 62

491 WILD FLOWERS IN VASE WITH LONG NECK
(VASE 11)   After 1912
Pastel 57×35 cm
Coll.: Paris, Ary Leblond; Paris, Louvre, 1954
Exhib.: Pu, No. 100; Pab, No. LVII, repr.
Lit.: Bacou, 1956, No. 90, repr.

492 WHITE LILIES IN BLACK-STRIPED VASE
(VASE 12)   1912–14 (1910)
Pastel 72×46 cm
Coll.: Buffalo, Albright Art Gallery
Exhib.: Nj, No. 24, repr.
Lit.: J. Canaday, Mainstreams of Modern Art, 1959, p. 389, repr.

493 LARGE BUNCH OF FLOWERS IN DARK VASE
(VASE 30)   1912–14
Pastel 88×70 cm
Coll.: Zürich, Werner Herold
Exhib.: Peinture Française en Suisse, Galerie des Beaux-Arts, Paris, 1938, No. 86, repr.

494 MIMOSA, ANEMONES AND LEAVES IN A BLUE
VASE (VASE 5)   After 1912
Pastel 75×59 cm
Coll.: Paris, J. Zoubaloff; Paris, Petit Palais, 1916
Exhib.: Pu, No. 99; Pab, No. LVIII, repr.
Lit.: Klaus Berger, The Art Quarterly, Summer 1958, p. 159, repr.

495 ANEMONES (VASE 14)   1914–15
Pastel 73.5×54 cm
Coll.: Switzerland, Maharanee of Baroda; Basel, Beyeler; New York, Alex Lewyt
Exhib.: Natures Mortes françaises, Charpentier, Paris, 1951, No. 15, repr.; Vier Eeuwen stilleven in Frankrijk, Boymans, Rotterdam, 1954, No. 105, repr.; Nj, No. 26, repr.

496 ANEMONES (VASE 30)   1914–15
Pastel
Coll.: New York, Kraushaar; New York, Thomas Cochram
Exhib.: Pq, No. 113; Pr; Ps; Nd, No 26; Ca, No. 23; Ne, No. 101

497 WHITE VASE WITH FLOWERS (VASE 7)   1916
(1908–10)
Pastel 73×54.5 cm
Coll.: New York, W. S. Paley; New York, Museum of Modern Art
Exhib.: Masterpieces of Art, World's Fair, New York, 1940, No. 353, repr.; Nj, No. 19, repr.; Nk, No. 61
Lit.: Alfred H. Barr, Masters of Modern Art, New York, 1954; Klaus Berger, College Art Journal, Fall 1956, p. 26, repr.

498 FLOWER VASE (VASE 32)   1916
Pastel 92×60.5 cm
Coll.: New York, R. Kahn; Cleveland Museum, Leonard C. Hanna Bequest, No. 30
Exhib.: Masterpieces of Art, New York World's Fair, 1940, No. 352, repr.; Ng, No. 15, repr.

Girls with Flowers   1900 - 1910

499 MEDITATION. IMAGINARY FLOWERS WITH
FIGURE OF A WOMAN (VASE 1)   1899
Pastel 46.5×55.5 cm
Coll.: Béziers, A. d'Andoque, 1899
Exhib.: Pab, No. XXXVII, repr.

500 RADIANT FLOWER WITH GIRL'S PROFILE
C. 1900
Pastel 60.5×49.5 cm

Coll.: New York, John Quinn; Beverly Hills, Charles Boyer
Exhib.: Carroll Galleries, New York, 1915, No. 14; Nc, No. 23 repr.

501 FERTILITY. AUSTERE WOMAN'S PROFILE IN CENTRE, SURROUNDED BY FLOWERS C. 1903
Pastel 29 × 21 cm
Coll.: Los Angeles, Harold English; Los Angeles County Museum, 1958

502 GIRL WITH COLUMN OF FLOWERS 1903
Pastel 58.5 × 48 cm
Coll.: Brooklyn, Dr. Theodore Leshner
Exhib.: Nk, No. 30

503 YOUNG GIRL IN THE MOUNTAINS C. 1905
Pastel 78 × 58.5 cm
Coll.: Paris, G. Benard; Germany, private ownership; New York, Wildenstein
Exhib.: Société des Amis du Luxembourg, Paris; Hôtel de la Curiosité, Paris, 1924, Nr. 64

504 FACE IN POINTED ARCH WITH FLOWERS IN THE BACKGROUND C. 1905
Pastel 78 × 66 cm
Coll.: Paris, O. Sainsère; Paris, Richet
Exhib.: Pq, No. 134; Ps, No. 152; Pab, No. 108
Lit.: Robert Rey: ›Odilon Redon‹, Art et Décoration, August 1920, p. 37, repr.

505 GIRL WITH CHRYSANTHEMUMS C. or after 1905
Pastel 66 × 52 cm
Coll.: Paris, Durand-Ruel; Haarlem, J. H. de Bois; Berlin-Babelsberg, Siegbert Stern; New York, Werner E. Josten

505a GIRL WITH FLOWERS IN HER HAIR
Pastel 32 × 23.6 cm
Coll.: Musashino-shi, R. Hirayama; Nishinomiya-shi, private ownership
Exhib.: European Masterpieces, Osaka, Gallery Fujikawa, 1953; Masterpieces from the Whole World, Osaka, 1955

506 BERNADETTE UNDER AN ARCH 1905–06
Pastel 65 × 53 cm
(Lost in World War II)
Coll.: Formerly Paris, Seligmann
Exhib.: Ne, No. 69

507 BERNADETTE AS AN APPARITION, WITH FLOWERS C. 1908
Pastel 69 × 54.5 cm
(Lost in Paris during World War II)
Coll.: New York, Seligmann

508 OPHELIA, THE BRIDE 1906–08
Pastel with Oil and Gouache 59.5 × 51 cm
Coll.: Domecy, Baroness Domecy; Geneva, Imbert; New York, Charles E. Slatkin

509 OPHELIA, SURROUNDED BY FLOWERS 1908 or earlier (1912)
Pastel 64 × 91 cm
Coll.: Paris, Armand Parent; Paris, Madame Mottart; Paris, César de Hauke; New York, Albert D. Lasker, 1949
Exhib.: Pq, No. 34 (als Aquarell); Pq, No. 132 (als Orpheus); Pr, No. 89; Ps, No. 144; French Art, London, 1932, No. 973, (repr. pl. CCIII); Pu, No. 81; Pw, No. 20; Pab, Nr. LV, repr.; Nk, No. 48, repr.
Lit.: Fegdal, 1929, pl. XVIII, repr.; Sandström, 1955, No. 133, repr.; Match, Paris, 24 Nov. 1956, No. 398, repr. in colour

510 GIRL'S PROFILE WITH RED VASE (VASE 6) 1908 (1913)
Pastel 73 × 65.5 cm
Coll.: Los Angeles, George Gard de Sylva; Los Angeles County Museum
Exhib.: Nj, No. 14, repr.
Lit.: Art News, N. Y., Sept. 1946, p. 30, repr. in colour

511 GIRL IN PROFILE WITH FLOWERS 1908–10
Pastel 64 × 50 cm
Coll.: Amsterdam, Cleyndert, (Loan to the Gemeentje Museum)
Exhib.: Hb, No. 148

512 FERTILITY. WOMAN'S PROFILE WITH FLOWERS Before 1909
Pastel 64 × 49,5 cm
Coll.: Paris, Hessel; New York, de Hauke; Chicago, Martin A. Ryerson; Chicago, Art Institute; New York, Francis Steegmuller
Exhib.: Pq, No. 116; Nd, No. 35; Ca, No. 22; Ne, No. 105
Lit.: Klaus Berger, College Art Journal, Fall 1956, p. 30, repr.

513 THE NYMPH ON THE CLOUDS   C. 1909
Pastel 51 × 37 cm
Coll.: Stockholm, Svensk-Franska
Konstgalleriet
Exhib.: Pq, No. 137; Galerie Beyeler, Basel,
1958, No. 4a

514 BOUQUET OF FLOWERS WITH WOMAN'S
PROFILE (Vase 35)   Before 1910
Pastel 53 × 45.5 cm
Coll.: Paris, Dr. J. Gosset
Exhib.: Bi, No. 210

515 WOMAN'S PROFILE WITH FLOWERS
Before 1910
Pastel 59.5 × 45 cm
Coll.: New York, Guggenheim Museum

516 WOMAN AMID FLOWERS   1909–10
Pastel 66 × 56 cm
Coll.: Paris, Joseph Hessel; Chicago, Martin
A. Ryerson; New York, Gomez de Vaez
(Sale Parke Bernet, 21. Febr. 1952); Geneva
Madame Marthe Nathan; New York,
Wildenstein; New York, Mrs, H. Harris
Jones
Exhib.: Pq, No. 112; Nd, No. 35; Ca, No.
22; Ne, No. 105; Bi, No. 195; Nk, No. 31,
repr.

Watercolours   1900 – 1912

517 MYSTERIOUS HEAD   1900
Watercolour 18.4 × 16.2 cm
Coll.: New York, John Rewald
Exhib.: Wb, No. 30; Ni, No. 30; Los
Angeles, 1959, No. 110
Lit.: Gazette des Beaux-Arts, November
1956, p. 87, repr.; Rewald, Post-Impressio-
nism, 1955, p. 173, repr.; John Rewald
Collection Sale, Sotheby's, London, 7. July
1960, No. 96, repr.

518 FIVE DUTCH WOMEN IN PROFILE
C. 1900 (1915)
Watercolour 18 × 25.5 cm
Coll.: Paris, Armand Parent; Chicago, John
A. Holabird
Exhib.: Pp, No. 41; Ps, No. 161; Nd, No. 45
Ca, No. 35; Ne, No. 83
Lit.: Mellerio, 1923, p. 107, col. repr.

519 DUTCH WOMAN IN PROFILE   C. 1900
Watercolour 18 × 17 cm
Coll.: Providence, USA., Charles Russell jr.;
New York, Wildenstein
Exhib.: Drawing through four Centuries,
Wildenstein, New York, 1949, No. 77

520 THE BARK   After 1900
Watercolour 20 × 17.5 cm
Coll.: Paris, A. Redon
Exhib.: Pp, No. 39; Ps, No. 163; Pu, No.
117; Pab, No. 196

521 SHIP OF THE DEAD (TWO-MASTER) After 1900
Watercolour 15.7 × 26.2 cm
Coll.: Basel, Kunstmuseum
Exhib.: Bi, No. 215; Ld, No. 40, repr.

522 TWO BUTTERFLIES   After 1900 (1890?)
Watercolour 21.5 × 19 cm
Coll.: London, private ownership
Exhib.: Ni, No. 28; Ld, No. 38, repr.

523 NUDE WITH RED CLOAK   C. 1904
Watercolour 23.5 × 15.5 cm
Coll.: Germany, private ownership; New
York, Wildenstein; New York, Mrs. Sam
Salz
Exhib.: Auction, Kunstkabinett, Stuttgart,
7. Nov. 1951, No. 1186; Nk, No. 66

524 NUDE AND BEGONIA
Watercolour 17.6 × 25.3 cm
Coll.: Atelier O. Redon; Winterthur, Hedy
Hahnloser-Bühler; Bern, Professor Hans R.
Hahnloser

525 GIRL WITH BENT HEAD (After Decamps)
C. 1904
Watercolour 20 × 16.5 cm
Coll.: Paris, A. Redon
Exhib.: Ps, No. 164; Pu, No. 116; Pab, No.
197; Nk, No. 73

526   ANEMONES WITH MASK   Before 1905
Aquarelle 24.5 × 17.5 cm
Coll.: Paris, A. Parent; Paris, César de Hauke
Exhib.: Ps, No. 161; Nd, No. 38; Ca, No. 29;
Pu, No. 119; Ld, No. 37, repr.
Lit.: Mellerio, 1923, p. 162, col. repr.

527   THREE LILIES IN A VASE   After 1905
Watercolour
Coll.: Gates Mills, Ohio, Mrs. William
Powell Jones

528   INSPIRATION
Watercolour
Coll.: Paris, Mme. Ary Leblond

529   MAGICAL CONJURATION
Watercolour
Coll.: Paris, A. Parent
Exhib.: Ps, No. 161

530   SEVEN BUTTERFLIES   1908–10
Watercolour
Coll.: New York, James W. Barney
Exhib.: Na, No. 277; Ps, Nd, No. 39; Ne,
No. 72
Lit.: Mellerio, 1923, p. 45, col. repr.

531   EIGHT BUTTERFLIES   1908–10
(Rewald: C. 1900)
Watercolour 26 × 19.5 cm
Coll.: New York, Mrs. Cornelius J. Sullivan;
New York, Louis E. Stern
Exhib.: Nineteenth Century French Draw-
ings, San Francisco, 1947, No. 120; Nk,
No. 69
Lit.: J. Rewald, Gazette des Beaux-Arts,
November 1956, No. 16, repr.

532   BUTTERFLIES WITH YELLOW FLOWER
1908–10
Watercolour 23 × 15 cm
Coll.: Paris, Jacques Zoubaloff; Paris, Petit
Palais, 1916
Exhib.: Pu, No. 104; Maîtres Français de la
collection du Petit Palais, Rotterdam, 1952,
No. 107; Pab, No. 200; Hb, No. 219; Bi,
No. 218; Nk, No. 71

533   FLOWERS WITH BUTTERFLIES AND CAT
Before 1910
Watercolour with Indian ink 15 × 23 cm

Coll.: Paris, Jacques Zoubaloff; Paris, Petit
Palais
Exhib:. Pu. No. 106; Maîtres Français de la
collection du Petit Palais, Rotterdam, 1952,
No. 106; Art Français, Tokyo, 1054; Pab,
No. 201; Hb, Nr. 218

534   THE MYSTICAL PERSONALITY OF SAINT
SEBASTIAN   Before 1910
Watercolour 24.5 × 15.5 cm
Coll.: New York, Grenville L. Winthrop;
Cambridge, USA, Fogg Art Museum, 1943
Exhib.: Pp, No. 32

535   THE RED BOUQUET   Before 1910
Gouache 42.8 × 38.5 cm
Coll.: Saarbrücken, Saarland-Museum
Exhib.: Französische Malerei von Delacroix
bis Picasso, Stadthalle, Wolfsburg, 1961,
No. 189, repr.

536   SIX BUTTERFLIES AND SEAHORSE   C. 1910
Aquarelle 15.5 × 23 cm
Coll.: New York, private ownership
Exhib.: Nk, No. 68, repr.

537   SEVEN STUDIES OF BUTTERFLIES   1910
(1905) (1914)
Watercolour 23 × 15 cm
Coll.: Paris, Jacques Zoubaloff; Paris,
Petit Palais
Exhib.: Ps, No. 160; Pu, No. 113; Maîtres
Français de la collection du Petit Palais,
Rotterdam, 1952, No. 118; Natures Mortes
de Géricault à nos Jours, St. Etienne, 1955,
No. 18; Pab, No. 205; Bi, No. 217

538   FACE IN A SHELL   C. 1910
Watercolour 15.5 × 22 cm
Coll.: New York, Louis Macmillan
Exhib.: Nk, No. 65

539   BUTTERFLIES, FLOWERS AND SNAKE
C. 1910
Watercolour 17 × 23.5 cm
Coll.: Paris, Jacques Zoubaloff; Paris, Petit
Palais
Exhib.: Pu, No. 112; Pab, No. 204; Bi, No.
216; Nk, No. 72, repr.

540   RED AND VIOLET FLOWERS   C. 1910
Watercolour 35.5 × 25.4 cm

Coll.: Winterthur, Hedy Hahnloser-Bühler; Bern, Professor H. R. Hahnloser
Exhib.: Hb, No. 224

541   SIX STUDIES OF FLOWERS   C. 1910
Watercolour 17 × 24.5 cm
Coll.: Paris, Jacques Zoubaloff; Paris, Petit Palais
Exhib.: Pu, No. 110; Maîtres Français de la collection du Petit Palais, Rotterdam, Geneva, Basel, La Chaux-de-Fonds, Bern, Zürich, 1952, No. 109; Natures Mortes de Géricault à nos Jours, St Etienne, 1955, No. 17, Pap, No. 202

542   EIGHT STUDIES OF FLOWERS   C. 1910
Watercolour 24.5 × 17 cm
Coll.: Paris, Jacques Zoubaloff; Paris, Petit Palais
Exhib.: Pu, No. 111; Pab, No. 203

543   LADY IN THE BOX   Perhaps c. 1910
Watercolour with oil 43 × 60.5 cm
Coll.: Chicago, Art Club; Chicago, Art Institute, 1952
Exhib.: Bd, No. 50; Pq, No. 15

544   BUST OF A WOMAN WITH OUTSTRETCHED HAND
Perhaps C. 1910
Watercolour 17.1 × 20.3 cm
Coll.: Paris, J. Zoubaloff; Paris, Petit Palais, 1916
Exhib.: Pu, No. 102; Meisterwerke aus Frankreichs Museen, Albertina, Vienna, 1950, No. 246; Exposition d'Art Français au Japon, Tokyo, 1954, No. 68; Bg, No. 774; Bh, No. 342; Bi, No. 219; Nk, No. 70

545   STUDIES WITH HEAD AND FLOWERS
C. 1910–12
Watercolour 27 × 21 cm
Coll.: Paris, Cabinet des Dessins du Musée du Louvre
Exhib.: Nk, No. 63

546   RIDER IN FLIGHT   1912
Watercolour 16.5 × 26.5 cm
Coll.: Paris, Ary Leblond
Exhib.: Hb, No. 204; Bi, No. 213

547   FISHES. IN MEMORY OF A VISIT TO THE AQUARIUM IN ARCACHON   1912
Watercolour 28 × 22 cm

Coll.: Paris, Marius Leblond; New York, John Rewald; New York, Alex M. Lewyt
Exhib.: Pu, No. 115; Pab, No. 199; Ni, No. 33, repr.; Los Angeles, 1959, No. 112; Nk, No. 74, col. repr.
Lit.: John Rewald collection sale, Sotheby's, London, 7 July 1960, No. 98, col. repr.

548   THE OYSTER   1912
Watercolour 23 × 14 cm
Coll.: Northampton, Smith College Museum of Art
Exhib.: Wb, No. 31

549   RABBITS   C. 1912
Watercolour 20 × 26 cm
Coll.: Paris, private ownership
Exhib.: Pr, No. 244; Pu, No. 114; Pab, No. 198; Ld, No. 39, repr.

550   DANTE'S VISION   C. 1914
Watercolour 18 × 25.5 cm
Coll.: Paris, Armand Parent; Chicago, John A. Holabird
Exhib.: Ps; Nd, No. 46; Cb, No. 36; Ne, No. 79
Lit.: Mellerio, 1923, p. 122, col. repr.

Charcoal Drawings 'My Black Pictures'

551   SELF PORTRAIT   C. 1888
Charcoal 34 × 22,5 cm
Coll.: The Hague, J. E. van der Meulen
Exhib.: Hb, No. 23, repr.; Ld, No. 1, repr.; Nk, No. 120, repr.

Early Nature Studies   *1862-80*

552   MOUNTAIN LANDSCAPE VIEWED BY SEATED MAN   1862, dated
Charcoal 29 × 22 cm
Coll.: Paris, Henri Mondor
Exhib.: Pab, No. 4
Lit.: Bacou, 1956, No. 4, repr.

553 LANDSCAPE WITH FOUR POPLARS
Before 1865
Charcoal
Coll.: Almen, Bonger

554 DANTE AND VIRGIL 1865 (Sandström: 1861)
Charcoal 24 × 37 cm
Coll.: Almen, Bonger, 1901
Exhib.: Pab, No. 6; Hb, No. 11; Bi, No. 5;
Ld, No. 2; Nk, No. 78
Lit.: J. Cohen-Gosschalk, Elseviers, 1909,
p. 84, repr.; J. Cohen-Gosschalk, Zeitschrift
für Bildende Kunst, 1910, p. 67, repr.;
Aubry: De Kroniek, 1919, repr.; Sand-
ström, 1955, No. 1, repr.; Bacou, 1956, No.
5, repr.

555 RIDER UNDER A TREE C. 1865
Charcoal 28 × 24 cm
Coll.: Béziers, Gustave Fayet, 1901; Paris,
Paul Bacou
Exhib.: Ps, No. 208; Pab, No. 7
Lit.: Bacou, 1956, No. 8, repr.

556 ADAM AND EVE C. 1865 (1875)
Charcoal 60 × 45 cm
Coll.: Béziers, Gustave Fayet; Paris, Paul
Bacou
Exhib.: Ps, No. 185
Lit.: Bacou, 1956, No. 9, repr.

557 GIRL UNDER A TREE
Charcoal 17 × 22 cm
Coll.: Basel Kunstmuseum
Exhib.: Bi, No. 6

558 OLD TREE 1870
Charcoal
Coll.: Paris, Ambroise Vollard; New York,
Jean Goriany; Chicago, Art Institute

559 TREE 1870
Charcoal
Coll.: Almen, Bonger
Lit.: Sandström, 1955, No. 8, repr.

560 BRUSHWOOD WITH TWO FIGURES BY A POND
1870–75
Charcoal 48 × 36.5 cm
Coll.: Almen, Bonger
Exhib.: Pab, No. 8; Hb, No. 2; Bi, No. 15
Lit.: Sandström, 1955, No. 9, repr.

561 TREE C. 1873
Charcoal 51 × 36 cm
Coll.: Otterlo, Kröller-Müller
Exhib.: Pab, No. XIX, repr.; Bi, No. 14;
Ld, No. 3, repr.
Lit.: R. Miedema, Odilon Redon en Al-
brecht Dürer, Amsterdam, 1928, No. 16, repr.

562 SUNSET 1870 or later
Charcoal 25 × 42.5 cm
Coll.: Paris, Roger-Marx; Chicago, Allan
Frumkin
Exhib.: Ps, No. 223; Nk, No. 80
Lit.: Fegdal, 1929, No. 4, repr.; Claude
Roger-Marx, Fusains, 1950, No. 15, repr.

563 TWO TREES C. 1875
Charcoal
Coll.: Paris, Ambroise Vollard; New York,
Jean Goriany; Chicago, Art Institute

564 THE TREES 1875–76
Charcoal 63 × 49 cm
Coll.: Paris, J. Dubourg
Exhib.: Pw, No. 28 (as 'Sous-bois'); Hb,
No. 3, repr.; Les Sources du XXᵉ Siècle,
Musée National d'Art Moderne, Paris, 1960,
No. 573, (as 'Deux Troncs d'Arbres')

565 TREES UNDER A STORMY SKY Before 1880
Charcoal
Coll.: Bordeaux, Piéchaud
Lit.: Sandström, 1955, No. 11, repr.

566 TREES Before 1880
Charcoal 62.5 × 48.5 cm
Coll.: Paris, Renand
Exhib.: Pac, No. 19
Lit.: Sandström, 1955, No. 10, repr.

Phantasy I 1870 - 80

567 THE BATTLE C. 1870 (see etching M. 5)
Charcoal 64.5 × 102 cm
Coll.: Paris, Jacques Dubourg
Exhib.: Bi, No. 16

568 GIRL OF A SAVAGE TRIBE
Charcoal
Coll.: Paris, A. Redon
Lit.: Mellerio, 1923, p. 130, repr.

569 NUDE IN THE OPEN AIR (DAWN OF CHAOS)
1870 or later
Charcoal
Coll.: Paris, Leblond
Exhib.: Ps, No. 213; Pu, No. 137
Lit.: Mellerio, 1923, p. 86, repr.

570 A MAN FLEES THE LIGHT (FEAR) 1872
Charcoal 38 × 35 cm
Coll.: Béziers, Gustave Fayet, 1901; Béziers,
A. d'Andoque
Exhib.: Pb; Ps, No. 200; Pab, No. 12
Lit.: Bacou, 1956, No. 10, repr.

571 CENTAUR WITH CELLO C. 1875
Charcoal 73 × 60 cm
Coll.: Paris, Ambroise Vollard; Paris,
J. Dubourg
Exhib.: Ps, No. 234; Pw, No. 24; Ng,
No. 31, repr.; Bi, No. 158
Lit.: Claude Roger-Marx, Fusains, 1950,
No. 5, repr.

572 MAN'S HEAD C. 1875
Charcoal 37.5 × 32 cm
Coll.: Otterlo, Kröller-Müller
Exhib.: Ld, No. 5, repr.

573 THE IDOL C. 1875 (Sandström: 1890)
Charcoal 52.5 × 37.5 cm
Coll.: Paris, Ambroise Vollard; New York,
Jean Goriany; Chicago, Art Institute
Exhib.: Nh, No. 15
Lit.: Sandström, 1955, No. 13 (as 'Rocher
humain'), repr.

574 EARTH SPIRIT WITH BLACK SUN C. 1875
Charcoal
Coll.: Paris, J. Dubourg
Exhib.: Pw, No. 36 (as 'Caliban')
Lit.: Sandström, 1955, No. 30, repr.

575 WITCH WITH WITCH'S CAULDRON 1875–80
Charcoal 40 × 37 cm
Coll.: Paris, Ambroise Vollard, 1899; New
York, Jean Goriany; Chicago, Art Institute,
1950
Exhib.: Pg, No. 37; Nh, No. 4; Pab,
No. 20; Hb, No. 7; Nk, No. 92
Lit.: Sandström, 1955, No. 29, repr.

576 EYES IN THE FOREST 1875–80
Charcoal 33.5 × 27.5 cm
Coll.: St. Louis, City Art Museum
Exhib.: Nk, No. 90, repr.

577 HEAD OF A MARTYR 1877
Charcoal 37 × 36 cm
Coll.: The Hague, J. Toorop; Otterlo,
Kröller-Müller
Exhib.: Ha, No. 8; Bd, No. 90; Pab,
No. 17, repr.; Hb, No. 16; Bi, No. 20
Lit.: Bacou, 1956, No. 26, repr.; Klaus
Berger, The Art Quarterly, Summer 1958,
p. 153, repr.

578 FOOL (OR INTUITION) 1877
Charcoal 39 × 33.5 cm
Coll.: Paris, J. Dubourg; Zürich, René
Malamoud
Exhib.: Bi, No. 19, repr.; Ld, No. 6, repr.
Lit.: Klaus Berger, French Master Drawings
of the Nineteenth Century, New York, 1950,
No. 51, repr.; Claude Roger-Marx, Fusains,
1950, No. 2, repr.

579 MEPHISTOPHELES (FOOLISHNESS, MADNESS)
C. 1877 (Sandström: 1885)
Charcoal 35 × 31 cm
Coll.: Paris, Ambroise Vollard; Paris,
Roger-Marx
Exhib.: Pv, repr.; Pab, No. 16, repr.; Hb,
No. 4; Pac, No. 6, repr.
Lit.: Mellerio, 1923, p. 123, repr.; Sand-
ström, 1955, No. 74, repr.; Bacou, 1956,
No. 41, repr.; Claude Roger-Marx, L'Œil,
May 1956, p. 21, repr.

580 THE BOWL 1878 or later
Charcoal 48.5 × 36.5 cm
Coll.: Paris, Ambroise Vollard; New York,
Jean Goriany; Chicago, Art Institute
Exhib.: Pab, No. VIII, repr.; Hb, No. 5

581 THE SPHERE (Described by J. K. Huysmans
in A Rebours, 1884) 1878
Charcoal 41 × 36 cm
Coll.: Paris, Emile Bernard, 1904; Almen,
Bonger
Exhib.: Pb; Pab, No. 19; Hb, No. 6; Ld,
No. 7, repr.
Lit.: J. Cohen-Gosschalk, Elseviers, 1909,
p. 81, repr.; Sandström, 1955, No. 32, repr.

582   MAN AND THE BALL OF THE EARTH   1884
or later
Charcoal 37.5×46.3 cm
Coll.: Paris, Ambroise Vollard; Paris, S.
Higgons
Exhib.: Pac, No. 28, repr.; Ld, No. 8, repr.

Demons   1880-81

583   WINGED DEMON BRINGING A MASK   C. 1878
Charcoal 45×33 cm
Coll.: Paris, J. Dubourg
Exhib.: Bh, No. 374; Bi, No. 22; Ld,
No. 12, repr.
Lit.: Claude Roger-Marx, Fusains, 1950,
No. 6, repr.

584   WINGED HEAD FLYING OVER THE SEA
Before 1879
Charcoal 45.5×37.5 cm
Coll.: Paris, Ambroise Vollard, 1899; New
York, Jean Goriany; Chicago, Art Institute,
1950
Exhib.: Modern Drawings, Museum of
Modern Art, New York, 1944, p. 32, repr.;
Nh, No. 5, repr.; Pab, No. 22; Hb, No. 8,
repr.; Nk, No. 88, repr.
Lit.: Hugh Edwards: Redon, Flaubert Vol-
lard, Bulletin, Art Institute, Chicago, 1942,
p. 4–6; Paul J. Sachs: Modern Prints and
Drawings, New York, 1954, Pl. 47, repr.;
Sandström, 1955, No. 134, repr.

584a WINGED HEAD ON THE CAPITAL OF A COLUMN
C. 1880
Charcoal 40.5×36 cm
Coll.: Tokyo, K. Nakagawa
Exhib.: Redon, Tokyo, Kyuryudo Gallery,
1954

585   WINGED HEAD   C. 1880
Charcoal 45×36 cm
Coll.: Paris, Jacques Dubourg
Exhib.: Hb, No. 14; Bi, No. 23, repr.

586   SKELETON IN THE FOREST   Before 1880
Charcoal 46.5×31 cm
Coll.: New York, John Rewald; Winnetka,
Illinois, James W. Alsdorf

Exhib.: Nk, No. 109
Lit.: Rewald, Post-Impressionism, 1956,
p. 177, repr.

587   FAUST AND MEPHISTOPHELES   1880
Charcoal 39×32 cm
Coll.: Paris, Joris-Karl Huysmans; Almen,
Bonger, 1894
Exhib.: Pb; Pg, No. 23; Ha, No. 11; Ng,
No. 29; Pab, No. 23; Hb, No. 9; Bi, No. 26;
Ld, No. 9, repr.
Lit.: J. Cohen-Gosschalk, Zeitschrift für
Bildende Kunst, 1910, No. 8, repr.; Sand-
ström, 1955, No. 73, repr.; Bacou, 1956
No. 40, repr.

588   THE THINKER AT THE WINDOW   C. 1880
Charcoal 37.5×50.5 cm
Coll.: Almen, Bonger
Exhib.: Ps, No. 180; Hb, No. 10

589   THE PRISONER BEHIND WINDOW BARS   1880
Charcoal 53.3×37.2 cm
Coll.: New York, Museum of Modern Art
Exhib.: Pab, No. 25, repr.
Lit.: Bacou, 1956, No. 33, repr.

590   THE PRISONER ENCIRCLED BY FLYING DEMONS
1881
Charcoal 38.8×36 cm
Coll.: Paris, Ambroise Vollard, 1897; Paris,
Roger-Marx
Exhib.: Pz, No. 23; Cent cinquante ans de
dessin française, Galerie Bernheim, Paris,
1952, No. 135; Pab, No. 26; Pac, No. 8,
repr.
Lit.: Claude Roger-Marx, Fusains, 1950,
No. 12, repr.; Bacou, 1956, No. 18, repr.

591   THE PRISONER BEHIND THE DORMER WINDOW
Before 1882 (1875–85)
Charcoal 36×51 cm
Coll.: Almen, Bonger; New York, E. Powis
Jones
Exhib.: Pab, No. 24; Bi, No. 25; Nk,
No. 95
Lit.: D. A. de Graaf, Apollo, 1940, p. 22,
repr.; Bacou, 1956, No. 32, repr.

592   DON QUIXOTE   C. 1880
Black conté crayon 30×21.5 cm
Coll.: Cambridge, USA, Fogg Art Museum,
Paul J. Sachs collection, 1945

Exhib.: Century Club of New York City, 1947
Lit.: Jean Seznec, Gazette des Beaux-Arts, Sept. 1948, p. 187, repr.; Paul J. Sachs, Modern Prints and Drawings, 1954, No. 49, repr.

593   EARTH SPIRIT   C. 1880
Charcoal 45×36 cm
Coll.: Paris, Ambroise Vollard; Paris, private ownership
Exhib.: Pac, No. 12, repr.

594   DEVIL LOOKING AT A SOUL   C. 1880
Charcoal 46.5×37 cm
Coll.: Paris, Ambroise Vollard; New York, Jean Goriany; Chicago, Art Institute
Exhib.: Nh, No. 5

595   HEAD OF A DECAPITATED MAN ON THE SCALES
C. 1880
Charcoal, vertical format
Coll.: Brussels, E. Picard
Exhib.: Bd, No. 105 (as 'Orpheus')
Lit.: Claude Roger-Marx, Fusains, 1950, No. 8, repr.

596   FIGURE WITH DEMONS (THREE MASKS)   1881
Charcoal 36×30 cm
Coll.: Béziers, Gustave Fayet, 1904; Béziers, A. d'Andoque
Exhib.: Pb; Ps, No. 203; Pab, No. 28; Bh, No. 343
Lit.: Bacou, 1956, No. 17, repr.

597   ORPHEUS' HEAD DRIFTING ON THE WATER
1881
Charcoal 41×31 cm
Coll.: Paris, E. Schuffenecker, 1891; Otterlo, Kröller-Müller
Exhib.: IVe Exposition des Peintres-Graveurs, Paris, 1892, No. 282; Pg, No. 16; Pq, No. 173; Pab, No. XI, repr.; Hb, No. 11; Bi, No. 24
Lit.: R. Miedema: Odilon Redon en Albrecht Dürer, Amsterdam, 1928, No. 26, repr.; Bacou, 1956, No. 35, repr.

598   WEEPING SPIDER   1881
Charcoal 48×36.5 cm
Coll.: Paris, Maurice Fabre; Béziers, Gustave Fayet; Paris, Bourgeat; Holland, J. F. G. Boom

Exhib.: Pg, No. 13; Ps, No. 182; Hb, No. 12, repr.; Nk, No. 97, repr.
Lit.: Claude Roger-Marx, 1925, p. 22, repr.

599   SMILING SPIDER (Described by Huysmans)
1881
Charcoal 49.5×39 cm
Coll.: Paris, André Mellerio, 1893; Paris, Cabinet des Dessins du Louvre, 1952
Exhib.: Pu, No. 123; French Drawings from Fouquet to Gauguin, London, 1952, No. 132; French Drawings, USA, 1952, No. 170, repr.; French Drawings, Masterpieces from seven Centuries, USA, 1956, No. 159; Pab, No. 29, repr.; Französische Zeichnungen, Hamburg, Cologne, Stuttgart, 1958, No. 185, repr.
Lit.: Denis Sutton, Burlington Magazine, März 1952, No. 28, repr.; Claude Roger-Marx, L'Œil, May 1956, p. 26, repr.; John Rewald, Post-Impressionism, 1956, p. 173, repr.

600   CALIBAN COWERING ON A BRANCH   1881
Charcoal 46×35 cm
Coll.: Paris, Emile Schuffenecker; Paris, Roger-Marx
Exhib.: Pg; Le dessin français de Fouquet à Cézanne, Paris, 1950, No. 222; Le dessin français de Watteau à Cézanne, Geneva, 1951, No. 184; Bh, No. 345; Pac, No. 16, repr.
Lit.: Claude Roger-Marx, Fusains, Paris, 1950, No. 14, repr.

601   DAVID AND GOLIATH
Charcoal 35×43 cm
Coll.: Paris, Michel Grilichess
Exhib.: Pac, No. 21

Visions 1882-85

602   TWO WOMENS' HEADS   C. 1882
Charcoal 33×33 cm
Coll.: Paris, Emile Bernard, 1904; Paris, Comte A. Doria
Exhib.: La Belle Epoque, Nice, 1950, No. 242; Pab, No. 35; Pac, No. 31

226

603 THE EYE LIKE A STRANGE BALLOON 1882
(see M. 38)
Charcoal
Coll.: New York, The New Gallery; New
York, Museum of Modern Art
Exhib.: Ni, No. 19, repr.; Nk, No. 101

604 SIREN 1882
Charcoal 50×36.5 cm
Coll.: Paris, Ambroise Vollard, 1899; Paris,
Roger-Marx
Exhib.: Pac, No. 15; Bh, No. 344
Lit.: Bacou, 1956, No. 11, repr.

605 THE RAVEN (Inspired by Edgar Allan Poe's
poem) 1882
Charcoal 50×35 cm
Coll.: Paris, Madame Albert Marquet
Exhib.: Ps, No. 231; Pab, No. IX, repr.;
Bh, No. 351; Pac, No. 7; Ld, No. 11, repr.
Lit.: René Huyghe: Le Dessin Français au
XIXᵉ siècle, Lausanne, 1948, Pl. 77, repr.;
Klaus Berger, The Reconversion of O. R.,
Art Quarterly, 1958, p. 154, repr.

606 THE FEMALE CENTAUR WITH DRAGON
Before 1883 (see M. 50)
Charcoal
Coll.: Paris, Roger-Marx
Lit.: Fegdal, 1929, No. 41, repr.; Claude
Roger-Marx, Fusains, 1950, No. 9, repr.

607 CYCLOPS Before 1883
Charcoal
Coll.: Béziers, Gustave Fayet; Paris, P.
Bacou
Exhib.: Ps, No. 204

608 FEMALE BODY IN SPIRAL CONVOLUTIONS
Before 1883 (see M. 48)
Charcoal
Coll.: Paris, S. Morin

609 THE MASQUE OF THE RED DEATH (After Edgar
Allan Poe) 1883
Charcoal 42×36 cm
Coll.: Brussels, Edmond Picard, 1886; Al-
men, Bonger, 1904; New York, The New
Gallery
Exhib.: Ba, Pg, No. 3; Ha, No. 34; Ps,
No. 179; Ng, No. 23; Pab, No. 31; Hb,
No. 15; Bi, No. 29, repr.; Ld, No. 14, repr.;
Nk, No. 102, repr.

Lit.: Mellerio, 1923, p. 58, repr.; Sandström, 1955, No. 89, repr.; Bacou, 1956,
No. 20, repr.

610 APPARITION 1883 (Sandström: 1876–79)
Charcoal 58×45 cm
Coll.: Paris, André Mellerio; Bordeaux,
Museum
Exhib.: Pg, No. 43; Ps, No. 214; Pu,
No. 125; Pab, No. 34
Lit.: Mellerio, Gazette des Beaux-Arts,
1920, p. 150; Sandström, 1955, No. 40,
repr.

611 SPHINX C. 1883
Black chalk 45×33.5 cm
Coll.: The Hague, Dr. H. P. Bremmer,
heirs
Exhib.: Hb, No. 20; Ld, No. 16, repr.

612 MARSH FLOWER 1884–85 (see M. 55)
Charcoal 49×33 cm
Coll.: Otterlo, Kröller-Müller
Exhib.: Pab, No. 32; Bi, No. 21
Lit.: Sandström, 1955, No. 53, repr.; Bacou,
1956, No. 25, repr.

613 MARSH FLOWER 1885
Charcoal 42.5×35.5 cm
Coll.: New York, H. Lawrence Herring
Exhib.: Nh, No. 6, repr.; Nk, No. 108, repr.
Lit.: Rewald, Post-Impressionism, 1956,
p. 174, repr.

614 MARSH FLOWER (BLOSSOM AS THE APPARITION
OF A GIRL) 1885
Charcoal 40.5×33 cm
Coll.: Paris, Ambroise Vollard; New York,
Jean Goriany; Chicago, Art Institute
Exhib.: Nh, No. 7, repr.; Nk, No. 107,
repr.

615 GHOST 1885
Charcoal 40.5×33 cm
Coll.: New York, Louis Macmillan
Lit.: Rewald, Post-Impressionism, New
York, 1956, p. 177, repr.

616 APPARITION C. 1885
Charcoal 42×29 cm
Coll.: The Hague, P. N. J. Bodes
Exhib.: Hb, No. 17

617 APPARITION   C. 1885
Charcoal 46×34.5 cm
Coll.: The Hague, G. Oudshoorn
Exhib.: Hb, No. 18

618 APPARITION   C. 1885
Charcoal 46.5×37.5 cm
Coll.: Holland, J. F. G. Boom
Exhib.: Hb, No. 19

619 DREAM POLYP   C. 1885
Charcoal 47.5×35.5 cm
Coll.: New York, Donald B. Strauss
Exhib.: Nk, No. 103

620 THE ROADSIDE MEMORIAL   1885
Charcoal 52×37.5 cm
Coll.: Philadelphia, Henri Dorra
Exhib.: Ng, No. 32, repr.; Nh, No. 20, repr.; Nk, No. 111, repr.

621 CACTUS HEAD   C. 1885/86 (1881?)
Charcoal 46.5×31.5 cm
Coll.: London, private ownership; New York, Jan Woodner
Exhib.: Ld, No. 15, repr.; Nk, No. 100, repr.

622 BLACK HORSE   C. 1883
Charcoal 42×39 cm
Coll.: Paris, J. Dubourg
Exhib.: Pw, No. 22; Bi, No. 27

623 RIDER   C. 1885
Charcoal 50.8×36.2 cm
Coll.: Béziers, Gustave Fayet; New York, Alexander M. Bing
Exhib.: Ps, No. 208; Nd; Nh, No. 8; Dessins français des collections américaines, Orangerie, Paris, 1958, No. 177, repr.

624 RAISING OF LAZARUS   C. 1885
Charcoal with white highlights 26×37.5 cm
Coll.: New York, John Rewald; Cambridge, Fogg Art Museum, Paul J. Sachs collection, 1955
Exhib.: Nh, No. 3; Wb, No. 69
Lit.: Art News, 50, Feb. 1952, p. 58, repr.; J. Rewald, Gazette des Beaux-Arts, November 1956, No. 5, repr.

Phantasy II   'painterly'   1885-90

625 MADAME REDON, PORTRAIT   1885, dated
Charcoal 38.5×32 cm
Coll.: Paris, A. Redon
Exhib.: Wa, No. 129; Pr, No. 269; Pab, No. 36; Französische Zeichnungen, Hamburg, Cologne, Stuttgart, 1958, No. 186
Lit.: Fegdal, 1929, Bl. XII, repr.

626 THE FRUIT OF THE HEATH   1885
Charcoal
Coll.: Paris, S. Morin

627 GIRL OF THE HEATH
Charcoal 47.5×34.5 cm
Coll.: The Hague, G. Oudshoorn
Exhib.: Bd, No. 89; Hb, No. 21

628 PROFILE IN LIGHT   1886 or shortly before (see M. 61)
Charcoal 38×28 cm
Coll.: Paris, Ambroise Vollard; Paris, Claude Roger-Marx; Paris, Asselain
Exhib.: Cent cinquante ans de Dessin français, Galerie Bernheim, Paris, 1952, No. 136; Pab, No. XIV, repr.; Pac, No. 11; Il Disegno Francese, Rom, 1959, No. 188; Sources du XXe Siècle, Musée d'Art Moderne, Paris, 1960, No. 574
Lit.: Bacou, 1956, No. 39, repr.

629 PROFILE IN LIGHT   C. 1886
Charcoal
Coll.: Paris, Petit Palais
Exhib.: Pu, No. 140
Lit.: Mellerio, 1923, p. 37, repr.

630 FALLEN ANGEL   Possibly before 1880
Charcoal 26×34 cm
Coll.: Paris, Ambroise Vollard; Paris, Asselain
Exhib.: Pac, No. 9
Lit.: Claude Roger-Marx, Fusains, 1950, No. 4, repr.

631 FALLEN ANGEL   C. 1885
Charcoal
Coll.: Paris, A. Mellerio; Paris, Marcel Kapferer
Exhib.: Ps, No. 210; Pu, No. 143
Lit.: Mellerio, 1923, p. 92, repr.

632   FALLEN ANGEL   1885/86 (Bacou: 1871) (see M. 64)
Charcoal 28×22.5 cm
Coll.: Paris, Ernest Chausson, 1894; Otterlo, Kröller-Müller, No. 646
Exhib.: Pab, Nr. III, repr.

633   ANGEL WITH BOOK
Charcoal
Exhib.: Bd, No. 91

634   SPRING   1886 (Bacou: 1883)
Charcoal 43×31 cm
Coll.: Brussels, Edouard Picard; Almen, Bonger; New York, Seligmann
Exhib.: Pg, No. 4; Ha, No. 36; Ps, No. 178; Ng, No. 21, repr.
Lit.: Bacou, 1956, No. 42, repr.

635   DRUID PRIESTESS   C. 1885 (see M. 63)
Charcoal 51.5×37.5 cm
Coll.: Paris, Ambroise Vollard; New York, Jean Goriany; Chicago, Art Institute
Exhib.: Nh, No. 9

636   ST ANTHONY SEEING A VISION   C. 1886
Charcoal 52.5×37 cm
Coll.: Paris, Ambroise Vollard; New York, Jean Goriany; Chicago, Art Institute
Exhib.: Nh, No. 11

637   THE WINDOW   C. 1886 (1892)
Charcoal 52.4×37.4 cm
Coll.: Paris, Ambroise Vollard, 1897; New York, Jean Goriany; Chicago, Art Institute
Exhib.: Nh, No. 10, repr.; Pab, No. XV, repr.; Hb, No. 34; Nk, No. 110

638   CALIBAN   1885–90
Charcoal
Coll.: Béziers, Gustave Fayet; Bordeaux, Lafargue
Exhib.: Pg, No. 25; Ps, No. 202
Lit.: Sandström, 1955, No. 83, repr.

639   TREE FACE   1885–90
Charcoal 47.5×33.5 cm
Coll.: Paris, Ambroise Vollard; New York, Jean Goriany; Chicago, Art Institute
Exhib.: Nh, No. 12; Nk, No. 96
Lit.: Sandström, 1955, No. 135, repr.

640   CENSER WITH DEMON   1885–90
Charcoal 34×31 cm
Coll.: New York, John Rewald
Exhib.: Wb, No. 68, repr.; Hc; Ni, No. 23, repr.; Los Angeles, 1959, No. 109; John Rewald collection sale, Sotheby's, London, 7 July 1960, No. 95, repr.
Lit.: Rewald, Post-Impressionism, 1956, p. 174, repr.

641   HEAD OF CHRIST   1885–87 (see M. 71)
Charcoal 31×28.5 cm
Coll.: Paris, J. Zoubaloff; Paris, Petit Palais
Exhib.: Pu, No. 131; Pab, No. 38

642   HEAD OF CHRIST WITH CLOSED EYES
Charcoal 31×28 cm
Coll.: Paris, Roger-Marx
Exhib.: Pac, No. 10, repr.
Lit.: Claude Roger-Marx, Fusains, 1950, cover, repr.

643   HEAD OF CHRIST WITH OPEN EYES
Charcoal 37×48 cm
Coll.: Béziers, Gustave Fayet; Béziers, d'Andoque
Exhib.: Ps, No. 188
Lit.: Bacou, 1956, No. 48, repr.

644   SUDARIUM
Charcoal 40.5×31 cm
Coll.: Paris, Dubourg
Exhib.: Pw, No. 33; Bi, No. 31

645   IN THE FONT   1887
Charcoal
Coll.: Almen, Bonger

646   THE NOVICE
Charcoal 41.5×37 cm
Coll.: De Steeg, S. van Deventer
Exhib.: Hb, No. 33

647   CHIMERA   After 1886
Charcoal 50.5×37.7 cm
Coll.: Paris, Claude-Emile Schuffenecker; Paris, Ambroise Vollard; Paris, Higgons; London, private ownership
Exhib.: Pg, No. 38; Pac, No. 14, repr.; Ld, No. 13, repr.

648   TEMPLE AND IDOLS OF THE BARBARIANS
1887
Charcoal
Coll.: Almen, Bonger

649–655   SEVEN DRAWINGS FOR THE LITHO-
GRAPHS FOR EDMOND PICARD'S ›LE JURÉ‹
1887
   1   A MAN OF THE PEOPLE AND A SAVAGE
      28×29.5 cm
   2   A SKELETON
      45×28 cm
   3   THE BELLS OF ST GUDULA
      51×30 cm
   4   THROUGH THE CRACK IN THE WALL
      43×30 cm
   5   DRUID PRIESTESS
      27×27 cm
   6   MUST THERE NOT BE AN INVISIBLE
      WORLD?
      50×35 cm
   7   THE DREAM IS CONSUMMATED IN DEATH
      54×36.5 cm
Coll.: for 1–6: Brussels, Edmond Picard; De
Steeg, S. van Deventer; for 7: Amsterdam,
Prentenkabinet
Exhib.: 2, 3: Pg, No. 30, 31; 1–7: Bd, No.
81–87; 7: Pab, No. 39, repr.; 1, 2, 5: Hb,
No. 22a, b, c; 6: Pac, No. 35; 1–6: Bi,
No. 33–38; 1–3, 5–7: Ld, No. 18–23, repr.
Lit.: 7: Sandström, 1955, No. 111, repr.

656   THE ARCHANGEL   C. 1888
Charcoal 50×36 cm
Coll.: Béziers, Gustave Fayet; Béziers, A.
d'Andoque
Exhib.: Ps, No. 184; Pab, No. 40
Lit.: Bacou, 1956, No. 36, repr.

657   METEOR
Charcoal 33.5×21 cm
Coll.: Paris, Ambroise Vollard; Paris,
Galerie de France; Bordeaux, private
ownership
Exhib.: Pv; Galerie Goya, Bordeaux, 1943,
No. 12; Bh, No. 348

658   MYSTIC DIALOGUE
Charcoal 44.5×32 cm
Coll.: Paris, private ownership
Exhib.: Pac, No. 24

659   RENUNCIATION   C. 1888
Charcoal 35×30 cm
Coll.: Paris, private ownership
Exhib.: Ld, No. 25, repr.

660   SLEEPY   1889
Charcoal 49×37 cm
Coll.: Almen, Bonger
Exhib.: Pe, No. 275, repr.; Pab, No. 41;
Hb, No. 24; Bi, No. 45; Ld, No. 26, repr.
Lit.: J. Cohen Gosschalk, Elseviers, 1909

661   MENACE   Before 1890
Charcoal 51×37.5 cm
Coll.: Montreal, H. Ernest

662   PEGASUS AND BELLEROPHON   1889
(1883–93)
Charcoal 53.7×35.9 cm
Coll.: Cambridge, Philip Hofer; New York,
Robert Lehmann
Exhib.: Ne, No. 95, repr.; Master Drawings,
Buffalo, 1935, No. 126, repr.; Nineteenth
Century French Drawings, California Palace
of the Legion of Honor, San Francisco, 1947,
No. 121, repr.; Dessins français des Col-
lections Américaines, Orangerie, Paris,
1958, No. 180, repr.; Nk, No. 115

663   SAINT IN THE TOILS OF A SERPENT
Before 1890 (see M. 108)
Charcoal 52.5×37.3 cm
Coll.: Paris, Ambroise Vollard; Paris, Hig-
gons
Exhib.: Pac, No. 29, repr.

664   FRIGHTENED CHILD STARING OUT OF A
DORMER-WINDOW   Before 1890
Charcoal 50.5×37.5 cm
Coll.: Paris, Ambroise Vollard, New York,
Jean Goriany; Chicago, Art Institute
Exhib.: Nh, No. 19; Nk, No. 118

Relaxation   1890-95

665   DRUID PRIESTESS   C. 1890 or earlier
Charcoal and black chalk
Coll.: Otterlo, Kröller-Müller
Lit.: Sandström, 1955, No. 12, repr.

666   THE WIND   1890
Charcoal
Coll.: New York, The New Gallery
Exhib.: Ni, No. 27, repr.

667   A FIRST ADUMBRATION OF HUMANITY IN THE
FLOWER   1890
Charcoal
Coll.: Bordeaux, M. J. Tauzin
Lit.: Sandström, 1955, No. 55, repr.

668   WOMAN WITH DEMON   1890
Charcoal 48.5×32.5 cm
Coll.: Otterlo, Kröller-Müller
Exhib.: Bi, No. 42
Lit.: Sandström, 1955, No. 64, repr.

669   WOMAN INHALING THE SCENT OF FLOWERS
C. 1890
Charcoal
Lit.: Claude Roger-Marx, Fusains, 1590,
No. 11, repr.

670   WOMAN WITH FLOWERS   C. 1890
Charcoal 52.5×37.5 cm
Coll.: Munich, private ownership
Exhib.: Ld, No. 32, repr.

671   WOMAN AT THE WINDOW   C. 1890
Charcoal 50.8×36.2 cm
Coll.: New York, Alexander M. Bing
Exhib.: Nh. No. 21; Dessins français des
Collections Américaines, Orangerie, Paris,
1958, No. 178, repr.

672   YOUNG GIRL   C. 1890
Charcoal 49×36 cm
Coll.: New York, Seligmann
Exhib.: Ng, No. 20; Nh, No. 20

673   GIRL'S HEAD   C. 1890 (C. 1885)
Charcoal 52.5×37.5 cm
Coll.: Paris, Ambroise Vollard; New York,
Jean Goriany; Chicago, Art Institute
Exhib.: Nh. No. 18
Lit.: Mellerio, 1923, p. 142, repr.

674   PAIN WITH CLOSED EYES   C. 1890
Charcoal 52×37 cm
Coll.: Paris, Roger-Marx
Exhib.: Bi, No. 30
Lit.: Claude Roger-Marx, Fusains, 1950,
No. 13, repr.

675   WITH HAIR LOOSE   C. 1890
Red chalk 40×36 cm
Coll.: Otterlo, Kröller-Müller, No. 644
Exhib.: Py, No. 159; Bi, No. 47; Ld, No. 27,
repr.

676   MUSIC (GIRL'S PROFILE LOOKING TO THE LEFT,
WITH FLOWERS   C. 1890
Charcoal
Lit.: Claude Roger-Marx, Fusains, 1950,
No. 16, repr.

677   BUST OF A GIRL IN PROFILE
After 1890
Charcoal 45.5×37 cm
Coll.: Otterlo, Kröller-Müller
Lit.: Rewald, Post-Impressionism, 1956,
p. 170, repr.

678   HEAD LOOKING TO THE RIGHT IN PROFILE
After 1890
Charcoal 49.5×36 cm
Exhib.: Ng, No. 26, repr.

679   FALLEN ANGEL   After 1890
Charcoal with pastel
Coll.: Paris, Petit Palais
Lit.: Mellerio, 1923, cover, repr. in colour

680   PEGASUS   After 1890
Black chalk 52.5×37.5 cm
Coll.: Paris, Ambroise Vollard; Bremen,
Kunsthalle
Exhib.: Ps, No. 236; Pw, No. 25; Bi, No. 28;
Ld, No. 10, repr.

681   IN THE SHADOW OF A WING   1891 (see
M. 113)
Black chalk 29×17 cm
Coll.: Béziers, Gustave Fayet, 1904 Béziers,
Madame A. d'Andoque
Exhib.: Ps, No. 205; Pab, No. 42; Bh, No. 349
Lit.: Bacou, 1956, No. 30, repr.

682   YOUTH   1891
Charcoal 48×37 cm
Coll.: Almen, Bonger, after 1894
Exhib.: Pg, No. 2; Ng, No. 27; Bi, No. 40

683   MEDITATION ON THE ABSOLUTE   1891
Charcoal 44×36.5 cm
Coll.: Almen, Bonger, 1901

Exhib.: Ps, No. 181; Pab, No. 44; Hb, No. 25, repr.
Lit.: D. A. de Graaf, Apollo, 1946, p. 27, repr. Sandström, 1955, No. 122, repr.

684 ARMOURED MAN IN PROFILE   C. 1890
Charcoal
Coll.: Paris, Petit Palais

685 ARMOURED MAN IN PROFILE 1891
Charcoal 50.7 × 36.8 cm
Coll.: Paris, Bailly, 1892; New York, Metropolitan Museum
Exhib.: Masterpieces of Drawing, Philadelphia Museum of Art, 1950, No. 106, repr.; Nh, No. 14, repr.; French Drawings, Masterpieces from Seven Centuries, USA, 1955, No. 160; Pab, No. XII, repr.; Nk, No. 104, repr.
Lit.: Claude-Roger-Marx, Fusains, 1950, No. 1, repr.; Rewald, Post-Impressionism, New York, 1956, p. 170, repr.; Bacou, 1956, No. 23, repr.; Rewald, Gazette des Beaux-Arts, November 1956, No. 14, repr.

686 GIRL (IN RIGHT PROFILE) WITH FLOWER
PEDESTAL   C. 1891
Charcoal 44 × 37 cm
Coll.: Otterlo, Kröller-Müller
Exhib.: Hb, No. 26, repr.; Bi, No. 41

687 MAN'S HEAD WITH LONG HAIR
Black chalk 31 × 20 cm
Coll.: Amsterdam, Prentenkabinet
Exhib.: Hb, No. 209

688 PROFILE IN FRAME
Charcoal 47.5 × 36.5 cm
Coll.: Almen, Bonger
Exhib.: Pab, No. 47; Hb, No. 28; Bi, No. 43

689 THE MUSE
Charcoal 37 × 37 cm
Coll.: Otterlo, Kröller-Müller
Exhib.: Bi, No. 44

690 EYE WITH POPPY-HEAD   1892
Charcoal 46 × 32 cm
Coll.: Paris, Ambroise Vollard; Paris, C. Roger-Marx

Exhib.: Pg, No. 15; Ha, No. 23; Ps, No. 229; Pz, No. 25; Pab, No. XVI, repr.; Pac, No. 17; Sources du XXᵉ Siècle, Musée d d'Art Moderne, Paris, 1960, No. 576
Lit.: Claude Roger-Marx, Fusains, 1950, No. 7, repr.

691 BLACK POPPY (GIRL IN PROFILE)   1893
Charcoal 51 × 37 cm
Coll.: Almen, Bonger, 1894
Exhib.: Pg, No. 40; Ha, No. 25; Ng, No. 25; Pab, No. 42; Hb, No. 27
Lit.: J. Cohen-Gosschalk, Zeitschrift f. bildende Kunst, Dez. 1910, No. 6, repr.; Mellerio, 1923, p. 148, repr.

692 PRAYER   1893 (preliminary drawing for M. 124)
Charcoal 34 × 24 cm
Coll.: Béziers, Gustave Fayet; Béziers, A. d'Andoque
Exhib.: Ps, No. 209
Lit.: Bacou, 1956, No. 45, repr.

693 WREATHED HEAD   C. 1894
Charcoal 50 × 36.5 cm
Coll.: Paris, André Gide; Paris, Baroness Alain de Gunzbourg
Exhib.: Pg, No. 47; Hb, No. 13, repr.; Bi, No. 39; Ld, No. 24, repr.

694 RACE HORSE   C. 1894 (see M. 129)
Charcoal 27.5 × 22.5 cm
Coll.: Rotterdam, Boymans Museum
Exhib.: Ld, No. 4, repr.; Hb, No. 206

695 HATCHING (WOMAN'S HEAD PEERING OUT OF A SPHERE)   Before 1894 (see M. 126)
Charcoal 51 × 36 cm
Coll.: Paris, J. Dubourg
Exhib.: Hb, No. 31; Bi, No. 32; Ld, No. 17, repr.; Sources du XXᵉ Siècle, Musée d'Art Moderne, Paris, 1960, No. 575, repr.
Lit.: Claude Roger-Marx, Fusains, 1950, No. 10, repr.

696 WOMAN'S HEAD BESIDE TREE TRUNK
C. 1894
Charcoal 52 × 37 cm
Coll.: Paris, J. Dubourg
Exhib.: Hb, No. 29; Bi, No. 50; Ld, No. 36, repr.

697 DELUSION OF THE SENSES C. 1895
Charcoal 29.5 × 23.5 cm
Coll.: Vienna, Würthle and Sohn; Worcester Art Museum, USA, Dial collection, 1921
Lit.: The Dial and the Dial Collection, Worcester, 1959, p. 107

Religious Mood   1895 - 1900

698 THE SERMON ON THE MOUNT   1895–1900
Charcoal
Coll.: Paris, Armand Parent
Exhib.: Ps, No. 216
Lit.: Fegdal, 1929, No. 23, repr.

699 MADONNA AND CHILD   1895–1900
Charcoal and pastel 45 × 35 cm
Coll.: Paris, S. Morin
Exhib.: Pab, repr. on the jacket of the catalogue
Lit.: Bacou, 1956, No. 52, repr.

700 CHRIST ON THE CROSS   1895–98
Charcoal 51 × 27 cm
Coll.: Paris, Ambroise Vollard; Paris, private ownership
Exhib.: Pab, Nr. 49; Ld, No. 34 rep.

701 CHRIST ON THE CROSS   1895–98
Charcoal 49.3 × 35 cm
Coll.: Paris, Ambroise Vollard; Paris, A. Leblond; Paris, Higgons; New Haven, Yale University Art Gallery, 1959
Exhib.: Pac, No. 18, repr.; Nk, No. 123

702 CHURCH INTERIOR   C. 1900
Charcoal 52.5 × 47.5 cm
Coll.: Paris, private ownership
Exhib.: Pw, No. 26; Pac, No. 20

703 THE CATHEDRAL   C. 1900 (see painting no. 211) Charcoal with pastel 87 × 68 cm
Coll.: Paris, Ricardo Vinés; Paris, private-ownership
Exhib.: Pm, No. 29; Pq, No. 135; Ps, No. 154; Pab, No. 74

704 JOHN THE BAPTIST'S HEAD IN A CHARGER 1900
Red chalk 45 × 55 cm, horizontal format

Coll.: Paris, Armand Parent; Paris, Roger-Marx
Exhib.: Pr; Pu, No. 130; Py, No. 155
Lit.: Fegdal, No. 25, repr.

Last Works   1895 - 1900

705 MYSTIC VEIL   1895
Charcoal 48.5 × 35 cm
Coll.: Almen, Bonger
Exhib.: Ng, No. 19; Pab, No. 48; Hb, No. 32
Lit.: J. Cohen-Gosschalk, Zeitschrift f. bildende Kunst, Dec. 1910, No. 6, repr.

706 GHOST   After 1895 (C. 1885) (see M. 161)
Charcoal 52.5 × 37.5 cm
Coll.: Paris, Ambroise Vollard; New York, Jean Goriany; Chicago, Art Institute
Exhib.: Nh, No. 16

707 WOMAN READING   C. 1895
Charcoal 60 × 50 cm
Coll.: Paris, A. Redon
Exhib.: Bd, No. 101; Py, No. 145, repr. as a painting
Lit.: Fegdal, 1929, No. 13, repr.

708 CHIMERA   1895–96 (Rewald: 1902)
Charcoal 55 × 39 cm
Coll.: Almen, Bonger
Exhib.: Ng, No. 24; Pab, No. 50; Hb, No. 30; Bi, No. 48; Ld, No. 35, repr.; Nk, No. 125, repr.
Lit.: D. A. de Graaf, Apollo, May 1946, p. 22, repr.

709 READING THE BRAHMANIC SCRIPTURES
After 1895
Charcoal 50.5 × 37 cm
Coll.: Paris, Ambroise Vollard; New York, Jean Goriany; Chicago, Art Institute, 1950
Exhib.: Pg, No. 27; Nh, No. 13, repr.; Paa, No. 42; Dessins français des Collections Américaines, Paris, 1958, No. 179, repr.
Lit.: Sandström, 1955, No. 95, repr.; Paul J. Sachs, Modern Prints and Drawings, 1954, No. 50, repr.

710 PHAETON'S DOWNFALL   Before 1896
(see M. 150)
Charcoal

Coll.: Saint-Germain-en-Laye, Maurice Denis; Saint-Germain-en-Laye, Dr. Denis
Exhib.: Pq, No. 158; Ps, No. 183; Pu, No. 135
Lit.: Bacou, 1956, No. 34, repr.

711 MOONSHINE Before 1896 (see M. 140)
Charcoal 49×36 cm
Coll.: Paris, Ambroise Vollard; Paris, Claude Roger-Marx
Exhib.: Pac, No. 27
Lit.: Claude Roger-Marx, Fusains, 1950, No. 3, repr.

712 WOMAN'S PROFILE AT NIGHT 1895 (1890?)
Charcoal 47×35.5 cm
Coll.: Paris, Ambroise Vollard; New York, Jean Goriany; Chicago, Art Institute
Exhib.: Nh, No. 17, repr.; Pab, No. XVIII, repr.; Hb, No. 35; Nk, No. 122

713 GIRL'S PROFILE WITH FLOWER C. 1895
Black chalk 49×35.5 cm
Coll.: New York, Wildenstein
Exhib.: Drawings through Four Centuries, Wildenstein, New York, 1949, No. 78

714 ILLUSION. GIRL'S PROFILE WITH FLOWERING BRANCH C. 1895
Black pencil with pastel 50 × 37 cm
Coll.: Otterlo, Kröller-Müller, No. 640
Exhib.: Py, No. 158 (as 'Songe'); Ld, No. 28, repr.
Lit.: Sandström, 1955, No. 123, repr.

715 WREATHED WOMAN'S PROFILE C. 1897
Charcoal 43×36 cm
Coll.: Boston, Swetzoff
Exhib.: Pg, No. 40; Pac, No. 22, repr.

716 HEAD OF A BOY IN PROFILE C. 1898
Chalk with charcoal 36×30 cm
Coll.: Paris, Jacques Ulmann
Exhib.: Pac, No. 23, repr.

717 DREAM C. 1898
Charcoal 52.5×37.5 cm
Coll.: Munich, private ownership
Exhib.: Bd, No. 92; Ld, No. 33, repr.

718 WOMAN'S PROFILE WITH LEAVES IN THE BACKGROUND 1898–1900
Charcoal 53.5×37 cm

Coll.: Chicago, Art Institute
Exhib.: Ng, No. 25, repr.; Nk, No. 121

718a THE SCALES (DEVIL WITH SERPENT) Used as cover design for the Moscow periodical 'The Scales', 1904, No. 1–6
Charcoal 44.5×28.5 cm
Coll.: Moscow, S. Poljakoff; Moscow, Museum for Modern Art; Moscow, Pushkin Museum

Drawings
Pencil, Pen and Ink

I 1860 - 1900

719 WOMAN RESTING UNDER A TREE 1860–65
Pencil
Coll.: Basel, Kunstmuseum
Lit.: Sandström, 1955, No. 4, repr.

720 WOMAN SITTING ON A BOULDER 1860–65
Pencil
Coll.: Winterthur, Museum
Lit.: Sandström, 1955, No. 6, repr.

721 THE PEYRELEBADE TREE 1862, dated
Pencil 20×26.5 cm
Coll.: Winterthur, Hedy Hahnloser-Bühler; Bern, Professor H. R. Hahnloser
Exhib.: Hb, No. 220

722 TWO WANDERERS IN THE HEATH 1863, dated
Ink 14.5×18.5 cm
Coll.: Bern, H. R. Hahnloser
Lit.: Sandström, 1955, No. 2, repr.

723 RIDER IN FLIGHT C. 1865 (see No. 179)
Ink and wash 30×46 cm
Coll.: Otterlo, Kröller-Müller
Exhib.: Bh, No. 350, repr.; Nk, No. 77
Lit.: Sandström, 1955, No. 25, repr.

724 PYRENEES LANDSCAPE WITH SEATED WOMAN
1865, dated
Pencil 28.5 × 26.8 cm
Coll.: Bern, H. R. Hahnloser
Lit.: Sandström, 1955, No. 5, repr.

725 ROLAND IN THE VALLEY OF RONCEVAUX 1865
Pen and ink 33.8 × 26 cm
Coll.: Paris, Ary Leblond; New York,
Charles K. Lock
Exhib.: Wa, No. 57; Pr. No. 296; Ps, No.
212; Pu, No. 120; Nk, No. 75; repr.
Lit.: Mellerio, 1923, p. 39, repr.; Bacou,
1956, p. 34

726 EVE DISCOVERS ABEL'S CORPSE C. 1865
(later version of 1880 in the collection:
Paris, Count Doria, formerly Paris, M.-A.
Leblond, exhib. in the Petit Palais, Paris,
1934, No. 133)
Pen and ink 15.4 × 16.3 cm
Coll.: Paris, Petit Palais
Lit.: Bacou, 1956, No. 3, repr.

727 MOUNTAIN LANDSCAPE WITH TWO FIGURES
C. 1865
Pen and ink 25 × 16.5 cm
Coll.: Paris, Petit Palais
Exhib.: Nk, No. 76, repr.

728 MOUNTAIN LANDSCAPE WITH TWO FIGURES
IN CONVERSATION C. 1865
Pen and ink 20.5 × 17 cm
Coll.: Paris, Petit Palais
Lit.: Bacou, 1956, No. 2, repr.

729 THE GIANT Before 1870
Pencil 24.8 × 28 cm
Coll.: New York, Philip Hofer; Cambridge,
Fogg Art Museum, No. 719, in catalogue
repr.; 1929
Exhib.: Wb, No. 63
Lit.: Sandström, 1955, No. 27, repr.

730 WOMAN WITH DEMON 1865–75
Pencil
Coll.: Paris, M. Lecomte
Lit.: Sandström, 1955, No. 80, repr.

731 LEAFLESS TREE 1870
Pencil 31 × 21.5 cm
Coll.: Paris, Henri Mondor
Lit.: Bacou, 1956, No. 12, repr.

732 APPARITION OF A WOMAN 1870–75
Pencil 19.3 × 19 cm
Coll.: New York, John Rewald; New York,
Charles E. Slatkin
Exhib.: Nh, No. 2; Wb, No. 64; Hc; Los
Angeles, 1959, No. 107; Nk, No. 83, repr.
Lit.: Gazette des Beaux-Arts, November
1956, p. 120; Rewald, Post-Impressionism,
1955, p. 169, repr.; John Rewald collection
sale, Sotheby's London, 7 July 1960, No. 94,
repr.

733 MAN WITH A LARGE HAT 1870
Black chalk 12 × 12.5 cm
Coll.: Paris, Louvre
Exhib.: Pab, No. 14; Nk, No. 86
Lit.: Bacou, 1956, No. 13, repr.

734 WOMAN PLAYING BOULE C. 1875
Pencil 12 × 15 cm
Coll.: Paris, Jacques Zoubaloff; Paris, Petit
Palais

735 THE ETERNAL SILENCE OF INFINITE SPACE
(PASCAL) 1878 (1862)
Pencil 22.5 × 27.5 cm
Coll.: Paris, Jacques Zoubaloff; Paris, Petit
Palais, 1916
Exhib.: Pu, No. 127; Pab, No. 3
Lit.: Mellerio, Gazette des Beaux-Arts,
1920, p. 143; Mellerio, 1923, p. 118, repr.

736 SLASHED BODY C. 1880
Ink 25.1 × 19.1 cm
Coll.: Béziers, Gustave Fayet, 1904;
Béziers, A. d'Andoque
Exhib.: Bh, No. 346

737 MASTER CALIBAN
Ink y brush 23.5 × 31.5 cm
Coll.: Winterthur, Hedy Hahnloser-Bühler;
Bern, Professor Hans R. Hahnloser

737a CENTAUR
Pencil 47.5 × 37 cm
Coll.: Tokyo, K. Nakagawa

738 CENTAURS FIGHTING 1880–89
Pencil
Coll.: Paris, A. Redon
Lit.: Mellerio, 1923 p. 83, repr.; Sand-
ström, 1955, No. 63, repr.

739 TREE 1892 (see M. 120)
Pen and watercolour 45.5×31 cm
Coll.: Dexter, Maine, Jerry Abbot
Exhib.: Nk, No. 119, repr.
Lit.: J. Rewald, Gazette des Beaux-Arts,
November 1956, No. 10, repr.

740–745 FROM THE SKETCHBOOK IN THE ART
INSTITUTE OF CHICAGO, WITH DEDICATION TO
RENÉ PHILIPPON 1895
  a TWO MASKS APPEARING OUT OF THE WALL
    C. 1887
    Black chalk
    Lit.: Bacou, 1956, No. 19, repr.
  b MAN WITH MASK C. 1890
    Black chalk
    Lit.: Bacou, 1956, No. 24, repr.
  c YOUNG WOMAN Shortly before 1895
    Black chalk
    Lit.: Bacou, 1956, No. 71, repr.
  d OWL Shortly before 1895
    Black chalk
    Lit.: Bacou, 1956, No. 89, repr.
  e AIR BALLOONS C. 1887
    (see No. 654 and M. 79)
    Black chalk
  f SAILING BOATS IN BRITTANY 1880
    Pencil and chalk
    Exhib.: Nk, No. 99

746 CRUCIFIXION 1895
Pencil
Coll.: Paris, A. Redon
Lit.: A. Mellerio, 1923, p. 41, repr.

747 YOUNG GIRL AT THE WINDOW After 1895
Chalk
Coll.: Linz, Neue Galerie
Exhib.: Lc, No. 61
Lit.: Sandström, 1955, No. 124, repr.

748 SHULAMITE WOMAN 1897 (see M. 167)
Ink 31.4×23.8 cm
Coll.: Winterthur, Hedy Hahnloser-Bühler;
Bern, Professor Hans R. Hahnloser
Exhib.: Hb, No. 221

749 GERMINATING SAPLING C. 1897
Pencil 32.7×22.7 cm
Coll.: Winterthur, Hedy Hahnloser-Bühler;
Bern, Professor H. R. Hahnloser
Lit.: DU, November 1956, p. 27, repr.

II 1900-1916

750 SELF PORTRAIT 1904, dated
Pencil 25×23 cm
Coll.: Paris, Georges Renand
Exhib.: Pq, Frontispiece of the Catalogue;
Pab, No. 192
Lit.: Mellerio, 1923, p. 79, repr.; Beaux-
Arts, 26/IV/1935, p. 2, repr.

751 ORPHEUS'S DESPAIR 1900
Coll.: Cleveland, Ted Coe
Lit.: J. Rewald, Gazette des Beaux-Arts,
November 1956, No. 15 A, repr.

752 HORSE AND GROOM C. 1900
(Perhaps influenced by a print by Géricault
or Carle Vernet)
Pen 20.5×26 cm
Coll.: Otterlo, Kröller-Müller
Exhib.: Ld, No. 30, repr.

753–772 PORTRAIT DRAWINGS OF HIS FRIENDS IN
RED CHALK:
  a EDOUARD VUILLARD 1900 (also as a
    lithograph) M, D
  b ARTHUR FONTAINE 1901, X
  c PIERRE BONNARD 1902 (also as a litho-
    graph) M
  d PAUL SÉRUSIER 1903 (also as a litho-
    graph) M
  e MAURICE DENIS 1903 (also as a litho-
    graph) M
  f RICARDO VINÉS 1903 (also as a lithograph)
  g ROGER-MARX 1904 (also as a lithogaph)
  h PRINCESS CYSTRIYA 1904
  i JULIETTE DODU 1904 (also as a litho-
    graph) M
  j OLIVIER SAINSÈRE 1905 X, M
  k LLOBET 1908 (also as lithograph)
  l GUSTAVE FAYET 1908
  m DR. P. E. WEILL 1911, X
  n MARIUS LEBLOND 1913, X, M
  o ARY LEBLOND 1913, M
  p ARMAND PARENT 1913, X, M
  q ERNEST CHAUSSON X
  r GEORGES COULON X
  s DR. SABOURAUD 1908, X, M, D
  t WALTNER X
  X *Exhibited:* Pq, No. 139–147
  M *Reproduced:* in Mellerio, 1923
  D *Exhibited:* Po, No. 47–48

773   EMILE BERNARD, PORTRAIT   1901, dated
Red chalk
Coll.: Paris, Altarriba
Lit.: J. Rewald, Gazette des Beaux-Arts,
November 1956, No. 15 B, repr.

773 a–m   THE MASK AND TWELVE OTHER INK
DRAWING'S FOR THE PERIODICAL 'WESI' (THE
SCALES) 1903/04
Coll.: Moscow, S. Poljakoff; Moscow, Museum for Modern Art; Moscow Pushkin
Museum

774   ANDRÉ BONGER   1904, dated
Red chalk 24 × 18 cm
Coll.: Almen, Bonger
Exhib.: Pab, No. 193; Hb, No. 208

775   NUDE   1904
Red chalk
Coll.: New York, Museum of Modern Art;
New York, Sam Salz; New York, Alex
M. Lewyt
Exhib.: Master Drawings, San Francisco,
1940, No. 79, repr.; Institute of Arts, Detroit, 1941; Modern Drawings, Museum of
Modern Art, New York, 1944; Nineteenth
Century French Drawings, San Francisco,
1947, No. 118; Nk, No. 126

776   THE ARTIST'S WIFE READING
Pencil 30.2 × 23.3 cm
Coll.: Winterthur, Hedy Hahnloser Bühler;
Bern, Professor Hans R. Hahnloser
Exhib.: Hauptwerke der Sammlung Hahnloser, Lucerne, 1940, No. 202; Hb, No. 225

777   APOLLO'S SUN CHARIOT
Pencil 18 × 15.3 cm
(Gift from the artist)
Coll.: Winterthur, Hedy Hahnloser Bühler;
Bern, Professor Hans R. Hahnloser

778   THE SUN CHARIOT   C. 1905
Red chalk 50 × 37.5 cm
Coll.: Geneva, private ownership
Exhib.: Ld, No. 29, repr.

779   PEGASUS   C. 1905
Ink 32.4 × 24.2 cm

Coll.: Amsterdam, Prentenkabinet
Exhib.: Hb, No. 212

780   NUDE WITH LONG HAIR AND FOUR FLOWERS
After 1905
Ink 24.7 × 12.3 cm
Coll.: Paris, Petit Palais
Exhib.: Pu, No. 106; Hb, No. 213
Lit.: A. Mellerio, 1923, p. 81, repr.

781   PERSEUS AND ANDROMEDA   C. 1908
Ink 16 × 28 cm
Coll.: The Hague, Dr. H. P. Bremmer,
heirs
Exhib.: Ld, No. 31, repr.

782   ROGER AND ANGELICA   Sketch for the New
York pastel, after Delacroix's picture in
the Louvre 1908–10
Ink 28.5 × 22 cm
Coll.: Paris, Jacques Zoubaloff; Paris, Petit
Palais, 1916
Exhib.: Pab, No. 194; Hb, No. 210
Lit.: Mellerio, 1923, p. 135, repr.

783   YOUNG GIRL IN PROFILE
Pencil 15 × 22.5 cm
Coll.: Winterthur, Hedy Hahnloser-Bühler;
Bern, Professor Hans R. Hahnloser
Exhib.: Hb, No. 222

784   YOUNG GIRL IN PROFILE 'SARACEN GIRL'
1910
Pencil 30 × 21 cm
Coll.: Paris, A. Redon
Exhib.: Wa, No. 128; Pr, No. 268; Pu, No.
149; Pab, Nr. 195

785   THREE NUDE STUDIES   C. 1910
Ink 22,9 × 18.1 cm
Coll.: Paris, Petit Palais
Exhib.: Hb, Nr. 215; Nk, No. 129
Lit.: A. Mellerio, 1923, p. 11, repr.

Mellerio's Catalogue of the graphic work showed
in 1923 a total of 223 prints: 42 etchings and
181 lithographs.

List of Illustrations

(O = oil, P = pastel, W = watercolour, L = lithograph, D = drawing, Ph = photograph; figures in brackets refer to the catalogue on pp. 182 ff.; figures preceded by M refer to the catalogue of André Mellerio, Bibl. No. 10)

I Plates Relating to the Biography

II Oil Paintings and Pastels

Black and White Plates

Sources of the Photographs

Index of Names

242

244